75¢

THE
PARTISAN
IMPERATIVE

THE
PARTISAN
IMPERATIVE

The Dynamics of American Politics
Before the Civil War

Joel H. Silbey

OXFORD UNIVERSITY PRESS
New York   Oxford

Oxford University Press
Oxford   New York   Toronto
Delhi   Bombay   Calcutta   Madras   Karachi
Petaling Jaya   Singapore   Hong Kong   Tokyo
Nairobi   Dar es Salaam   Cape Town
Melbourne   Auckland

and associated companies in
Beirut   Berlin   Ibadan   Nicosia

First Published in 1985 by Oxford University Press, Inc.,
200 Madison Avenue, New York, New York 10016
First issued as an Oxford University Press paperback, 1987

Oxford is a registered trademark of Oxford University Press

Library of Congress Cataloging in Publication Data
Silbey, Joel H.
The partisan imperative.
Includes index.
1. United States—Politics and government—
1815–1861—Addresses, essays, lectures.   I. Title.
E338.S55   1985   320.973   84-20691
ISBN 0-19-503551-8
ISBN 0-19-504157-7 (pbk.)

Printing (last digit): 9 8 7 6 5 4 3 2 1
Printed in the United States of America

63,378

*To Lee Benson
and Samuel T. McSeveney*

ACKNOWLEDGMENTS

The chapters in this book that have been previously published appear in this volume with the kind permission of the journals and publications in which they first appeared: "The Civil War Synthesis in American Political History," from *Civil War History*, Vol. 10, No. 2 (June 1964), 130–40; "'Delegates Fresh from the People': American Congressional and Legislative Behavior," from *The Journal of Interdisciplinary History*, Vol. 13 (1983), 603–27, copyright © 1983 and reprinted by permission of M.I.T. Press; "Parties and Politics in Mid-Nineteenth-Century America," from *Capital Studies* (Fall 1972); "'The Salt of the Nation': Political Parties in Antebellum America," from Richard L. McCormick, ed., *Political Parties and the Modern State* (New Brunswick: Rutgers University Press, 1984); "'Let The People See': Reflections on Ethnoreligious Forces in American Politics," from *Journal of Libertarian Studies*, Vol. 6 (Summer/Fall 1982), 333–47; "'There Are Other Questions Beside That of Slavery Merely': The Democratic Party and Antislavery Politics," from Alan M. Kraut, *Crusaders and Compromisers: Essays on the Relationship of the Antislavery Struggle to the Antebellum Party System* (Westport, Conn.: Greenwood Press, 1983); "The Southern National Democrats, 1845–1861," from *Mid-America*, Vol. 47 (July 1965), 176–90; "'The Surge of Republican Power': Partisan Antipathy, American Social Conflict, and the Coming of the Civil War," from Stephen E. Maizlish and John J. Kushma, eds., *Essays on American Antebellum Politics, 1840–1860* (College Station: Texas A & M University Press, 1982).

PREFACE

All but one of the essays included here originally appeared in various professional journals and thematic collections edited by others, but they are closely bound together by an argument and several themes. Each is part of a twenty-five-year effort on my part to understand and explain the thrust and texture of mid-nineteenth-century American politics—an attempt to come to terms with the political dynamics of the generation before the Civil War. The essays present a perspective on how politics was conceived and conducted then. They lay out the era's central tendencies, set forth the evidence on behalf of the argument offered, and knit the whole together into a specific overview of the existing political culture within which Americans responded to the events of the day.

My position on the matters discussed here did not originate nor has it developed in an intellectual vacuum or by my own efforts alone. It reflects, rather, a happy and persistent intellectual interaction with other scholars interested in the same era and its politics—a dialogue that has included both supportive friends and those who disagree with me. In fact, one of the main joys of my long exploration of these topics has been the constant contact with the work of others engaged in the same task, learning from them in innumerable ways. In the footnotes of each of the essays included here their work is listed and their impact on the whole can be traced.

It is impossible to list all of the scholars who have stimulated and instructed me. But several particularly stand out in my memory for their critical role: my teachers, Allan G. Bogue, William O. Aydelotte, and Samuel P. Hays; the pioneers in exploring the boundaries of the new political history: Thomas P. Alexander, Ronald P. Formisano, Michael Holt, Paul Kleppner, Richard P. McCormick, and the late John

Shover; Phyllis Field, Alan Kraut, Robert Hampel, and M. Philip Lucas, who studied with me and taught me as well; and a number of first-rate scholars: William Gienapp, Marc Kruman, and Richard L. McCormick, whose work has been so stimulating from their days as graduate students to the present, when their mature findings are redefining and expanding the field. In a special category is Eric Foner, whose insight into this period, almost always in disagreement with my own, has been so challenging as to provide the best kind of intellectual provocation and excitement.

In bringing these essays together I have been greatly aided in many ways by a web of personal support. My family's toleration, patience, good humor, and warmth provided the kind of environment that made the rest possible. At Cornell, my colleagues, especially Walter LaFeber and Glenn Altschuler, the History Department's formidable support staff led by Anita Reed, the research financing provided by successive department heads, the Provost's office and by the Return Jonathan Meigs research fund, all contributed far beyond the call of duty, as they always have. The Cornell University Library is not what it once was, but remains, because of its staff and its collections, a first-rate home base in which to conduct research in American history.

Sheldon Meyer and Leona Capeless of Oxford University Press have been encouraging, discerning, and splendid editors during the process of turning this manuscript into a finished book. I am deeply grateful to them as I am to Jane Dieckmann who compiled the index with diligence and care.

Finally, but not least, has been the stimulation, good sense, knowledge, and friendship of the two fine scholars to whom this book is dedicated. They have given me much, and have meant more over a very long time indeed.

Ithaca   J. S.
July 1984

CONTENTS

INTRODUCTION

Scholars have devoted a great deal of attention to the pre-Civil War era in the United States, never more so than at present. Throughout the period from the end of the second war with England in 1815 until the firing on Fort Sumter in 1861, Americans were preoccupied by the need to deal with the forces generated by the pressures of internal development and rapid physical and economic growth. Politically, this meant that they were engaged in attempts to work out the meaning of the American experience, to define who they were, where they were going, and to ascertain just what tools of political management and direction they needed to control and guide a pluralist country of continental proportions, democratic realities (and pretensions), and mass political involvement. These monumental tasks produced powerful and well-articulated political tensions in the United States in the first half of the nineteenth century. Economic, social, regional, cultural, and sectional impulses vied for dominance and spilled over into the legislative halls, onto the campaign hustings, and at the polls on election day. Turbulent political confrontation was a constant norm of American life.[1]

It was not so long ago that most historians readily believed that they had a good grasp of the politics in the years that culminated in the American Civil War. They agreed that intimations of that bloody conflict bestrode the whole period before it, casting its shadow everywhere. With their eyes focused primarily on the outcome of the American experience in 1861, most historians usually asserted that the predominant influence in political life was the unrelenting pressure of frag-

1. No one monograph covers the entire field in these terms. Good places to begin to think about the whole include, Lee Benson, *The Concept of Jacksonian Democracy: New York As a Test Case* (Princeton: 1961); and David M. Potter, *The Impending Crisis, 1848–1861* (New York, 1976).

menting sectional political forces fueled by sharp and persistent systemic differences between North and South. As these two sections "increasingly took different paths of economic and social development," Eric Foner has recently summed up, "and as, from the 1830s onward, antagonistic value systems and ideologies grounded in the question of slavery emerged in these sections, the political system inevitably came under severe disruptive pressures." These new pressures could not "be contained within the existing inter-sectional political system."[2]

Since conflict between the two main sections was the critical focus of American political life, fragile political parties scrambled to mirror that basic conflict. Despite their nationalizing pretensions, parties actually incorporated and drew their main sustenance from different alignments of the sectional blocs present on the scene. Whatever national qualities the parties possessed proved weak and unable to sustain themselves in the face of the strong currents that threatened them as the Civil War drew near. The voters primarily mirrored sectional attitudes as well as did representatives in Congress and other state and national policy makers as well. The Civil War was the logical, perhaps inevitable, outcome of such persistent sectional confrontation.[3]

At the same time, historians of the period (as of other periods in the American past) rooted their analysis in what has been labeled the "Progressive" interpretation of American politics. In Charles A. Beard's forceful if inelegant dictum, they believed that in the political world, "economics explains the mostest."[4] Contrasting economic needs— clashes between economic haves and have-nots in the society—and the challenges between different political programs stemming from economic differences underlay political and sectional conflict. These economic matters formed the substance of party warfare in antebellum society. At one level they led individuals to seek out the party that best represented their specific economic interests. At another level, the sum of thousands of such choices evolved into large-scale, economically defined, sectionally rooted blocs. Economics divided sections from each other as it did individuals. It was the motor of political conflict.[5]

In the 1950s, when I began my research into the period, these two perspectives still ordered and explained the events of the time to most

2. Eric Foner, *Politics and Ideology in the Age of the Civil War* (New York, 1980), 35.

3. For a fuller description of these points see, Joel H. Silbey: *The Shrine of Party: Congressional Voting Behavior, 1841–1852* (Pittsburgh, 1967), chap. I: "Sectional Complexity and Interplay."

4. Quoted in John Higham *et al.*, *History* (Englewood Cliffs, N.J., 1965), 230.

5. Richard Hofstadter, *The Progressive Historians: Turner, Beard, Parrington* (New York, 1968).

historians. But their day was largely past. It was becoming clear to many students of the period that the sectionalist perspective had become too loosely and widely applied and, in fact, distorted some important aspects of the reality of the time. Similarly, the research of some historians as well as scholars in other disciplines began to pose a challenge to the socioeconomic determinism that infused so much of the writing of the history of American politics. These scholars argued that despite frequent resentment of social privilege and economic inequities, political conflict rooted in such was never central in the American experience, in fact, was rarer than suggested and, most critically, never sustained for very long.

Such questioning was not simply the product of another reading of the familiar sources with a fresh and skeptical eye. It largely drew sustenance from something else—the development of what has come to be called the new political history—an approach to analysis that involved interweaving of historical research with the methods and speculations of the social sciences. In this view, research was to focus on persistent underlying historical structures rather than on single dramatic episodes; it was to involve consciously subjecting our explanatory propositions to rigorous testing, generally through the systematic statistical manipulation of quantitative evidence. Finally, middle-range sociological and psychological theories about contemporary human behavior were to be cautiously and judiciously fitted to the historical evidence where appropriate to provide helpful explanatory insights. In short, the new political historians sought a more structured, precise, and complete understanding of the past than was thought possible of achievement with the more traditional methods of the historian, fraught as they were with loose taxonomies of causation and proof by haphazard quotation and/or persuasive rhetoric.[6]

The methodological considerations undergirding this approach to past politics have been fully explored by Allan Bogue and others.[7] For my purposes, the methods of the new political historians proved attractive because of their relevance, indeed indispensability, in understanding what went on in the United States in the first half of the nineteenth century. That understanding and its dimensions are the subject of these essays. When I began my examination of this period as a

6. For introductions to these epistemological points, see Lee Benson, *Toward the Scientific Study of History: Selected Essays* (Philadelphia, 1972); and John Higham, *History: Professional Scholarship in America* (Baltimore, 1983).

7. Bogue's writing on this subject provides the clearest introduction to the new political history. See, *Clio and the Bitch Goddess: Quantification in American Political History* (Beverly Hills, Calif., 1983).

graduate student, I was stuck, as others had been, by the strong evidence of the nonsectional, noneconomic sensibilities at play in the political world. As my research deepened and my knowledge of the period grew, I came to agree with and adopt the insights of other new political historians, most notably Lee Benson, who led in forging a new comprehension of the period. The new political historians varied in their methods, interpretations, and emphases to some degree. Nevertheless, their general thrust was clear. Aware that there have been different dominant styles and substances to American politics in different periods, they argued that amidst a number of contradictions and some ambiguities, certain specific strong and determinative patterns particularly characterized antebellum American politics. Their work persuaded me and helped me, in turn, to contribute to their growing perspective. All of the essays included here follow the directions they originally sketched out.

To begin with, each of these pieces is rooted in quantitative analyses of political behavior: the comprehensive measurement of many popular elections and legislative and congressional voting behavior decisions over a long period of time. As with the other new political historians, I sought means to grasp the total behavior of all of the actors in the political universe, rather than relying only on the statements, actions, and behavior of prominent leaders and observers of politics.[8] But the results of that numerical operation were only a first step. They provided the main building blocks that allowed subsequent development of a much different understanding of what was going on in the political world, how people perceived what was at stake in specific elections and legislative decisions, and who and why they reacted as they did.

My research interests came to center most particularly on the nature of political parties in the pre-Civil War era and the reasons for the strong commitments to them then. Exploring these issues led to a much different view about many aspects of politics and of parties than historians usually had held. Three factors distinguish the politics of the period, I argue. First, the shape and thrust of the era's popular politics originated in local and personal, not national, elements. This was not a political world without ideas, conflicts, and differing perspectives about what constituted the general welfare. But the source of those ideas lay outside the traditionally noted places. People defined themselves and sorted themselves out politically because of perceptions growing out of beliefs, experiences, and memories rooted in their home communities. This did not mean that those great issues, the Bank of the United

8. Silbey, *Shrine of Party.*

States, the tariff, and slavery, for example, which have so preoccupied historians, were absent or irrelevant. It did mean that such matters were often filtered through the prism of local outlooks, or took secondary place to local issues among many voters or, on occasion, while present, were not crucial in the political decision making of a large number of Americans. It also meant that Americans constantly made connections between their local perspectives and community anxieties and their perception of national issues and the framework of national political conflict.

Second, national political parties played a primary role in organizing, shaping, and giving life to antebellum politics, not as reflectors of sectional forces but as direct and persistent alternatives to them. Parties organized and overwhelmingly dominated the political dynamics of the age. Political parties were (and are) imperfect institutions. But they developed in antebellum America to meet a specific need: to combine popular expression, collective action, and the always present leadership element of the society, in a relationship designed to forge certain ends in the political system. As they matured the parties took on other, intense qualities as well—what I label a partisan imperative grew in the consciousness of most Americans to shape and direct their politics. That imperative made it clear that political life and individual political choice were partisan; that little could exist in American politics that was not partisan. As a result, those involved in politics, from voters to congressmen, acted less and less as individuals and more and more as parts of a well-defined, collective group with conscious and well-understood ideas and outlooks. As they emerged, issues—even, for a very long time, sectional issues—were tamed and channeled by these same partisan impulses. Those sectional forces, and there were many, had to fit themselves alongside other, more national, issues—they had to give way to the forces of national partisanship, until quite late in the period. Partisan, not sectional, perspectives, in short, more often controlled the American political landscape of the time than did any other basis of division.

Third, party warfare was not devoid of ideological content. But divisions based on socioeconomic tensions within the society fueled partisan conflict only in part. Rather, political forces reflected perspectives rooted in different ethnic and religious attitudes and the persistent hostilities they created. These attitudes repeatedly spilled over onto the political landscape. They shaped popular and legislative voting, party behavior and outlooks, and the way Americans defined and understood issues—that is, much of the texture of antebellum political life. It was not that economic differences did not play a role in political warfare.

They could and often did. But, like sectional influences, they were more intermittent, less overwhelming, less the everyday stuff of political warfare than previously suggested by most historians.

As in most times, then, there was, in these years, general agreement about the style, substance, organization, and boundaries of conventional politics. Within that agreement the parties squared off against one another over specific policies and ways of thinking about the nation's present needs and future prospects. In so doing they gained the support of the bulk of the American electorate. A few people, at the same time, remained outside this partisan consensus. These people sought to think and organize in other ways and to push different matters. Many of them promoted a sectional orientation in politics. Others thought primarily in classic terms of class differences and economic determinism. All of them had some place and played some role in American politics. But they were a minor eddy in the normal flow of political life for much of the antebellum period.

These essays spell out and develop these points.[9] In the first two, written almost twenty years apart, I sought to establish the shape of the political world and the nature of its behavior and organization by engaging in a historiographic presentation of the insights of the new political historians. The record of such research was not very large when the first essay appeared in 1964, and the argument was, therefore, thinner and more tentative than I wanted—if suggestive. By 1983, on the other hand, the amount of work produced allowed the interpre-

---

9. These essays originally appeared as follows: "The Civil War Synthesis in American Political History," *Civil War History* X (June 1964), 130–40; "'Delegates Fresh from the People,': American Congressional and Legislative Behavior," *Journal of Interdisciplinary History* XIII (Spring 1983), 603–27; "Parties and Politics in Mid-Nineteenth Century America," *Capitol Studies* I (Fall 1972), 9–27; "'The Salt of the Nation': Political Parties in Ante-Bellum American," in Richard L. McCormick (ed.), *Political Parties and the Modern State* (New Brunswick, 1984), 21–51; "'Let the People See:' Reflections on Ethnoreligious Forces in American Politics," *Journal of Libertarian Studies* VI (Summer/Fall 1982), 333–47; "'There Are Other Questions Beside That of Slavery Merely': The Democratic Party and Antislavery Politics," in Alan M. Kraut (ed.), *Crusaders and Compromisers: Essays on the Relationship of the Antislavery Struggle to the Antebellum Party System* (Westport, Conn., 1983), 143–75; "The Southern National Democrats, 1845–1861," *Mid-America* XLVII (July 1965), 176–90; "'The Surge of Republican Power': Partisan Antipathy, American Social Conflict, and the Coming of the Civil War," in Stephen E. Maizlish and John J. Kushmas (eds.), *Essays on American Antebellum Politics, 1840–1860* (College Station, Texas, 1982), 199–229. "'The Undisguised Connection,' Know Nothings into Republicans: New York As a Test Case," previously unpublished, was delivered to the annual meeting of the Organization of American Historians in Los Angeles, California, in April 1984.

tation to be moved much further along, although still firmly along the same lines suggested two decades earlier.

The articles of the second set are my attempt to move beyond historiographic presentations and add to the extant research by examining in detail what exactly the partisan imperative was and what it meant to antebellum Americans. Parties and partisan domination did not emerge all at once. One of the major recent findings of the new political historians is the rather extended length of the process of party evolution and partisan digging in.[10] By the late 1830s, however, partisan choices were largely clarified and had increasingly penetrated the minds of those involved in politics. Political elites, thoroughly partisan in their orientation and behavior, led the way. But they were not alone. The masses participated widely in partisan activities, accepted the imperatives of the partisan new order and watched happily as partisan organizations set the agenda of politics. In the Congresses of the 1840s, one can see and appreciate the full dimensions of this potent political force as it flowered, both there in the legislative halls and on the campaign hustings outside as well.

Undergirding what was happening was the basic substance fueling antebellum political warfare—the persistent importance of ethnocultural conflict in America and its deep penetration onto the political scene especially in this part of the nineteenth century.[11] The last essay in this section suggests how such hostilities were able to cut across other differences present and readily incite political confrontation. Certainly, in the years before the Civil War, social stratification, as one main engine of political activity, was repeatedly challenged and undercut by this other most critical and elemental political force.

As the new political historians developed these ideas, other scholars, outside the faith, have rarely wavered in their own commitments. Many have continued to challenge the revisionist perspective in favor of reemphasizing, refining, and making more sophisticated the traditional argument for the primacy of sectional forces and economic differences in the politics of the era.[12] They find the Civil War synthesis reasonable, and still persuasive, if in need of some limited modification. They generally mention the perspectives of the new political historians but

10. Ronald P. Formisano, *The Transformation of Political Culture: Massachusetts Parties, 1790s–1840s* (New York, 1983); M. Philip Lucas, "The Development of the Second Party System in Mississippi, 1817–1846" (Ph.D. diss., Cornell University, 1983).

11. Robert Kelley, *The Cultural Pattern in American Politics: The First Century* (New York, 1979).

12. Foner, *Politics and Ideology*.

their own emphasis remains as it was, on the sectional elements in the political arena. Southern politics, as one prime example, was "the politics of slavery"—that is, primarily of sectional concerns and tensions even if encased within a two-party structure.[13]

This continued emphasis is directly confronted and weighed in the final essays included here. Both in Congress and elsewhere, Americans involved in antebellum politics felt the strength of the sectional breezes blowing through American life in the 1840s and 1850s. But their reaction to those breezes suggests the toughness and dominance of the partisan imperative. Legislators, party leaders, and voters proved reluctant to shuck the way they approached politics, that is through their party identification. Democrats (who comprised a majority of the electorate until near the very end of the period) in particular remained resistant to the pressures of sectional tides and spokesmen. As a result, few Americans, even those most exposed, as among the Democrats in the South, readily fell into line as sectionalism heated up. Other forces and reactions could still be brought into play, effectively and persistently, if not permanently, among these men.

Those historians who continue to argue for the primacy of sectional forces and the slavery issues in antebellum America are especially caustic about the relationship between the findings of the new political history and the central event that culminated the era—the secession crisis and the ensuing Civil War. How can ethnocultural conflict, for example, help us understand the working out of a phenomenon rooted in the economics, psychology, and sociology of the slave system? What happened to the allegedly powerful political parties with their antisectional perspectives during the crisis of the Union? The Civil War's outbreak, in this view, clearly indicated, as it always had, what was really at stake and what shaped politics on the American scene at the end of the day.[14]

The last two essays in this collection seek to address that particular challenge. The rise of the Republican party in the 1850s has been traditionally seen as the capstone of sectional politics—and in many ways it was. But the rest of the equation does not necessarily follow. The Republican party articulated a strong sectionalist, anti-Southern perspective. But it also drew a great deal of sustenance from the per-

13. William J. Cooper, Jr., *The South and the Politics of Slavery, 1828–1856* (Baton Rouge, 1978); and Cooper, *Liberty and Slavery: Southern Politics to 1860* (New York: 1983).

14. "The new interpretation [of the new political historians] leaves a yawning gap between political processes and the outbreak of war." Foner, *Politics and Ideology,* 19.

sistence of the traditional divisions over ethnic and religious matters in American society. So did other Northerners, not in the Republican party, who refused to allow the onset of sectional confrontation to divert their attention from their customary partisan concerns and loyalties. Quite the contrary in fact.[15]

Similarly, on the other side of Mason and Dixon's line, Southern secessionists capped their political experience in this era by testifying to the strength of party loyalties in defining the secession crisis, and to the continuing importance of ethnoreligious attitudes in helping them make sense of the Republican onslaught. As Marc Kruman has recently stated, in words that effectively argue what I have sketched out here, party politics in North Carolina "molded what North Carolinians expected from government, how they democratized their political system, how they understood the sectional conflict, how they responded to the secession crisis. . . . On every vital matter affecting the society, party politics substantially influenced what white North Carolinians believed and how they behaved from the late 1830s to the end of the Civil War."[16] Southern behavior in the secession crisis, it seems to me, demonstrated how the forces other than sectionalism defined reactions to events involving nonpartisan elements in this particular political culture.

Taken as a whole, these essays suggest something of the capacity of the new political history to rethink, recast, and reweave our understanding of the pre-Civil War era in particular, and of the general shape and thrust of American politics in general. The partisan imperative is a major key to comprehending the period after 1815 and confronting historical controversy about it. Still, although forcefully articulated (and strongly demonstrated), as here and elsewhere, as in Kruman's work, the argument remains incomplete. These essays elaborate a viewpoint rooted in a particular style of historical research. They are nowhere near the last word on these matters—nor can they be. Rather, they seek to provide an insight into the forces that shaped that particular political world and the reactions of the participants. Others have also called attention to some of what I discuss here.[17] No one has, as yet, offered a

15. Joel H. Silbey, *A Respectable Minority: The Democratic Party in the Civil War, 1860-1868* (New York, 1977).

16. Marc Kruman, *Parties and Politics in North Carolina, 1836-1865* (Baton Rouge, 1983), xiv.

17. Robert P. Swierenga (ed.), *Beyond the Civil War Synthesis: Political Essays of the Civil War Era* (Westport, Conn., 1975); Richard L. McCormick, "The Party Period and Public Policy: An Exploratory Hypothesis," *Journal of American History* LVI (September 1979), 279-98.

coherent perspective, an organic whole, on these matters. Thus, the system's anatomy is suggested, but its connecting tissue and the exact configurations of its thousands of cells have not been fully examined. A sustained, in depth description and analysis is still needed—a full mapping of the whole—before all parts of the picture will be clear. Much of the evidence for such a finished description exists, and the act of bringing it together is presently engaging a number of historians including myself. In the interim, these essays, by defining, clarifying, and taking stock on where we are, may prove useful to those interested in understanding the central core of the critical antebellum years of American political history.

ONE:
THE HISTORIOGRAPHIC
FOUNDATION

1

THE CIVIL WAR SYNTHESIS IN AMERICAN POLITICAL HISTORY
(1964)

The Civil War has dominated our studies of the period between the Age of Jackson and 1861. Most historians of the era have devoted their principal attention to investigating and analyzing the reasons for differences between the North and South, the resulting sectional conflict, and the degeneration of this strife into a complete breakdown of our political system in war. Because of this focus, most scholars have accepted, without question, that differences between the North and the South were the major political influences at work among the American people in the years between the mid-1840s and the war.[1] Despite occasional warnings about the dangers of overemphasizing sectional influences, the sectional interpretation holds an honored and secure place in the historiography of the antebellum years.[2] We now possess a formidable number of works which, in one way or another, center attention on the politics of sectionalism and clearly demonstrate how much the Civil War dominates our study of American political history before 1861.[3]

Obviously nothing is wrong in such emphasis if sectionalism was indeed the dominant political influence in the antebellum era. However, there is the danger in such emphasis of claiming too much, that in centering attention on the war and its causes we may ignore or play down other contemporary political influences and fail to weigh adequately the importance of nonsectional forces in antebellum politics. And, in fact, several recent studies of American political behavior have raised serious doubts about the importance of sectional differences as far as most Americans were concerned. These have even suggested that the sectional emphasis has created a false synthesis in our study of history which increases the importance of one factor, ignores the significance of other factors, and ultimately distorts the reality of American political life between 1844 and 1861.

I

Scholars long have used the presidential election of 1844 as one of their major starting points for the sectional analysis of American political history. In a general sense they have considered American expansion into Texas to be the most important issue of that campaign. The issue stemmed from the fact that Texas was a slave area and many articulate Northerners attacked the movement to annex Texas as a slave plot designed to enhance Southern influence within the Union. Allegedly because of these attacks, and the Southerners' defending themselves, many people in both North and South found themselves caught up in such sectional bitterness that the United States took a major step toward civil war.[4] Part of this bitterness can be seen, it is pointed out, in the popular vote in New York State where the Whig candidate for the presidency, Henry Clay, lost votes to the abolitionist Liberty party because he was a slaveholder.[5] The loss of these votes cost him New York and ultimately the election. As a result of Clay's defeat, historians have concluded that as early as 1844 the problem of slavery extension was important enough to arouse people to act primarily in sectional terms and thus for this episode to be a milestone on the road to war.

Recently Professor Lee Benson published a study of New York State politics in the Jacksonian era.[6] Although Benson mainly concerned himself with other problems, some of his findings directly challenge the conception that slavery and sectional matters were of major importance in New York in 1844. In his analysis Benson utilized a more systematic statistical compilation of data than have previous workers in the field of political history.[7] Observing that scholars traditionally have looked at what people said they did rather than at what they actually did, Benson compiled a great number of election returns for New York State in this period. His purpose was to see who actually voted for whom and to place the election in historical perspective by pinpointing changes in voting over time and thus identifying the basic trends of political behavior. Through such analysis Benson arrived at a major revision of the nature of New York State voting in 1844.

Benson pointed out, first of all, that the abolitionist, anti-Texas Liberty party whose vote total should have increased if the New York population wanted to strike against a slave plot in Texas, actually lost votes over what it had received in the most immediate previous election, that of 1843.[8] Further analysis indicated that there was no widespread reaction to the Texas issue in New York state on the part of any large group of voters, although a high degree of anti-Texas feeling indeed existed among certain limited groups in the population. Such sentiment, however, did not affect voting margins in New York State.[9] Finally, Benson concluded that mass voting in New York in 1844 pivoted not on the sectional issue but rather on more traditional divisions between ethnic and religious groups whose voting was a reaction to matters closer to home. These proved of a more personal and psychological nature than that of Texas and its related issue of slavery extension.[10] Sectional bitterness, contrary to previous historical conceptions, neither dominated nor seriously influenced the 1844 vote in New York. Although Benson confined his study to one state, his conclusions introduce doubts about the influence of sectionalism in other supposedly less pivotal states.

II

Another aspect of the sectional interpretation of American politics in the pre-Civil War era involves Congress. Political historians have considered that body to be both a forum wherein leaders personally expressed attitudes that intensified sectional bitterness, as well as an arena which reflected the general pattern of influences operative in the country at large.[11] Therefore, writers on the period have considered the behavior of congressmen to have been more and more dominated by sectionalism, particularly after David Wilmot introduced his antislavery extension proviso into the House of Representatives in 1846. Although there may have been other issues and influences present, it is accepted that these were almost completely overborne in the late 1840s and 1850s in favor of a widespread reaction to sectional differences.[12]

In a recently completed study, I have analyzed congressional voting in the allegedly crucial pivotal decade 1841–52, the period which historians identify as embodying the transition from nationalism to sectionalism in congressional behavior.[13] This examination indicates that a picture of the decade as one in which sectional influences steadily grew stronger, overwhelmed all other bases of divisions, and became a permanent feature of the voting behavior of a majority of congressmen, is grossly oversimplified and a distortion of reality. In brief, although sectional influences, issues, and voting did exist, particularly between 1846 and 1850, sectional matters were not the only problems confronting congressmen. In the period before the introduction of the Wilmot Proviso in 1846, national issues such as the tariff, financial policy, foreign affairs, and land policy divided congressmen along political, not sectional, lines.[14] Furthermore, in this earlier period issues which many believed to have shown a high degree of sectional content, such as admittance of Texas and Oregon, reveal highly partisan national divisions and little sectional voting.[15]

Even after the rise of the slavery-extension issue, other questions of a national character remained important. Slavery was but one of several issues before Congress and it was quite possible for congressmen to vote against one another as Northern and Southern sectionalists on an issue and then to join together, regardless of section, against other Northerners and Southerners on another matter. Certainly some men from both geographic areas were primarily influenced by sectional considerations at all times on all issues, but they were a minority of all congressmen in the period. The majority of congressmen were not so overwhelmingly influenced by their being Northerners or Southerners, but continued to think and act in national terms, and even resisted attempts by several sectionally minded congressmen to forge coalitions, regardless of party, against the other section.[16]

A careful study of congressional voting in these years also demonstrates that another assumption of historians about the nature of politics is oversimplified: the period around 1846 did *not* begin the steady forward movement of congressional politics toward sectionalism and war. Rather, it was quite possible in the period between 1846 and 1852 for congressmen to assail one another bitterly in sectional terms, physically attack one another, and even threaten secession, and still for the majority of them to return in the following session to a different approach—that of nonsectional political differences with a concomitant restoration of nonsectional coalitions. For example, it was possible in 1850, after several years of sectional fighting, for a national coalition of Senators and Representatives to join together and settle in compromise terms the differences between North and South over expansion. And they were able to do this despite the simultaneous existence of a great deal of sectional maneuvering by some congressmen in an attempt to prevent any such compromise. Furthermore, during this same session Congress also dealt with matters of railroad land grants in a way that eschewed sectional biases.[17] Obviously the usual picture of an inexorable growth of sectional partisanship after 1846 is quite overdone. And lest these examples appeared to be isolated phenomena, preliminary research both by Gerald Wolff and by myself demonstrates that as late as 1854 there was still no complete or overwhelming sectional voting even on such an issue as the Kansas-Nebraska Act.[18]

Such analyses of congressional behavior in an alleged transition period reinforce what Lee Benson's work on New York politics demonstrated:

many varieties and many complexities existed with respect to political behavior in the antebellum period, so that even slavery failed to be a dominating influence among all people at all times—or even among most people at most times—during the 1840s and early 1850s. Again, our previous image of American politics in this period must be reconsidered in light of this fact and despite the emergence of a Civil War in 1861.

III

Perhaps no aspect of antebellum politics should demonstrate more fully the overpowering importance of sectional influences than the presidential election of 1860. In the preliminaries to that contest the Democratic party split on the rock of slavery, the Republican party emerged as a power in the Northern states with a good chance of winning the presidency, and loud voices in the Southern states called for secession because of Northern attacks on their institutions.[19] In dealing with these events, historians, as in their treatment of other aspects of antebellum politics, have devoted their primary attention to sectional bickering and maneuvering among party leaders, because they considered this activity to be the most important facet of the campaign and the key to explaining the election.[20] Although such a focus obviously has merit if one is thinking in terms of the armed conflict which broke out only five months after the election, once again, as in the earlier cases considered here, recent research has raised pertinent questions about the political realities of the situation. We may indeed ask what were the issues of the campaign as seen by the majority of voters.

Earlier studies of the 1860 election, in concerning themselves primarily with the responses and activities of political leaders, have taken popular voting behavior for granted. This aspect has either been ignored or else characterized as reflecting the same influences and attitudes as that of the leadership. Therefore, the mass of men, it is alleged, voted in response to sectional influences in 1860. For instance, several scholars concerned with the Germans in the Middle West in this period have characterized the attitudes of that group as overwhelmingly antislavery. Thus the Republican party attracted the mass of the German vote because the liberal "Forty-Eighters" saw casting a Lincoln vote as a way to strike a blow against slavery in the United States.[21] Going beyond this, some historians have reached similar conclusions about other Middle Western immigrant groups.[22] As a result, according to most historians, although narrowly divided, the area went for Lincoln thanks in large part to its newest citizens, who were Northern sectionalists in their political behavior. Such conclusions obviously reinforce the apparent importance of geographic partisanship in 1860.

Testing this hypothesis, two recent scholars systematically studied and analyzed election returns in Iowa during 1860. Such examinations are important because they should reveal, if the sectional theory is correct, preoccupation among Iowa voters—especially immigrants—with the slavery question and the increasingly bitter differences between North and South. Only one of these studies, that of Professor George H. Daniels of Northwestern University, has appeared in print.[23] But Daniels's findings shatter earlier interpretations which pin-pointed sectional concerns as the central theme of the 1860 election.

Briefly stated, Daniels isolated the predominantly German townships in Iowa and, following Lee Benson's methodological lead, analyzed their vote. He found that, far from being solidly Republican voters, or moved primarily by the slavery question, the Germans of Iowa voted overwhelmingly in favor of the Democratic party. And Daniels discovered that the primary issue motivating the Germans in 1860 was an ethnic one. They were conscious of the anti-alien Know-Nothing movement which had been so strong in the United States during the 1850s and they identified the Republican party as the heir and last refuge of Know-Nothingism.[24] If the Germans of Iowa were attracted to the Republicans by the latter's antislavery attitudes, such attraction was more than overcome by the Republicans' aura of antiforeignism.[25] Furthermore, the Republicans were also identified in the minds of the Iowa Germans as the party of prohibitionism, a social view strongly opposed by most Germans.[26] Thus, as Daniels concludes, ". . . The rank and file Germans who did the bulk of the voting considered their own liberty to be of paramount importance. Apparently ignoring the advice of their leaders, they cast their ballots for the party which consistently promised them liberty from prohibition and native-American legislation."[27] As a result, the Germans of Iowa voted Democratic, not Republican, in 1860.

Lest this appear to be an isolated case, the research of Robert Swierenga on Dutch voting behavior in Iowa in 1860 confirms Daniels's findings. Swierenga demonstrated that the Dutch also voted Democratic despite their vaunted antislavery attitudes; again, revulsion from certain Republican ideals overpowered any attraction toward that party on the slavery issue.[28]

Such research into the election of 1860, as in the earlier cases of the election of 1844 and congressional voting behavior in the 1840s and early 1850s, suggests how far the sectional and slavery preconceptions of American historians have distorted reality. Many nonsectional issues were apparently more immediately important to the groups involved than any imminent concern with Northern-Southern differences. Once again, the Civil War synthesis appears to be historically inaccurate and in need of serious revision.

IV

Several other provocative studies recently have appeared which, while dealing with nonpolitical subjects, support the conclusion that sectional problems, the slavery issue, and increasing bitterness between North and South were not always uppermost concerns to most Americans in the fifteen years before the outbreak of the war. Building upon the work of Leon Litwack, which emphasizes the general Northern antagonism toward the Negro before 1860, and that of Larry Gara demonstrating the fallacy of the idea that a well-organized and widespread underground railroad existed in the North,[29] Professor C. Vann Woodward has cautioned students against an easy acceptance of a "North-Star" image—a picture of a universally militant Northern population determined to ease the burden of the slave in America.[30] Rather, as Woodward points out, a great many Northerners remained indifferent to the plight of the slave and hostile to the would-be antislavery reformer in their midst.[31]

In this same tenor, Milton Powell of Michigan State University has challenged long-held assumptions that the Northern Methodist church was a bulwark of antislavery sentiment after splitting with its Southern branch in 1844. As Powell makes clear, Northern Methodists were concerned about many other problems in which slavery played no part, as well as being beset by conditions which served to tone down any antislavery attitudes they may have held. More importantly, this led many of them to ignore slavery as an issue because of its latent tendency to divide the organization to which they belonged.[32] Thus, even in areas outside of the political realm, the actual conditions of antebellum society challenge the validity of the sectional concept in its most general and far-reaching form.

V

This review of recent research indicates that much of our previous work on the prewar period should be reexamined free from the bias caused by looking first at the fact of the Civil War and then turning back to view the events of the previous decade in relation only to that fact. Although it is true that the studies discussed here are few in number and by no means include the entire realm of American politics in the antebellum era, their diversity in time and their revisionist conclusions do strongly suggest the fallacy of many previous assumptions. No longer should any historian blithely accept the traditional concept of a universal preoccupation with the sectional issue.

But a larger matter is also pointed up by this recent research and the destruction of this particular myth about political sectionalism. For a question immediately arises as to how historians generally could have accepted so readily and for so long such oversimplifications and inaccuracies. Fortunately for future research, answers to this question have been implicitly given by the scholars under review, and involve methodological problems concerning evidence and a certain naïveté about the political process.

Historians generally have utilized as evidence the writings and commentaries of contemporary observers of, and participants in, the events being examined. But, as both Benson and Daniels emphasize, this can endanger our understanding of reality. For instance, not enough attention has been paid to who actually said what, or of the motives of a given reporter or the position he was in to know and understand what was going on around him. Most particularly, scholars have not always been properly skeptical about whether the observer's comments truly reflected actuality. As Daniels pointed out in his article on German voting behavior, "contemporary opinion, including that of newspapers, is a poor guide."[33]

If such is true, and the evidence presented by these studies indicates that it is, a question is raised as to how a historian is to discover contemporary opinion if newspapers are not always reliable as sources. The work of Benson, Daniels, and myself suggests an answer: the wider use of statistics. When we talk of public opinion (that is, how the mass of men acted or thought) we are talking in terms of aggregate numbers, of majorities. One way of determining what the public thought is by measuring majority opinion in certain circumstances—elections, for example, or the voting of congressmen—and then analyzing the content and breakdown of the figures derived. If, for example, 80 percent of the Germans in Iowa voted Democratic in 1860, this tells us more about German public opinion in 1860 than does a sprightly quote from one of the Germans in the other 20 percent who voted Republican "to uphold freedom." Historians are making much more use of statistics than formerly and are utilizing more sophisticated techniques of quantitative analysis. And such usage seems to be prelude to, judging by the works discussed here, a fuller and more accurate understanding of our past.

There are also other ways of approaching the problems posed by the 1850s. Not enough attention has been paid, it seems to me, to the fact that there are many different levels of political behavior—mass voting, legislative activity, leadership manipulation, for example—and that what is influential and important on one level of politics may not be on another. Certainly the Germans and Dutch of Iowa in 1860 were not paying much attention to the desires of their leaders. They were responding to influences deemed more important than those influences shaping the responses of their leaders. As Swierenga pointed out in his analysis of Dutch voting:

> While Scholte [a leader of the Dutch community] fulminated against Democrats as slave mongers, as opponents of the Pacific Railroad and Homestead Bills, and as destroyers of the Constitution, the Dutch citizens blithely ignored him and the national issues he propounded and voted their personal prejudices against Republican nativists and prohibitionists.[34]

Obviously, when historians generalize about the nature of political behavior they must also be sure which group and level of political activity they mean, and so identify it, and not confuse different levels or assume positive correlations between the actions of people on one level with those on another level. Such precision will contribute greatly to accuracy and overcome tendencies toward distortion.

Finally, based on the work under discussion here, it is clear that historians must become more aware of the complexities of human behavior. All people, even of the same stratum of society or living in the same geographic area, do not respond with the same intensity to the same social or political stimuli. Not everyone perceives his best interests in the same way, or considers the same things to be the most important problems confronting him. Depending upon time and circumstances, one man may respond primarily to economic influences; another one, at the same time and place, to religious influences; and so on. Sometimes most people in a given community will respond to the same influences equally, but we must be careful to observe *when* this is true and not generalize from it that this is *always* true. Single-factor explanations for human behavior do not seem to work, and we must remain aware of that fact.

With improved methodological tools and concepts historians may begin to engage in more systematic and complete analyses of popular voting, legislative voting, and the motivations and actions of political leaders. They will be able to weigh the relative influence of sectional problems against other items of interest and concern on all levels of political behavior. Until this is done, however, we do know on the basis of what already has been suggested that we cannot really accept glib explanations about the antebellum period. The Civil War has had a pernicious influence on the study of American political development that preceded it—pernicious because it has distorted the reality of political behavior in the era and has caused an overemphasis on sectionalism. It has led us to look not for what was occurring in American politics in those years, but rather for what was occurring in American politics that tended toward sectional breakdown and civil war—a quite different matter.

2

"DELEGATES FRESH FROM THE PEOPLE": AMERICAN CONGRESSIONAL AND LEGISLATIVE BEHAVIOR (1983)

Systematic quantitative research in congressional and state legislative history has the same virtues as similar research in other areas: the ability to examine the behavior of large masses of individuals with great precision and to uncover insights and relationships hitherto unknown or only partially understood. History of this kind attempts to refine crude generalizations and impressionistic hunches, to clarify old and contentious problems, and to open up new ideas and problems. If political history is only "surface history," as researchers of the Annales school have suggested, that surface still needs to be clearly marked and understood for other purposes.[1]

Most students of legislative history would reject the Annales stereotype, however. Andrew Jackson once referred to members of a Democratic national convention as "delegates fresh from the people." The same imagery with the same meaning reflects one of the prime motivations stimulating recent work in congressional-legislative voting behavior by historians. Most research has been guided by the idea that "the study of Congress can be much more than the study of a political institution and its functions; it can also be a study of the political life of the entire society."[2]

Legislative voting behavior, in this view, is not the ritualistic recording of decisions made elsewhere. Rather, it is part of the battleground between contending forces in the society. Congress and the state legislatures, in the way they behave, reflect these external forces battling for specific public policies. But the legislative bodies contribute to that battle as well as being possessors of power and influence in their own right. Important decisions occur there. At each stage in the process of shaping public policy, including battles at the legislative level, much happens to

alter and affect the societal forces in combat. Thus, the behavior of
Congress and its state equivalents deserves independent analysis as part
of the larger process of understanding a political system constantly in
conflict, at the polls, in the bureaucratic offices, in the White House and
governors' mansions, and in legislative chambers as well.

In his essay on historians and the study of legislative behavior Allan
Bogue suggests a formal model of legislative activity that reflects this
point of view. The model is divided into three stages, two of them
before the actual vote on a bill, the third, the vote itself. The first stage
consists of the preliminary set of sociopolitical forces shaping the way
that the individual legislator approaches a voting decision. It focuses on
the milieu, personal and environmental, out of which a political tendency,
a thrust toward a particular choice, is formed. The second stage consists
of the immediate framing of the choice at a specific moment—when a
congressman, with his intellectual baggage, reacts to the pressures that
are present and makes his decision. This stage includes the cues and
pressures within Congress: from one's colleagues, his party, and committee leaders. The whole process of decision making is not a unitary
one, given its several parts and the possible interplay of many forces at
each step. The actual vote is the result of the interplay of all of these
forces on each individual legislator.[3]

It cannot be said that historians of congressional and legislative behavior have followed through on all of the elements of this model.
Rather, the work of the past generation of quantitative studies of
congressional and legislative behavior has involved primarily the final
stage: the examination of roll-call voting behavior. In 1967, the first
book-length roll-call studies of the American Congress utilizing the
new systematic commitments and quantitative methods appeared. In
the next few years there were several articles, a few additional books,
and a number of doctoral dissertations completed on various eras of the
American legislative experience. They have unevenly covered (or at least
touched on) every period of American history since the late colonial era,
ranging from Henderson's study of the Continental Congress under the
Articles of Confederation, to Hilty's study of New Deal congressional
behavior and Reichard's analysis of Dwight Eisenhower's first Congress.[4]

The earliest roll-call studies were inclusive: their scope was the total
behavior in the individual sessions of a single or series of Congresses.
Thus, I began with all of the members and all of the roll-calls in the eras
that I considered, and I tried to delineate the nature of the patterns
present. But not all of the published roll-call studies attempt such coverage. Often their focus is on a bloc within the whole, the Radical Repub-

licans in the Civil War era, for example; on a single bill, such as Kansas-Nebraska; or on a specific policy area, such as banking or agricultural policy, either in the short term or over a longer period. They do not attempt to understand the totality of congressional behavior as the earlier books have done. Some have isolated and placed blocs and individuals within the larger patterns of the voting of the entire legislature: where Harry Truman, the Southern Democrats, the liberals in the House, or the conservative coalition stood in relation to the whole.[5]

Finally, there is a set of studies where congressional behavior itself is not the main focus of research. Rather, roll-calls are used, where appropriate, to draw out evidence on matters which are the primary concern. Students of farm protests in the 1930s or American relations with Panama, for example, include some legislative analysis to elucidate vital points. Although they are not primarily legislative studies of the kind discussed here, they ought to be mentioned as part of the ongoing development of studies of congressional and legislative behavior.[6]

Although these studies have touched upon most eras of American history, they have tended to be episodic, clustering around a few moments and important subjects: the War of 1812, the era of sectional controversy, Reconstruction, the Populist-Progressive years, and the New Deal. Topically, there is heavy emphasis on foreign affairs in studies of the War of 1812, on economic affairs in the Reconstruction period, and on southern behavior throughout. The reason for such coverage lies in what these studies do in the first instance. They have generally been tests of previously held judgments and assumptions deeply imbedded in the existing literature but never previously based on strong empirical foundations.[7]

Roll-call studies of state legislative behavior have also increasingly appeared in the last decade, although not in the same profusion as the congressional studies. "The American state legislatures," Campbell wrote five years ago, "are an underdeveloped historical resource." Nevertheless, much seems now to be happening. Beginning with Davis's important article in 1970, several other historians have contributed important studies. There is not as yet, however, wide or systematic coverage in these works of all states or all periods of American history.[8]

Roll-call studies do not involve only quantitative manipulation. Historians have gone beyond the delimiting and ordering of behavior to examine, classify, and evaluate the patterns revealed. All of the roll-call studies have linked the voting alignments to the social and political dynamics likely to shape the behavior of the congressmen. The assumptions about this relationship have always been clear: that the roll-calls reflect some type of personal or group attribute and that the important question for the roll-call analyst is to discover which elements, alone or in combination, best explain the quantitative patterns present.

In keeping with the accepted assumption that a pluralism of political forces has generally existed in the United States, each capable of influencing an individual legislator's or a bloc's behavior, analysts have primarily tested for the range of explanatory forces which had previously been articulated in the literature as the primary behavioral elements at work. First, the power of sectional alignments in American politics, always a central concern of American political historians, and second, the strength of partisan voting, given the power and persistence of parties throughout our history, were the primary elements examined in the early congressional studies. Logically following from this came consideration of subsectional and regional groupings as well as different factions within the larger blocs. At the same time, a number of studies also tried to relate the patterns to other forces: the nature of the economic and social forces in specific constituencies, or the level of political competition between the parties within districts as determinants of individual voting behavior.

In all of these efforts, the quantitative techniques used have been borrowed largely from the social sciences. Methods have varied widely in degree of sophistication and in application. Nevertheless, historians have moved beyond simple percentaging or adding of yeas and nays in unsystematic fashion. Cluster blocs, indices of cohesion, agreement and disagreement, factor analysis, and, most particularly, Guttman scaling, have been the tools of this methodological foray. At first a single method was used but, increasingly in recent work, a wider range of methods has been found relevant. There has been some argument over the appropriateness of one method as against another for the best and most precise results. Not all of these disagreements have been resolved. Nevertheless, one can take the optimistic view and argue that each method and approach has made some contribution to this vast and expanding enterprise of the roll-call analysis of congressional and legislative behavior.

No survey of recent investigation of congressional behavior by historians is complete if focused solely on roll-call studies. There have been other types of analysis by quantitative means. The most vigorous research beyond the roll-call deals with the recruitment and social background of legislators. Scholars have asked who was recruited to serve in particular Congresses and legislatures and how they differed from one another socially and biographically. They have considered class (and caste), region, and cultural characteristics, particularly social background, wealth, ethnoreligious identification, political experience, and role for large universes of legislators with the assumption that these are key indicators, both to behavior and to the nature of the representative institutions themselves. Again, the emphasis has usually been on covering the entire group at a particular time, as in Alexander and Beringer's study of the members of the Confederate Congress, or Main's analysis of the membership of the upper houses of the colonial legislatures.[9]

The way American legislatures behave has not only been shaped by forces in the external environment interplaying with the individual legislator. Congress and state legislatures often contain complex internal mechanisms: leadership positions and committee structures that influence individual and group decisions. From the beginning of Congress some senators and representatives have had more power than others. Lobbying and similar activities have also contributed to the final shape of legislation. Although political scientists have filled shelves with studies of these forces and of the impact that they have on congressional behavior in the complex legislative world of recent eras, historians have barely touched on these activities and institutions in any systematic fashion.[10] For one thing, the political science studies have come primarily through a method unavailable to historians: the systematic interviewing of congressmen about matters. Much of that kind of activity is not recoverable in anything more than anecdotal and random form. Nevertheless, a number of historians are now engaged in attempts to develop an understanding of these elements.[11]

What has all of the work done over the past two decades added up to substantively? Clearly, the classification of roll-call behavior has sharpened and clarified our knowledge substantially. Historians are asking new questions and thinking in new ways about the evidence available. Students of legislative behavior have also dramatically recast aspects of our vision of the political world. Some findings have been surprising, some much less so. Most suggest repeatedly how structured, not random, were the patterns of response by individual legislators to the issues of their day, and how much continuity there has been to that structure. That is because the rhythms of Congress have usually been partisan. Party membership has generally been the strongest influence in shaping the way representatives voted. The same has also been true for the far different world of various state legislatures.

Such conclusions are not surprising in a political environment increasingly permeated by partisan institutions and outlooks. Although fully developed partisan structures and attitudes did not emerge at the beginning of national politics, in the Continental Congress and from the first Congress onward two separate blocs appeared that repeatedly voted against one another. Over the years party labels became attached to these blocs and remained. The blocs themselves hardened into distinct sides. As Mary Ryan sums up her work on the 1790s, "by 1796 all classes of issues before Congress had become foci of party loyalty."[12]

Although such partisan patterns never reached into every aspect of congressional activity and rose and fell in importance, party labels continued to be the best predictors of congressional behavior at critical points over the next decade. For example, in the many studies of Congress's decision to vote for war in 1812, party divisions dominated the findings. As Hatzenbuehler has written, "Republican party unity was the determining factor in the decision of the House of Representatives to declare war on Great Britain." Nor was this pattern surprising, sudden, or new. Congressional voting, partisan as it was, Bell argues, "was substantially the same [in 1812] . . . as it has been over two decades."[13]

Even as Federalism collapsed in the aftermath of the War of 1812, partisan memories continued to "make a difference" and affect some legislative behavior well into the Era of Good Feelings, although partisan commitments no longer played the "commanding role" that they had earlier. Nielsen found consistent voting blocs existing in 1819 and continuing to build up thereafter. Their development was neither uniform nor present on all matters before the House. Nevertheless, it was in the House of Representatives in this period that Congressman Churchill Cambreleng of New York argued that parties were "indispensable to every Administration . . . essential to the existence of our institutions."[14]

Partisan clues were abundant. In his pioneering study of the Washington environment in the first quarter of the nineteenth century, Young stressed the importance of boarding house groups on Capitol Hill in shaping congressional behavior in committee and on the floor. He argued that the particular housing arrangements of congressmen were based on local, regional, and sectional tendencies and contributed to a fractured, nonorganized political situation. But Bogue and Marlaire showed, contrary to Young's assertion, that these boarding house groups had a definite partisan cast. If they were important influences on congressional behavior, as Young had argued, they were adding to and reinforcing a growing partisan quality to legislative life in Washington, not merely reflecting or intensifying sectional, regional, or local impulses. To Bogue and Marlaire "some sense of party affiliation can apparently be attributed to the majority of the congressmen of 1821–1822."[15]

By 1825–1827, Nielsen further argues, a clear two-coalition situation was evident in Congress. With a great deal of consistency men were voting with one another against a similarly consistent bloc of congressmen on the other side of the aisle. The significance of these voting blocs has to be underscored. There was as yet little in the way of a highly developed party structure either in the external political environment or in either house of Congress, but more than randomness or accident was frequently at work. And as the proto-partisan organizations in existence continued to develop into wide-ranging, cue-giving structures, at first fitfully and then with a rush through the 1830s, the impact was clear: as party structures developed rapidly and extensively outside Congress, partisanship permeated everywhere, reinforcing the tendency to act in a partisan manner once on Capitol Hill. Congressmen were elected as partisans, carried specific party labels into office with them, and reflected partisan battles over issues and candidates at the local level.[16]

In the 1840s, partisan behavior reached its greatest heights to that time. Despite extensive differences among districts and regions electing the congressmen, "in the actual roll-call voting, the heterogeneity was compressed, with only a few dissenters, within a stable, wide-ranging, and large-scale system of national parties." And these votes reflected real differences over issues—that is, the parties divided from one another on a whole range of issue areas, consistently and repeatedly. One can define where the parties stood on issues by the behavior of each party's representatives on roll-calls in economic areas, social policy, and usually in foreign affairs. Legislative voting behavior squared consistently with rhetorical positions taken by party representatives in pamphlets, editorials, and on the hustings.[17]

Once clearly established, the basic partisan pattern remained. Even during the growing sectional tensions of the 1850s, party continued to play an important role in congressional behavior. Wolff found the pulls of partisanship still at work during the session of Congress that produced the Kansas-Nebraska Act. Later, whether in the Civil War Senate, or both houses in the 1870s, 1880s, and 1890s, the party divisions that had taken such deep root in American culture continued to affect legislative voting. Shade sums up the years after the Civil War as an era of "continuous, high, and fairly stable partisanship in the United States Senate running up to the turn of the century."[18]

In the Progressive era during the early twentieth century, despite Republican insurgency and the alleged introduction of new ideological divisions along a progressive-conservative continuum, several historians have shown, as Clubb and Allen put it, that "the issues of the Progressive Era were fought out within the framework of traditional partisan alignments." Although such partisan cohesion in Congress declined during the twentieth century, most markedly after 1945, it continued to manifest itself throughout the era. In the 1920s and 1930s, partisanship continually played an important structuring role. In the former decade, as one example, Olssen suggests that "bipartisan cooperation" was "difficult" for progressive Democrats, despite the similarity of their views to those held by progressive Republicans and the opportunity often offered for both groups to work together in bipartisan fashion against the conservative elements in Congress. Hilty concludes his study of the Senate in the 1930s in words familiar through repetition: "Perhaps the most striking feature of Senate voting during the New Deal was the recurrent partisanship." Despite decline thereafter, it still appears. As recently as the Panama Canal debates in 1976, House voting reflected strong partisan stances with support for the treaty coming from Democrats and opposition from Republicans, although there were some defections.[19]

The same pattern emerges in the available studies of state legislative voting from the Confederation period onward. Countryman found persistent sharp divisions, which he defines as partisan, as early as the 1770s in New York State. Partisanship "gave structure and direction," he concludes, "to the operations of the legislature." In the 1830s, party divisions had the same kind of effect in state legislative activity as they did in Congress. Davis, in his study of Illinois, and Ershkowitz and Shade, in a study of six states, all found a high degree of partisan differences in roll-call behavior. In New Jersey, Levine found party identification not only to be the most salient influence on roll-call behavior, but he also traced its permeation into all areas of legislative activities: voting for minor legislative offices, committee assignments, and the like. At first various officers and committees were chosen with other, nonpartisan matters in mind. But partisanship crept into these choices as well, and then the development of a full roster of partisan norms followed.[20]

Most critically, this partisanship stretched over a range of issues that ultimately defined where the parties stood. Erickson stressed "the importance of party" in shaping the way Iowa legislators voted on banking policy in the middle of the nineteenth century. Ershkowitz and Shade found partisanship stretching into areas of moral legislation as well. Field found similar divisions on black suffrage issues in New York State. "Whigs and Democrats," Ershkowitz and Shade argue, "disagreed over the proper role of government in securing liberal republican ends and in shaping American culture. Their legislative behavior illustrates the dimensions of this conflict." Nor did such behavior decline thereafter in the nineteenth century.[21]

Partisan voting has always existed in congressional and legislative behavior but there have been other elements as well. There was, for example, a frequent limiting effect due to issue positions taken by individual legislators. Party voting varied in intensity and amount from issue area to issue area. There were few times when all of the issues of a session fell on a single, partisan-defined, voting dimension. Votes on banking and currency usually had the highest partisan cohesion in the pre-Civil War era, for example. A sharp drop off in partisanship occurred on internal improvements issues at critical moments. Sectional issues such as slavery usually received a sectional response in Congress, although even then some partisan cast usually appeared. As a result there have been voting blocs based on nonpartisan, often issue-defined groups —southerners, Scalawags, regional blocs, Radical and moderate Republicans, etc.—in every era of legislative voting. Much attention has consequently been paid to them.

Such nuances are interesting in their own right, especially in historians' topic-specific studies, but these nonpartisan blocs have clearly not been present as frequently or been as important as group behavior defined by partisan commitments. The former were exceptions or deviations from the pattern. They were present at intermittent, if often important, moments, but did not have the staying power and reach of the larger partisan quality. Historians have correctly and fruitfully expended much effort studying such nonpartisan blocs. But there still remains the other fact: if Congress is pictured as a series of snapshots taken at different times, the dominant character of each photograph is usually the amount of partisanship in the vote. Despite deviations, party remains more important more often than was generally acknowledged before the days of systematic quantitative analysis.

The most significant substantive finding of the roll-call studies in relation to this research revolves around the relatively lesser importance of sectional influences from the 1770s onward into the present. Their relative lack of dominance—albeit constant presence activated at different times—is astonishing. To summarize, party, not sectional, voting was the constant, repeated norm, especially from the 1820s onward; partisanship more than sectionalism was invigorated and reinforced by external factors present in the political environment and by internal factors, particularly leadership and partisan cues, within the legislative environment.[22]

The primary problem, therefore, is to take the party voting standard and to consider the amount, nature, and timing of any variation from it.

We have to delineate with exactness the conditions under which any nonpartisan deviations occur. The national electoral situation, the internal distribution of power in Congress, the nature of Congress as an institution, and the stage of party development, all come to mind as matters worth considering. There are others. Bogue found, for one example of the kind of work needed, that party cohesion among Republican Senators was lower during the Civil War years than in other periods. Party "was an omnipresent influence," he wrote. But other matters were also important determinants of voting: section, constituency, and ideological differences within Republicanism. Why were the latter more effective then than at other times? Bogue suggests a number of reasons to account for this deviation from the norm, among them the absence of an effective and significant opposition to the Republicans within the Senate. Such a special condition is one way to try to explain an abnormal condition. There may be others worth exploring.[23]

The second major area of historical research into legislative behavior, after the classification of roll-call behavior, has emphasized a different kind of pattern. Prosopographical studies, as indicated earlier, have the same purpose and sources as elite studies do elsewhere in political and social history. Historians engaged in such research in Congress and state legislatures have produced two major findings. The first is that "modern legislatures are populated by individuals who are not representative of the population at large, in that they are not collectively a mirror of the population sociologically. Recruitment to legislatures is characterized by the selection of persons of high social status and intense political experience." This is hardly surprising: it is congruent with the findings of collateral biographical studies of the origins of American political leadership generally.[24]

The second finding is more compelling. Since the early research of Beard, many historians have viewed America's elite leadership as divided and representing different socioeconomic forces within the society. They have housed themselves in different parties throughout our history. Here recent systematic research has produced mixed results. Goodman, for example, found that in the House of Representatives from 1797 to 1804, there were some socioeconomic differences between Republicans and Federalists from the Middle Atlantic and New England states. The Republicans tended to be more recently arrived in the country, less educated, lower on the economic scale, and from non-English ethnic groups. Similarly, Campbell found significant ethnic distinctions among state legislators in the late nineteenth-century Midwest. However, Goodman found few such distinctions among Southern congressmen at the beginning of the nineteenth century and Campbell found little in the way of occupational distinctions between legislators of the different parties.[25]

The conclusions to be drawn from this work suggest some variations in sociopartisan distinctions, but of an intermittent kind. The variations are usually milder than expected and not the basis for hard judgments. Nevertheless, it appears that elite leadership divides more along ethnocultural than economic lines, prefiguring and reflecting the nature of the party coalitions that they represent. Partisan differences in the larger society, rather than class differences, primarily shaped the recruitment of legislators.

As already noted, historians have not expended much effort on questions about the internal workings and structural influences of legislatures, areas to which political scientists have long been attracted. A number have, however, tried to adapt some of the political scientists' guidelines to look at the internal structure and locus of power in different Congresses to determine the pattern and importance of each at different moments in our past. Bogue's analysis of power in the Civil War Senate serves as a model for further endeavors of this kind. Bogue asked the simple and usual question: who, among the Republican Senators, had the most power? He borrowed a number of measuring techniques for determining the answer from related political science literature. He isolated a number of Senators as the possessors of substantial power, able to shape and direct the way that the Senate operated more than most of their colleagues. In addition, Bogue made some judgments about how the relative power of the different Republican factions operated in relation to each other, why certain things did or did not occur due to such power relationships, and, finally, how such relationships shifted to affect legislation and Republican behavior in successive sessions of the Senate. Many shrewd guesses had been made about these matters previously; Bogue was the first to apply quantitative methods to focus and sharpen our understanding of an elusive concept.[26]

In 1970, one historian, fresh from some quantitative research of his own, fretted that some tendencies in the work of quantitative historians could radically alter historical studies. A growing dichotomy existed between those who used quantitative methods to deal with specific and traditional questions that had long bothered historians (of the type focused on thus far in this article) and "those who advocate total immersion in computer and quantitative techniques in hopes that completely different kinds of questions will eventually be posed and answered." At the time his suggestion seemed exaggerated. Historians had shown little inclination to shift focus away from their traditional concerns.[27]

A decade later, Hackney's perception seems closer to reality. A number of historians now do wish to move history away from its topic-specific focus and recast it into different, much more theoretical, social scientific channels. These scholars are very critical of the present state of the art. They argue, as one example, that the large number of discrete topical studies have not produced a critical mass of elements that could be welded into a model of legislation and legislative behavior throughout American history. In the realignment-critical election organizing scheme, students of popular voting behavior have found a useful model for understanding the nature of stability and change in the electoral process. In addition, the ethnocultural axiom in popular voting behavior research promises the development of a theory of substantive behavior and sociopolitical conflict as well. Legislative studies have had nothing comparable because scholars have not done the longitudinal studies of change and patterns of behavior needed to develop and articulate similar, nonstatic models of behavior.

Because historians have treated Congress statically (as individual snapshots), and not as a dynamic, ongoing process, we have been unable to put the pieces together coherently. The episodic treatments, although abundant, are largely noncomparable with each other. That is not good enough. Such critics advocate, and try to demonstrate by example, the need for a more developed understanding of Congress and legislative behavior as a process rooted in a larger matrix of change, and not just as a series of particular, random episodes understood in their own terms alone. Bogue, for example, argued that since "dozens of scholars have been working upon aspects of American legislative history during the last fifteen years," it was now time "that we began to fit the findings into a theory of the historical development of legislative behavior in America."[28]

Such suggestions have had an effect. Studies of a different nature have begun to appear in congressional and legislative history, although so far in only a few articles and unpublished essays. The focus of these has been macropolitical and longitudinal rather than micropolitical and episodic. A second step followed, which moved beyond the specifying of patterns to the application of theoretical constructs explicitly to explain and organize cross-time processes as well: modernization, institutionalization, and bureaucratization. The point of the efforts, as has been said about one such study, is that "when institutions persist through time it is possible that the attributes of the individuals serving within those institutions may change and those changes in turn may tell much about the institution and larger environment within which it exists."[29]

One group of these studies deals with cross-time analyses of a familiar problem: the extent of, and changes in various crucial elements of congressional life—partisan cleavages, recruitment patterns, etc. Clubb, for example, led a team that decoded the long-range patterns discernible in congressional roll-call behavior in the first session of every Congress from 1861 to 1974, the better, they argued, to put any topical findings at any point along the continuum into clear and precise perspective. Brady, a political scientist, has also looked at long-range trends, this time from the 50th to 90th Congresses (1887–1968). In both studies, the extent of partisan voting is the key variable on which the analysis turns. Both find a long-range trend downward in it. The trend is not a straight line, however. Brady discerns three different eras: a highly partisan one at the beginning of the period, a transition, and a lower partisanship era. Using somewhat different terms, Clubb reports an occasional and temporary upbeat in party voting from time to time within the long-range downward trend. Both find the reasons for this downward movement in the external factors associated by other scholars with the decline of party in the American political process. In other words, roll-call voting, the dependent variable, reflects long-term shifts in the way politics itself is carried on in the larger American society and in how such external characteristics change over time. Clubb also finds some short-term internal explanation for the partisan fall off, that is, the collapse of the power of the internal power structure of Congress beginning in 1910.[30]

In these and similar studies, some attempts have been made to fit critical election-realignment theory, derived from research in electoral behavior, to patterns of legislative voting. The results are interesting, if still incomplete. The electoral cycle goes through a number of distinct periods, each with different ideological intensity and amounts of party-line voting, among other characteristics. Why should legislative behavior not show similar patterns? Specifically, should there not be stronger ideological voting patterns the closer Congress is to an electoral realignment, and a weakening of such as Congress moves into a period of stability? There should be comparable changes in the amount of party voting as well. Bogue and Clubb made tentative explorations of these themes and found such patterns. Although the results are tentative, the efforts are important both in developing ideas as to why Congress was acting the way it was at specific moments, and in moving toward combining what was going on in different areas of the political world into a single theory for a more unified understanding of the total process.[31]

Bogue, allied with Clubb and Traugott, engaged in an even more ambitious longitudinal study, this time of the recruitment patterns in the House of Representatives from 1789 to 1970. This is the most far-reaching study yet done in terms of chronological sweep and the most radical in terms of the conscious use of theoretical underpinnings to test and help explain the data. Based on information culled from the *Biographical Directory of the American Congress*—occupation and experiential data, family patterns, and age—Bogue et al. sought a pattern of modernization in the way in which Congress was recruited over two centuries. Modernization theory suggests development toward complexity in organization, regularity in service and promotion, a pattern of structured career development, and also socially different sources of legislative recruitment evolving over time as the United States modernized from a colonial rural landscape to a post-industrial megalith.[32]

When the results were in, shifts and changes did appear in the social resources from which congressmen were recruited over time. But, surprisingly, the amount of change did not appear "impressive" to the authors. Furthermore, the velocity of whatever changes there were was glacial rather than sudden and dramatic. Great external events—internal growth, civil war, the industrial revolution, and great electoral over-turns—did not immediately and dramatically affect congressional recruitment. The tides were calmer and slower than expected.

Modernization theory fared better in a number of studies by political scientists that analyzed developments in the internal structuring of Congress. Polsby's studies of internal institutionalization, of the regularization of congressional careers, and of the way in which Congress conducted its activities over time also tested the idea of modernization. He found that throughout the history of the House of Representatives since 1789, there was a general trend toward "impersonal, automatic and universalistic methods of conducting business" associated with movement toward "institutional maturity." There was a growth of internal complexity, seniority as a norm defining leadership, increased numbers of specialized committees, and finally, longer terms for con-gressmen, all in contrast with the underdeveloped, haphazard, and erratic patterns at the beginning of the nineteenth century. In similar work on the Senate, Price found congruent patterns of growth and development, and the emergence of complexity, regularity, and general norms of operations.[33]

In the researches of Bogue, Clubb, Brady, Polsby, Price, and their associates, much depth, breadth, and, particularly, comparative strength, has been added to our understanding of Congress. If few of the findings have been startling in themselves, they provide a perspective and a solidity of information beyond stopped moments in time: fluid, dynamic processes are revealed rather than the more caught-at-a-moment analysis characteristic of topic specific studies. They provide information useful in a systematic way to scholars seeking insight into matters outside the realm of legislative activity, such as long-range trends in society at large.

The findings of these studies raise intriguing questions about the nature of political change in the American past, for example. One of the major findings of the new political history has been the emphasis on great shifts around the 1890s. In popular voting behavior, a realignment, not only of voting forces but also of the structure of electoral politics, occurred. There was a short burst of dislocation followed quickly by profound changes in voting patterns. In public policy areas as well, the 1890s provide a convenient watershed for different ways of doing governmental business in this country. In congressional and legislative studies, however, such an overturn is much less clear. Macropolitically our studies have largely, if not completely, emphasized continuity and gradual change—beginning with a rumbling below the surface and only gradually, and in quiet ripples, appearing on the floor and in committee rooms of the various legislative bodies. This was certainly true of 1896, for example, where in Congress changes were not immediately apparent. Whatever was changing in politics worked itself onto the floor over a longer period than the electoral studies suggest.[34]

In contrast to the macrolongitudinal studies as a way of understanding congressional behavior at any specific moment, Zemsky, in a few brief articles, has offered an alternative for comparative understanding: this time a microvision. To accomplish some of the same comparative ends as the macropolitical studies, he suggests beginning with the understanding that Congress, or any legislature, is a system: a patterned and interactive institution of people, constraints, opportunities, effects, and operations that can be caught, generalized, and specified with a great deal of precision. Concerned that we may have misunderstood congressional behavior and the relative significance of such things as partisan behavior because they may have meant different things at different times to different people, Zemsky argues that we should specify as precisely as possible a model of legislative action and interaction at one moment and then test that highly specified model against similarly specified behavior at other times. Then we will be able to detail what actually changes and what are the proportions of change in the various subsumed elements within a system and its model. Zemsky began to develop such a model first for the non-rigidly institutionalized colonial legislature of Massachusetts, and then for Congress in the Grant era. In the latter case, he and his students tested the model's predictive ability against actual behavior in that session as a prelude to the more ambitious efforts.[35]

All of these studies are a long way from the topic-specific material discussed in the first part of this article that led one student or another to inquire into patterns of voting on the War of 1812, or antebellum banking policy. They reflect a quite different cast of mind. They are all in an early and still exploratory stage. They have been intriguing and promising, while adding much information and useful ways of analyzing our data. Along with the topic-specific studies of other quantitative-behavioral historians, they suggest the kinds of different roads traveled as this particular subfield has developed and learned the boundaries and problems that need to be mastered and explored.

Fifteen years of effort have produced a substantial, if incomplete, corpus of work in quantitative American congressional and legislative history. As elsewhere, the quality of the work varies, mistakes have been made, and problems of focus, methods, and relationships remain to be resolved, as do questions of comparability. Furthermore, despite these efforts, too much legislative history remains wedded to nonquantitative approaches, even when the material cries out for quantitative analysis. And even where quantitative expertise has been applied, there have often been divergent research goals. Finally, the quantitative analysis of the behavior of state legislatures still remains relatively undeveloped.

Some commentators on the new political history, including congressional and legislative history, have been negative and pessimistic about what has been done. They argue that the high hopes of two decades of effort have not been met. They suggest that although more and more work appears, the research has lost focus and there has not been much growth in reach and understanding.[36]

One might argue, however, that much has been accomplished. American legislative history is not without its rich resources and end products, nor entirely bereft of ideas about where to go next. There are useful clues to some of the larger aspects of politics and the society discernible in the legislative studies: repeated, consistent, pluralist legislative conflict despite the homogeneity found among the members; a legislative politics that reflected patterns of continuity more than change; an organizational structure rooted in parties of tremendous strength usually reflecting ideological differences between them; and suggestions of an interactive relationship with, rather than isolation from, the electorate. Instead of mindless optimism, or stirrings of black despair, therefore, a more balanced view of the work done so far suggests both accomplishments and unsolved problems. The body of this article has endeavored to deal with the former. In trying to reach a fair assessment, it seems appropriate now to concentrate on the chief categories of unresolved problems.

First is the matter of comparison of phenomena; for example, evaluating shifts in the extent of party voting in different eras and situations. Such critically important work is still too difficult to do. Despite the chronological reach of the roll-call studies, the same questions have not always been asked at different points, nor have the same categories or methods been used. Structuring comparable elements is sometimes essayed, but generally such attempts are woefully incomplete. Part of the reason for this is disagreement over which are the proper methods and what questions should be asked. Part relates to historical fascination with only limited and different parts of the legislative process. Shannon correctly refers to the "intellectual individualism" of researchers which has led to "confusion and ambiguity" in results. Benson, for one, has strongly articulated a call for better organized joint efforts to confront certain categories of historical problems. But it remains unclear how far scholars in American legislative history are prepared to go in harness together.[37]

Some historians find the repeated emphasis on party unsatisfactory, arguing that party voting is an opaque, blunt detail that says little about its source, composition, and power. Further, even when there is agreement about the importance of party in structuring legislatures, the basic question as to what that says about the nature of parties is argued about with as yet little resolution. Some scholars want to know much more about that nature and the reasons for party strength before they will admit its centrality. Parties, they argue, cannot exist as reified abstractions, and they believe that they have been used in that way.[38]

Behind the partisan blocs of legislators lies a dense network of individual and group relationships, beliefs, pressures, and forces. The network is many-stranded. All parts of it influence specific behavior under the general rubric of party loyalty. Why, then, should party be isolated as the basic determinant? Fair enough. But one can also suggest in rebuttal that sometimes the power of the external environment is enough of an explanation of individual voting. As legislators grew up in, breathed, reacted to, and were affected by a particular environment, they acted, unsurprisingly, in terms of the norms, pressures, and directions of the environment. And if that idea is correct, it suggests a pattern of research focusing outside the legislative halls in order to understand the persistence of partisanship within them.

The problem of relating constituency forces either to partisan or sectional outlooks or to subsequent behavior directly has been barely touched upon. It is a major and acceptable assumption of these studies that congressmen, elites though they may be, reflect the popular will, or at least interact with the popular will, as they perceive it, and do not totally ignore it. But this is a difficult generalization to analyze with a great amount of coverage or complexity. As a result, the easiest part of such influences, the electoral connection—the size of majorities in a district, that is the level of partisan competition—has been the most frequently emphasized. But clearly, much more remains to be done.[39]

There is also the question of the output from this array of legislative activities: the policies, laws, and bills that are the end of months of work. How does Congress define what it will do and how does this definition shift from era to era? Here again, the amount of historical analysis is limited. Only a start has been made in dealing with this question; systematic quantitative analysis is still largely not done. Nevertheless, historians have not lost sight of that aspect of legislative activity. Rather, they have placed it second to other matters.

Finally, as already noted, the unifying insight into all of this activity continues to elude us. No grand synthesis has emerged out of the work done comparable to the realignment and ethnocultural organizing themes in electoral history (even though the findings thus far do suggest some middle level generalizations and point to some of the directions in which to go). The role of model building in addressing this problem remains controversial and largely unexplored, with no agreement as to the next step to be taken.

There is, then, a full range of unfinished business in the study of American legislative history. We have mastered certain topics and established a quantitative bedrock of useful information. We have been less successful in the pursuit of other elements, equally useful and important. There is, in sum, reason for optimism. At the very least, scholarly activity in this area has refined many of the important questions, suggested many of the answers, and begun to explore much that should prove fruitful in the future. We are far from where we started and better off. Our sights are much more clearly focused than they were, as is our expertise and the base on which we stand. That is not a negligible achievement.

TWO:
PARTIES AND
POLITICAL CONFLICT

3

PARTIES AND POLITICS IN MID-NINETEENTH-CENTURY AMERICA (1972)

Early in 1849, a Georgia newspaper editor, angrily viewing the failure of the Southern congressional unity movement, complained that by their actions, Southern congressmen had once more cruelly sacrificed the rights and interests of their section on a shrine for false gods: the political parties.[1] A decade later, the persistent Southern firebrand, Robert Barnwell Rhett, similarly charged that devotion to national parties frustrated attempts to secure Southern rights and institutions against rampaging, abolitionist Northerners.[2] The unhappy utterances of both men reflected the belief that something unnatural and artificial was the source of their frustration. To Rhett and men of similar outlook, the antebellum political parties were unimportant, unnecessary, and obsolete institutions, which somehow continued to turn public attention away from the vital conflict of the day: the extension of slavery.[3] Contending with sham parties during the recurring sectional crises, the fire-eaters believed, revealed nothing more than the baseness of most politicians and the delusions of their followers.

The constant complaints of these sectional leaders about the persistence of party loyalty raises certain questions concerning the nature of political activity and political divisions in the antebellum United States. Such vehement Southern critics of the parties as Rhett, William Lowndes Yancey, and John C. Calhoun never satisfactorily explained how the parties maintained their strength within the American political system. None of these men, for example, fully considered the possibility that the national parties had real and substantial meaning to many people. Calhoun contemptuously labeled people "party hacks" who were faithful Democrats and Whigs not because they only sought the spoils of office, as he believed, but for the more deeply seated reasons of public policy. Such reasons retained a remarkable hold despite the rising exigencies of sectional conflict.[4]

Historians have generally shared Calhoun's skepticism about political parties in antebellum America. They have repeatedly stressed the sectional nature of the society and the subordination of institutions to that arrangement. Frederick Jackson Turner set the tone when he argued that the United States has always been "an empire, a federation of sections"—a fact affecting everything else, including political parties. Even in Congress, Turner noted, "party voting has more often broken down than maintained itself on fundamental issues; that when . . . [roll-call] votes are mapped or tabulated . . . a persistent sectional pattern emerges."[5] Furthermore, the parties themselves were really sectional coalitions. "Sectional interests," agreed political scientist V. O. Key, "have constituted important building blocks for American parties. Each party has had its roots deep in sectional interest and each has sought to build intersectional combinations powerful enough to govern."[6] Historians, therefore have concluded, that the conflicts between the national parties were unreal and not reflective of basic differences in the society. Charles Sydnor, in his classic study of the South between 1819 and 1848, asserted that "since neither Whigs nor Democrats offered a program that was thoroughly satisfactory to large segments of Southern political thought . . . party conflict south of the Potomac from nullification to the late 1840s had the hollow sound of a stage duel fought with tin swords."[7] Glyndon Van Deusen also stressed this point in the conclusion to his study of Whig thought and theory, insisting that depsite the differences in outlook between the Whigs and their Democratic rivals, "the political conflicts of the Jacksonian period were fought more often with a view to gaining control of the government than out of devotion to diametrically opposed political and social ideals."[8]

The origins of many of these ideas are clearly rooted in the study of pre-Civil War politics, particularly those of such men as Calhoun and his friends. Historians have repeatedly stressed the presence of sectional cleavages, the resulting disruption of national institutions, and the polarization of the Union due to the basic sectional structure of the society. Given this, the powerful national institutions that occasionally developed in the pre-Civil War period were, at best, artificial contrivances that were helpless before the onrush of sectional conflict and destined to be swept away in the rush toward civil war.[9]

It is evident that there was a great deal of localism and sectionalism in American politics in the nineteenth century, particularly in the two decades preceding the Civil War. But the fact of sectional conflict does not necessarily reveal either the full range or all of the most salient aspects of American politics in the period before the war.[10] Rather, concentration on the failure of the political system at that time may have led us to ignore much else operating within the American political structure and to misinterpret, somewhat, the significance of sectionalism within the political process.

James Young has shown that the political structure of early nineteenth-century America was highly localized. Certainly, presidential elections were local affairs, national totals being built, as in 1824, the classic of this type, on enormous margins in a few states.[11] It is also true that, in the 1850s, sectionalism played an increasingly important part in American politics. The repeated statements of the Rhetts, Yanceys, and Calhouns about the strength and tenacity of national party commitments indicate that American politics in the pre-Civil War era cannot be explained in terms of localism and sectionalism. Sectional polarization did indeed occur in American politics in the antebellum period. But, a national structure, dominated by national political parties and giving rise to national outlooks, was a major aspect of American politics for much of the antebellum period. This structure shaped, or significantly challenged, other behavioral variables. It had the basic strength and recuperative powers to survive reforms and the rise of sectional pressures, largely because of traditionally held national considerations and attitudes.

The American people were both highly politicized and highly partisan in the 1830s and 1840s. This is confirmed, in part, by the level of popular participation in elections. The work of such scholars as Charles G. Sellers, Richard P. McCormick, and Walter Dean Burnham has shown that the rate of turnout for elections in the period after the establishment of a two-party system throughout the Union was quite high— higher than today's figures, and higher, also, in partisan races between Whigs and Democrats than in contests for such sectionally oriented matters as elections of delegates to the Nashville Convention or to the secession conventions of the South. Furthermore, of those who voted, a remarkably high number were "core" voters, constantly committed to one or another of the two major parties, while relatively few people were "swing" or independent voters. Finally, this description of the American political system was true nationwide. In the decade before 1840, in response to a series of sharp political conflicts, a deeply divided and highly competitive electorate emerged. Both parties could summon substantial numbers of voters everywhere in the country, and neither party could count on many safe states or regions. For the first time, an era of a truly national two-party system existed in the United States. By

1840, as Professor McCormick has pointed out, a closely competitive two-party system existed in every state.[12]

There was no particular sectional or local cast to party appeals in this period. In his recent study of the second American party system, Professor McCormick has described an essentially localistic system, in which the parties in the different states evolved for diverse reasons, in large part unrelated to what was happening in other states at the same time. But to see the two parties in the 1840s as only some sort of loose confederation of local units is to overstress greatly the decentralizing tendencies of the political culture of the time.[13] Although their organizational structure may have been decentralized, the two parties and their representatives, in formulating their outlook on matters of public policy and, more pertinently, in acting in terms of that outlook, succeeded in establishing a national framework of contrasting ideas, beliefs, and behavior. Close investigation of party platforms, political pamphlets, and campaign speeches clearly indicate this. And these appeals were, as one Whig congressman pointed out, not words to be ignored, but principles "worth fighting for . . . the rules of our action."[14] In Congress, most of all, the national quality and strength of the two parties were shown.

Congressional voting throughout the 1840s and beyond shows a persistent cleavage along nationally partisan lines. Each party had significant numbers of congressmen from the different regions of the country most of the time, so that voting cleavages did not reflect a sectional cast.[15] The percentage of party cohesion was dramatically high. Nor was this unity confined to just a few issues. Partisan commitments extended over almost the whole range of congressional activity, including such issues as the tariff, foreign affairs, finance, land, expansion, and government operations of various kinds. If one submits to intensive quantitative analysis the more than two thousand roll-call votes in Congress in the decade after the two parties became firmly established throughout the country, one finds that the overwhelming mass of each party's congressmen voted together and in positions opposite to those taken by the mass of the other party's congressmen. This pattern was true regardless of the alleged viewpoints of any sectional group within either party. Most Southern Whigs voted with their Northern colleagues for higher tariffs than did most Democrats, Northern, Southern, or Western. Most Northern Democrats were as expansionistic in their voting behavior as their Western and Southern colleagues, whether the votes concerned Texas, Oregon, California, or Cuba. Of course, a few maverick congressmen dissented from what may be defined as their party's position, but their numbers were quite small on most issues and did not detract from the quite well-defined party positions. Furthermore, whatever dissension existed was of a transient quality. From issue to issue, a different group of individuals dissented.[16]

A specific example of party cohesion can be found in an examination of the voting patterns on the tariff of 1846, an issue and a session of Congress traditionally identified by historians as significantly revealing the underlying sectionalism of American politics. The administration of James K. Polk, in keeping with traditional Democratic statements on the matter, entered office pledged to lower tariff duties. On July 28, 1846, a new low-tariff bill passed the Senate by a vote of 28 to 27. Before that, however, there was a series of roll calls on various amendments, as congressmen tried to raise or lower duties, or impose or remove specific rates on specific goods. Eighty percent of the Democratic senators consistently voted together at the low-tariff end of the scale of attitudes, while 96 percent of the Whig senators similarly united in the high-tariff position.[17]

Table 3-1. Tariff Scale, Senate, 29th Congress, 1846

Position	Scale Type*	Democrats		Whigs	
		No.	%	No.	%
Low	(0–2)	20	80	—	—
Moderate	(3–4)	1	4	1	4
High	(5–6)	4	16	24	96

*Scale positions were clustered for interpretive purposes into three groupings.

In the House of Representatives, as in the Senate, both Democrats and Whigs held together remarkably well. In the House over two-thirds of the Democrats voted together in favor of a low tariff; an additional 15 percent took a middle of the road position. Over 98 percent of the Whig representatives banded together in favor of a more protective tariff.[18] In 1846, incidentally, Democrats in the House were less unified on the tariff issue and on other policy questions than was normally the case.

A closer look at the factional groupings within the parties on this issue indicates the lack of a significant sectional component. Senators in the most low-tariff position on the scale (scale type 0), included two Democrats from New England, one from New York, two from the Border South, one from Alabama, and two from the Middle West. Among the Northerners were one man later to be a Free Soiler and one subsequent Doughface (pro-Southern in his orientation). In the next most low-tariff scale position were all but a few of the remaining Democrats, including three Southerners, four Midwesterners, and the remaining New York senator. Among these men were two prominent Doughfaces, two national Southerners, and two more sectionally minded Southerners.

At the other end of the scale, in the most high-tariff position, there were eight slave state Whigs, eight New England Whigs, and both Whig senators from the supposedly low-tariff Midwest. Among the four high-tariff Democrats were the two Pennsylvanians, and senators from Connecticut and Mississippi. The partisanship so prevalent in much of this can also be seen in the split among senators from the partisanly divided states of Maine, New Hampshire, Ohio, and Virginia where the Democratic senators were in the low-tariff position while the Whigs from the same states supported a high tariff. The only exception to this was Connecticut, whose Whig and Democratic senators both supported a high tariff.

Similar results occurred in the House of Representatives, where most of the factions were nonsectional. There were exceptions, of course. One can see evidence of the traditional image of Northern high-tariffism in the actions of the Pennsylvania delegation. All but one Pennsylvania Democrat voted in the most high-tariff position. The same is true of several New York Democratic congressmen. But other New York Democrats, both from the city and upstate, voted consistently for low tariffs, as did both of New York's senators. Only Pennsylvania's delegation voted together regardless of party. It is possible that further refinements of these patterns would indicate the relevance of some economic or functional division, but two points should be stressed. In most cases, Democrats from a section were more low tariff than were their Whig counterparts. Neither the exception of Pennsylvania nor the possible presence of functional groupings materially detracts from the essentially partisan quality of the vote on the tariff. Nor was there anything atypical about the party cohesion manifested on this particular issue. The voting patterns on other issues revealed similar consistencies of national party cohesion throughout the 1840s.[19]

There were other issues on which the level of partisan cohesion was not as dramatically high as on these particular examples. Nevertheless, before the rise of the slavery-extension controversy, there was only one real deviation from the general partisan cast of congressional voting patterns. Occasionally both parties, but particularly the Democrats, fragmented on internal improvements legislation—though a partisan cast remained in the voting on that issue as well.[20] The Whigs were

Table 3-2. Party Cohesion, Selected Issues, 1841–1846

Issue	Democrats*	Whigs
Finance, H.R., 27th Congress	94.4%	86.5%
Expansion, S., 28th Congress	95.7	93.1
War Issue, S., 29th Congress	92.6	84.2

*This figure indicates the highest number of party members in one area of the scale.

usually united and most Democrats differed to some degree from the Whig position. The internal groupings on this issue were a complex amalgam. Occasionally they were regional, occasionally functional, and always there was something of a partisan quality. In most cases, Democrats from one section or region differed in their voting behavior from Whigs of the same area. Most important, there were often groups of congressmen from all sections who voted as their party position dictated, regardless of local or sectional considerations. This can be seen in one particular instance. Although many Western Democrats favored an expanded program of federal internal improvements, several changed their minds, or at least their votes, when their party leader, President Polk, stingingly vetoed the Rivers and Harbors Bill of 1846.[21] Finally, the fragmentation that did occur had little discernible effect on party unity on other issues, either in that or in subsequent Congresses.

The overwhelming partisanship that characterized congressional voting behavior in the 1840s can be readily seen in the fact that on all issues considered between 1841 and 1849, except those dealing with slavery in the territories (involving only a small fraction of the total number of issues considered), party unity averaged just over 80 percent. Most of the dissenting 20 percent, furthermore, did not cast their vote with the other party. A few, of course, did: John C. Calhoun on Mexican War policy, and John Quincy Adams on matters of expansion, for example. Stressing the exceptions, however, distorts the reality of a situation in which voting by party best demonstrates the shape of congressional voting behavior.

Another point worth noticing is that the level of party cohesion remained fairly stable throughout the 1840s. From 1841 through 1846, party cohesion averaged 81.8 percent; in the period from 1846 through 1849, despite the fight within the Democratic party over Oregon and internal improvements, overall cohesion dropped only slightly, to 80.7 percent.

Even on matters concerning the Negro and slavery, some partisan considerations were present despite strong sectional pressures. As early as 1841, some matters involving Negro rights, questions of the slave trade in the District of Columbia, the gag rule against the reception of abolitionist petitions, and related questions, were voted on in the House of Representatives. Many Northern Democrats voted with the Northern Whigs on the antislavery side of the issue. Others voted consistently with their fellow Democrats from the South. At the same time, nine of the thirty-one Southern Whigs broke with their section's philosophy and voted either with their Northern colleagues or took a middle of the road position. The reasons offered by the congressmen for such sectional deviation reflected partisan commitments: the fear of splitting the party or the conviction that raising the slavery issue was a trick on the part of one party to destroy the unity of the other.[22]

In the last years of the 1840s there was a noticeable rise of sectional pressures in Congress as issues connected with slavery in the territories increasingly came to the forefront. But, even as sectional tensions rose along with increased sectional voting, the partisan quality of congressional behavior was still evident. Many Northern Democrats continued to be distinctly less antislavery in their voting behavior than were the Northern Whigs. In the South, the reverse was true: Southern Whigs were usually more moderate in their voting behavior on sectional issues than were their Southern Democratic colleagues.[23] Partisanship could, it seems, still partially influence voting on sectional issues. Despite the differences on these matters manifested after 1846, sectionalism did not carry over to affect other issues. Here, traditional and sharp partisanship still prevailed.[24]

The meaning of this seems clear: the party representatives in Congress, by tenaciously, vociferously, and intensely reflecting partisan outlooks, helped to deepen and further a political culture in which the mainspring of choice was expressed through the medium of national party coalitions. The occasional local and regional tendencies in congressmen's behavior remained quixotic exceptions to the generally partisan cast of congressional activity.

Furthermore, this essentially national and partisan system of politics had an ability to survive the rise of interest in and fighting over "puny sectional questions and petty strifes about slavery," as Senator Thomas Hart Benton of Missouri characterized them.[25] Partisan conflict was intense, elections were bitterly fought everywhere, and the hostility between members of the opposing parties carried over beyond the elections into subsequent relations in Congress and elsewhere. After being at each other's throats over matters of serious concern, it was quite difficult for the members of each party, even if they were sectional colleagues, to work together. Rather, most of the members of each party stuck together against the other coalition, regardless of regional or local considerations. The editor of the *Charleston Mercury* succinctly and accurately summed up the general political situation in Congress in this period when he noted, in 1849, that "the antipathies of Whig and Democrat are too strong in Washington . . . their exercise forms too much the habit of men's lives there."[26]

The difficulties such an outlook and political structure posed for the non-national leaders can be seen in the frustrating experience of John C. Calhoun in 1849, when he attempted to mold a sectional bloc out of the raw materials of the Southern representatives and senators in Congress. In response to the passage of a resolution against the slave trade in the District of Columbia by the House of Representatives, Calhoun called a meeting of all Southern congressmen to consider a course of action.[27] He hoped that they would strongly assert their sectional unity against such action by the North, regardless of other considerations.

Despite a great deal of editorial support, the meeting failed. Only 69 of 121 Southern congressmen attended the first meeting, and Calhoun and his supporters found they could not control the caucus. A moderate Whig, who was an avowed opponent of sectional action, was elected chairman of the meeting. Other anti-Calhoun moderates attended the meeting to prevent rash action. Their arguments in favor of moderation are revealing. Most denied that there was any justification for holding the meeting, and reiterated previous arguments against sectional political divisions. Furthermore, with a new Whig president (Zachary Taylor) about to enter the White House, many members of that party apparently felt that the president should be left free to deal with the territorial issue without the South forcing his hand. President Polk also intervened to convince Southern Democrats not to be a party to the movement. He deplored agitation on the slavery question and asserted that, to him, the whole sectional unity movement was "ill-advised."[28]

Because of the opposition to sectional unity, Calhoun and the sectionalists could not achieve their purpose in the caucus. Calhoun prepared an address listing the South's grievances against the North, but many of those attending considered the document too strong. After bitter debate, they modified the draft considerably. Even then, only 48 of the 121 Southern congressmen signed this more moderate public statement. Many of the most prominent Democrats refused to sign and only two Southern Whigs of thirty-four in Congress supported the message. Howell Cobb, a Democrat from Georgia, who was one of those who refused to sign, wrote shortly afterwards that my "opinion is that my course will ultimately meet with the approval of a large majority of the

Southern Democracy. And I entertain no doubt that the true interest and policy of the South requires the preservation of the Democratic party of the Union, which is hopeless under the lead of Mr. Calhoun."[29]

Such attitudes, with their strong partisan underpinning, as expressed in the caucus episode of 1849, continued to operate even as national politics came under strong sectional pressures in the 1850s. Thomas B. Alexander's study of roll-call voting in the House of Representatives in that decade, repeatedly indicates the persistence of much partisanship despite the increasing sectional thrust of the period. Throughout the decade, Whigs, for example, continued to reveal "a definite reluctance to be classed with the Democrats" as "partisan antagonisms in the House . . . resumed some of their former characteristics" after the strong sectional pressures of the late forties.[30] Part of this can be readily seen in Gerald Wolff's analysis of the 1854 Senate session, wherein sectional voting unity still did not readily manifest itself even in response to what historians have traditionally believed were signals of sectional polarization.[31] Wolff found that, despite the alleged Southern hostility to free land for Western settlers, and the sectional political unity supposedly forged during that year by the debates over the extension of slavery into Kansas, the Southern senators fell into a voting pattern which revealed, once again, their basic disunity. He demonstrated that partisan differences continued to affect them, and that more mundane variables, such as constituency pressures had more significant impact on voting behavior and the creation of factions than North-South sectional polarization. "Despite one of the durable myths of agricultural history," Wolff concludes, "a substantial number of southern senators supported the Homestead bill. . . ." Whatever the reasons for the bill's defeat, "it is clear that a selfishly united slavocracy was not to blame."[32] In fact, as late as the congressional session of 1859–60, partisan influences were still present in congressional voting.[33]

There was, however, an increasing sectional polarization in Congress in the 1850s. In the middle of that decade a significant realignment of political forces in the country began to occur, with major impact on the subsequent distribution of congressional seats. American electoral politics occasionally undergoes a realigning period, a time when "the underlying pattern of party identification is substantially and durably altered."[34] Some voters leave their traditional party home and join the other coalition in response to some critical pressure or deeply felt crisis. As a result, a new majority party emerges, enjoying the support of most of the voters in the country or in a particular region. The other party can only win, in this new situation, a minority of the votes cast in a given election. In time, if the pattern is fairly constant throughout a region, it has a significant impact on the number of congressional seats and other offices each party wins. As a result of the realignment of political forces in the 1850s, the Whig party declined and the Republican party emerged. In these years the South sent mostly Democrats to Congress, the North increasing numbers of Republicans. There was a concomitant increase in the sectional quality of the roll-call voting in Congress, a fact reflected in the angry debates and editorial exchanges between sectional spokesmen. North and South seemed locked in bitter sectional confrontation, with little room for their considerations to affect the political structure.[35]

Despite the increased sectional polarization reflected in congressional voting behavior, other dimensions of the political environment also must be noted for full appreciation of the political culture of the time. In addition to the sectional polarization, an older, partisan tradition still remained as an important aspect of American politics. Popular voting behavior certainly reflected this fact. Neither section became the exclusive province of one party as a result of the realignment, despite the nature of the congressional delegations. Rather, there was constant competitive challenge to the majority party by members of the opposition in each section, despite the pressure toward sectional unity and sectional outlook. Old attitudes and patterns of behavior were not easily overcome. Some of the underlying reasons for the political realignment in the North stemmed from causes not sectional in nature, although they appeared, at first, to be so.

In the South, for example, despite the growing power of the Democracy as the defender of that region, there remained a substantial bloc of voters and politicians who resisted the party of Jackson and fought under various names against the sectionally oriented Democrats. These men talked, walked, and acted like Whigs, and for the most part, were Whigs, still fighting against the party their forebears had first opposed in the bitter days of King Andrew. They did quite well, too. There continued to be significant pockets of anti-Democratic voters who vigorously contested elections, bitterly fought the Democrats, and succeeded, through their actions, in maintaining a two-party system. In the presidential election of 1856, for example, Millard Fillmore, former president and Whig House leader, picked up about 43 percent of the vote in fire-eating Mississippi, which compared favorably with earlier Whig totals in that state. He did even better in the Border States and Upper South. Nor were these Southern Whigs inarticulate about their anti-Democratic attitudes. The ex-Whig representative, Henry Hilliard of Alabama, himself convinced that "old issues are dead and gone," found it difficult to persuade his fellow Southern Whigs of that fact. He pleaded with them to conquer their partisan prejudices against

Southern Democrats so that both groups could unite in support of the Buchanan administration and against the Northern Republicans. The tone of his plea made it clear that he realized conquest of ingrained anti-Democratic prejudices was no easy task.[36] In fact, as Professor Alexander indicates, there was much talk among these Southern Whigs "about a fusion [with the Northern Republicans] which would essentially restore the national unity of the former Whigs."[37]

The Southern Democrats expressed similar doubts about their Whig sectional brethren. Even when the Southern Whigs joined the Democratic party to defend Southern interests, past divisions and loyalties were expressed. After thanking the Southern Whigs for their support of Buchanan in 1856 against the dangers of John C. Frémont and antislavery Republicanism, the editor of the *Richmond Enquirer* sternly added that "fidelity to the South is not the sole test of Democracy." There were other principles to be accepted before one became a Democrat, and no one could remain in the party unless he accepted those principles.[38] The constant repetition of similar attitudes helped to exacerbate traditional partisan tensions in the South throughout the fifties, despite the countervailing pressures towards sectional unity.

On the other side of Mason and Dixon's line, too, the impact of sectional factors may not have been as pronounced as it seems at first glance. The realignment in the North in the 1850s saw the movement of many hitherto committed Democrats, and the introduction of new voters into the emerging Republican coalition, which was, as is well known, a sectional party. But the growth and dominance of the Republicans in the North can also be closely identified with a behavioral phenomenon quite nonsectional in character: ethnocultural conflict. The Republicans, adopting the outlook and image of the Know Nothings, attracted to their cause many Democrats and new voters responding to fears of the rising tide of German and Irish-Catholic immigration, the growing political power and social activities of these immigrants, and the identification of the Democratic party with their well being and support. Again, although other matters, including slavery, played important roles in the realignment, one historian has suggested that opposition to the alien threat was "largely responsible for the political revolution' that began in 1854"[39] Although such ethnic antagonism was primarily confined to the North in this period, it can be most fruitfully considered as something other than a sectional phenomenon.

There is a further dimension to the Northern political situation in the 1850s. As is the case with most realignments, relatively few people shifted their position. The Democrats continued to manifest great strength in the Northern states, albeit they were now the minority party there. In the presidential election of 1860, for example, they won 46.3 percent of the vote in New York State, a figure which compared favorably with their percentage of 48.9 in 1844 at the height of the partisan confrontation in American politics.[40] In other Northern states they also did well.

In the closely competitive political situation of the time, a shift of only a few percentage points in the popular vote totals was enough to give the Republicans control in most Northern states. But the North still remained a two-party area with a competitive Democratic party vigorously contesting the Republican hegemony throughout the region. Partisan divisions had neither died nor become enfeebled by the rise of sectionalism.

Table 3–3. Democratic Strength,
Nationally and in Selected Northern States,
1844 and 1860

	1844	1860*
National	49.6%	47.6%
New York	48.9	46.3
Connecticut	46.2	42.0
New Jersey	49.4	51.9
Ohio	47.8	44.9
Indiana	50.1	47.0
Illinois	54.4	47.9

*The two Democratic tickets are put together here, where necessary, since their total reflected the whole Democratic vote, despite their split over candidates.

This situation, reflecting deep and tenacious partisan commitment, persisted throughout the fifties into the election of 1860. Furthermore, intersectional relationships and brokerage between members of the same party continued to be a factor in political life. It is too simple, for example, to characterize the contending factions of the Democracy in the election of 1860 as entirely sectional in orientation, and leave it at that. Although the basic thrust of each party may have been sectional, there were limitations which underscore the persistence of national partisan attitudes. Many Southern Democrats supported Stephen A. Douglas as a means of keeping the national party together. As Howell Cobb of Georgia put it, in addressing a Democratic meeting in 1856, "I care not whether the Democratic orator who preceded me hails from the North, or the West, or the South, if he stands on this platform, the truthful exponent of Democratic principles, he speaks one voice with me." A year before he hanged John Brown, Virginia fire-eater Henry A. Wise commiserated with Douglas's campaign manager (just after Douglas had been removed from his chairmanship of the Senate Committee on the Territories), on their attempt "to maintain conservative nationality against embittered and implacable sectionalism."[41] Such men were still present and active in the South in 1860.

The persistence of party attachments among Southerners is also attested to by the anger of such leading sectionalists as Robert Barnwell Rhett of South Carolina, who complained in 1860 that "the fact is that, from party contact at Washington, the courage of southern representatives . . . oozes out. . . . So long as the Democratic party, as a 'National' organization, exists in power at the South, and so long as our public men trim their sails with an eye to either its favor or enmity, just so long must we hope for no southern action for our disenthrallment and security."[42] In many Southern states in 1860 there were bitter conflicts for control of the party machinery and for the name "Democrat" on the ballot. This was because of the full realization of the importance of these factors as determinants of support from many voters, and despite the long-time, angry attacks by sectionalists against the national party organization. Thus, these Southern Democrats held out against those pressures and refused to sectionalize. They did this for the same reasons that bring parties together originally and maintain them despite the cross-pressures of nonpartisan factors in political life. Many of them had always been Democrats and wanted to remain so. Others saw in the Democratic party a means of achieving their policy ends. All had developed a pattern of ideas, based on the role and importance of national political parties in their culture and lives, which they still maintained and used to challenge the assumptions and assertions of the sectional unifiers. Their behavior cannot be simply dismissed as unique, quixotic, or irrelevant. Although their numbers dwindled, they always existed on the Southern scene and, for a long period they were powerful enough, first to frustrate and then to delay the plans of the sectionalists.

"Most members of the Electorate," a leading student of voting behavior recently wrote, "feel some degree of psychological attachment to one of the major parties. This partisan identification is remarkably resistant to passing political events and typically remains constant through the life of the individual. It exercises an important influence on perceptions, attitudes, and behavior."[43] The same thing can probably be said about the political scene in the 1840s and 1850s. The strength of this party identification helps explain the persistence of traditional partisan loyalty, "the cursed bonds of party" as James Seddon, a Southern sectionalist, characterized the phenomenon, which one continues to see throughout the antebellum period. Such attachments may have been, as some contemporaries claimed, the result of simple conservatism, dough-facery, or plain hunkering after the spoils of office. But it is also reasonable to see this as the behavior of men continuing to think and act in terms of the traditional values and institutions of their political culture. Congressman William Bissell of Illinois, fighting the day to day battles of the crisis period of 1850, felt it was incumbent upon all men, despite the furor over the slavery question, "to preserve the integrity of our party."[44] In the same year, the editor of the Rochester *Daily Advertiser* set forth a similar theme. "All here," he wrote, "are anxious to terminate at the earliest possible moment the blighting domination of whiggery; and to that end, to make any reasonable sacrifices in reference to matters of subordinate concern."[45]

People chose, in the first instance, to vote for one of the two national parties since it fulfilled, in their minds, their self-interest in a way that the other party definitely could not. Their descendants continued to support the same party because they continued to believe that that party still reflected their interests, while the other party still did not. The result of such behavior, and the forces underlying it, was the presence of a strong national party structure clung to tenaciously and with a deep-seated loyalty that seemed to preclude the possibility of change. Horace Greeley, continually hamstrung in his efforts to wean Democratic voters away from their leaders, once unhappily noted that the latter "may have roast baby for breakfast every morning, with missionary steaks for dinner, and yet rule the country forever."[46] Given such, the impact of the sectional controversy was severely limited by the presence and strength of the party system.

The depth of commitment helps to explain the rapid comeback of the Democratic party in the North during the Civil War, despite its alleged Southernism and connection with rebellion, and in the face of bitter Republican bloody-shirt campaigns against it. Though rent, twisted, and weakened by the events of the previous half-decade, the Democracy still had loyal legions of followers behind its policies, principles, and organization.[47] The elections of 1862 were a Democratic triumph and both the presidential contests of 1864 and 1868 were fiercely and closely fought despite the absence of Southern votes that might have further aided the Democrats. In 1864 the Democrats won about 45 percent of the national vote. They did even better four years later against the popular war hero, Ulysses S. Grant. In such crucial large states as New York, Pennsylvania, and Ohio they often fought the Republicans to a standstill in local and state elections as well as national contests.[48]

The persistent and intense party loyalty felt by Democrats was the base on which the party built its strength and asserted itself after 1860. "Party and party organization," the Republican secretary of the navy, Gideon Welles complained, "rose above country, or duty [during the war]. In fact, party was a substitute for country." People considered public policies "not in terms of good for the country but in terms of good for and needs of the party."[49] Such deeply ingrained partisanship, of course, aided the Democrats, as with their substantial popular following they were able to challenge the Republicans constantly, pose policy alternatives, successfully appeal for votes, and generally perform the functions of a major competitive party within a two-party system. In the aftermath of the election of 1868, the Republican leader, James G. Blaine, unhappily but accurately summed up the history of political parties during the Civil War decade. At first glance, he noted, the results seemed to be "an overwhelming victory for the Republican party . . . [but] certain facts tended to qualify the sense of gratulation and triumph." A great war hero had barely been able to defeat a disloyal governor (Horatio Seymour of New York, the Democratic candidate, had been particularly abused by the Republicans as a friend and ally of the Confederacy). "Considering the time of the election, considering the record and achievements of the rival candidates," Blaine concluded, "the Presidential election of 1868 must be regarded as the most remarkable and most unaccountable in our political annals."[50]

These trends continued in the post-Civil War era. Several recent studies of Congress and of the larger political environment after the war, indicate that party remained a crucial force at work in Congress and elsewhere, often despite the apparent salience of other forces, including sectionalism. Allen Weinstein, for example, in closely studying the roll-call voting in the original fight over silver remonetization in the early 1870s, noted that despite the usual assertion that the forces arrayed on both sides of the question were sectional in character, "silver politics began as a partisan rather than a sectional issue and remained one until after passage of the Bland-Allison Act."[51] Other scholars, such as Robert Wiebe, Walter Dean Burnham, and David Rothman noted the continuance of intense partisanship in the society generally, the closely competitive electoral structure, and the development of a much more sophisticated structure of party leadership and organization.[52] But none of this is surprising to anyone who is aware of first, the functions parties performed within the American electoral system and second, the actual situation of political life in mid-nineteenth-century America.

"The capacity of party identification to color perceptions," Donald Stokes has written, "holds the key to understanding why the unfolding of new events, the emergence of new issues, the appearance of new political figures, fails to produce wider swings of party fortune. To a remarkable extent these swings are dampened by processes of selective perception."[53] Despite the alleged importance of the great issues of the nineteenth century, such as slavery and silver, when historians calculate causes, consequences, and reasonable explanations of the political realities of the era, they must include in their equations what often seems to be an irrational fact: the traditional and usually unshakable adherence of many Americans to the party of their fathers, come what may. In 1848, Representative Howell Cobb spoke in Congress on "the necessity for party organization" in response to Southern Whig efforts to win Democratic support for the slaveholder, Zachary Taylor. Party was not, Cobb remarked,

a mere catchword used to delude, deceive and impose upon the honest people of the land. . . . [Rather], it is an association of men acting in concert with each other to carry out great fundamental principles in the administration of Government. . . . It enables the people to declare their will in practical form. We stand here today indebted in party organization for all the important measures of national reform and constitutional rights which mark the brilliant administrations of Jefferson, Madison and Jackson. . . .

We are now called upon to renounce a system from which all these blessings have flown—to disband the Democratic party—to throw our cherished principles to the winds. . . . [This] effort to break down party organization is a blow at the very corner-stone of our whole political system. It strikes at the fundamental principle of self-government, and seeks to paralyze the arm of the people by relieving their agents and representatives from all responsibility to them as the source from which all power emanates.[54]

Cobb obviously spoke for a generation that never considered party battles to be mere hollow duels, simple contests for office, or the reflection of petty animosities and concerns.

4

"THE SALT OF THE NATION": POLITICAL PARTIES IN ANTEBELLUM AMERICA (1984)

It seems ironic indeed that at the very time when political parties have been in decline as effective forces on the contemporary American scene, they have been reborn among political historians. Since the 1960s our knowledge of the ideological, behavioral, and organizational aspects of party history has widened and deepened in significant ways. In that fateful decade alone, four different books collectively and significantly redefined the landscape. Lee Benson in 1961, Richard P. McCormick in 1966, William N. Chambers and Walter Dean Burnham in 1967, and Bernard Bailyn the same year, each helped shift our emphases and modify our perceptions.[1] The many who followed them built on their work to sharpen and sort further, classify more completely, and fill in the spaces within the guidelines. The McCormick generation of American political historians has contributed an extraordinarily rich legacy to American political history.[2]

Many of these scholars worked in new ways, argued new truths, and suggested new directions. Those labeled new political historians moved away from an elite-dominated, descriptive, chronological focus and the repetitive look at great national issues refracting through the political system. One of the major tasks of political history, they argued, was to deal not only with dramatic crises, dominant personalities, great events and movements, and the struggle for power among party activists, but to consider and dissect central aspects of normal and routine political discourse, behavior, and patterns as well. As a result they have been lumpers rather than splitters.[3] They focused their primary attention on structure, context, political calculus, electoral, legislative, and institutional behavior, rather than on individual events and great personalities. Certain kinds of theoretical musings, usually drawn from outside of history, informed their work, explicitly and otherwise.

At the same time, others working along more traditional lines, less quantitative and behavioral in their approach, also enriched our understanding and expanded our grasp of what was involved in past politics. Following the path marked by Bailyn and Eugene Genovese, they sought out the mind sets and the ideological perspectives that permeated the political scene and influenced the way events unfolded.[4] They successfully demonstrated ways of connecting even the most banal political pronouncement to larger and deeply ingrained belief systems.

Out of all of this work both traditional and innovative in approach, has emerged a picture of politics and political parties increasingly at variance with many previously well-established truths, one that, as John Higham once accurately suggested, has restored complexity to our understanding of past politics.[5] Reviewing the elements of that understanding, especially for the antebellum years, suggests how much has been changed by recent scholarship. Research rethinking the basis of voting choice, the actions of congressmen and state legislators and the persistence and pervasiveness of party in this period, has thoroughly documented the need for new perspectives on the discrete elements of the political process.

More than appreciating the change in the individual aspects of political life is possible, however. Ronald Formisano, while appraising the recent literature of the Jacksonian era a few years ago, argued that "the old syntheses are gone or modified beyond recognition," but that a new one had not yet emerged about that multifaceted era.[6] The first part of that characterization is certainly true in the study of politics and political parties in the years before the Civil War. However, despite incompleteness, unexplored corners, and ragged edges, the second part need no longer be true. The outlines of the situation then have been particularly well marked by historians' efforts. A synthesis of them into a fuller, more clear-cut understanding of the whole is possible and can be attempted. Except for Michael Holt's chapter in *The Political Crisis of the 1850s*, Richard L. McCormick's effective overview identification of the period and its public policy dimension, and William Gienapp's essay describing the style and thrust of politics in this era, such a synthesis has not yet been done.[7] Recent research describes a very particular world, establishes its boundaries, and suggests its character. But only part of the ground is mapped, the rest of the topography still needs to be developed.

I want to use this occasion, therefore, to draw out of both my own ongoing research into electoral behavior, party operations, and the dynamics of the political process in the "party period" in American history, a work tentatively titled, "Fresh from the People: The Dynamics of the American Political Order, 1838–1893," as well as the work of others, to address some persistent controversies, elucidate some obscure matters, offer some clarifying and linking suggestions, and by so doing, to refine and extend our understanding of a crucial part of the American political experience.

Much of the focus of the quantitative-behavioral studies has been definitional and boundary-setting. Scholars have concentrated not only on the sequences of national events from the Revolution to the Civil War and beyond as filtered through the parties, but how and when parties conceptualized their role and style of operation, organized certain elements, and established certain patterns. Four particular findings are generally familiar to all of us.

First, recent scholarship has established the chronological boundaries of party systems as shaped by mass electoral behavior. There has been a temporal variation in the course of American electoral politics. The nation's political system has lasted a long time. But the institutions, behavior, and perspectives making up the electoral dimension of that system have not always been the same. They have, rather, altered or been realigned several times in turnout patterns, in the nature of party competition, and in the makeup of the contending coalitions to form five distinct party systems.[8] Thus, for example, mass participation was limited in the first system, extensive in the second and third. Turnout to vote was high in the second and third, progressively lower in the fourth and fifth party systems. The Southern electorate was split between the parties in several of the systems, united in one-partyism in several others.[9]

Second, scholars lately have been much more careful in defining what we mean by political parties. They have identified and labeled various elements and characteristics such as the state of organizational development, the existence of voter stability, and the way parties functioned in office. These critical aspects have to reach a certain state of maturity before it can be said that parties and party systems existed. Party organizations did not fully develop at first, for example. Their influence on appointments to office, or the way legislators behaved, has varied at different moments. The understanding of these variations has allowed scholars to catch subtle but important differences in attitudes toward parties, pre-party political cultures, and the state of American political development at a particular moment.[10]

Third, political historians used to believe, or at least stress, that parties persistently were troubled by the problem of maintaining their unity and those difficulties were the important matters of scholarly concern. Their eyes were often caught by factionalism, explosive extremes, and the threats posed to party stability.[11] The Free Soilers, Mugwumps, and insurgents have all been the subject of much attention.[12] Historians have now rethought that to some degree. Factions, while often remaining important and of some interest, have lost much centrality, and scholars now emphasize stability, that is, continuities of party support, party structure, and party strength and "the larger allegiances that overrode the ubiquitous factions." Parties were more stable than not in their appeal and voter support. Cross-cutting issues such as slavery and sectionalism did not automatically overwhelm them, parties were still able to go about their traditional business in their traditional ways. Parties may often have been faction-ridden but they did not crumble readily as a result.[13]

Fourth, scholars used to believe that unadorned economic and class differences basically determined all mass political choice and party warfare. They now are aware of a different kind of central influence and the importance of other kinds of values and perceptions. The American political system has often had a high ethnoreligious content to it, especially in voter attitudes. Economic divisions have existed as well but not anywhere near as centrally as once thought. Ethnoreligious forces were rooted in historical and community experiences that deeply affected most Americans. They were less intermittent than were economic forces. Such ethnoreligious influences have varied in power over time but they have always been present and potent and throughout the nineteenth century were particularly powerful.[14] Many of the battles over equality, freedom, and the power of government had ethnocultural resonance.[15] The major political shift of 1854, which ultimately led to the triumph of the Republican party, for example, had a very heavy ethnoreligious component.

These ideas and generalizations, and others as well, inform a particular vision of our partisan past. They have been well incorporated into the common discourse of scholars. But further research remains crucial. Some further details are obviously needed and some revision of one of the outstanding generalizations as well. Scholars still need to clarify certain things about America's various political universes, how they did business and their chronological boundaries, for two. In the first, historians have not really examined adequately how party organizations fulfilled their functions and made their linkages. How, specifically, they carry on their job in a particular political environment. Nor have they related such matters to some of the larger questions that help define the political system in any era: how their activities are circumscribed by the belief systems and "givens," the political culture of particular moments. To answer such questions historians have to turn more of their attention inward, inside parties, to pursue the way specific activities were carried on.

In the matter of descriptive generalizations, Lee Benson and I have challenged the idea of five sequential party-systems based on electoral coalitions, arguing instead for an organizing scheme rooted in stages of national development.[16] We agree that politics in America always reflects and refracts larger economic and social concerns of the country yet never in quite the same way. Particular political environments have not been permanent. But we have gone beyond the electoral bases of defining the resulting differences. Despite what often appear to be unchanging values, ideas, and institutions, there have been important discontinuities in our political experience, different textures at different moments and sharp boundaries between different epochs. Sometimes politics has been a central concern of Americans, other times not. At different times there have been different processes, different rules and customs, different institutions operating in different ways. Public business was carried on differently at different moments, institutions were sustained or supported differently, differences existed in restraints, in style, and in substance, policy was made differently, popular and elite expectations varied, politics was linked to the rest of the system in different ways. At various times parties influenced voting behavior differently, represented interests and groups differently, recruited for and organized the government differently, in short, on different political terrain there have been different ways of thinking, organizing, and operating.

We argue that the concept of party systems does not catch all these elements. A changing political culture—or era—is more than the results of shifting voter choices. The concept of party systems particularly does not underscore, as fully as is necessary, the distinctive political culture of the years between the 1830s and the 1890s. A substitute concept, that of political eras, does. It provides an effective framework for analysis of the discrete elements comprising the political system and allows an attempt to tie them together in an intelligible way.

The American political system in the years from the late 1830s to almost the end of the century was qualitatively distinct from what preceded it and from what followed it in marked, important, deterministic ways. The "party period" reflected a particular stage of our history, similar in many respects to others but ultimately unique to its historical moment. A web of relationships and processes came together in specific ways to shape a particular system. Politics then revolved around the needs of a continental, pluralist nation containing a mass electorate with a weak formal interest-group structure, that needed to be organized and mobilized, all of which led to strong parties and particular ways of doing business. Political leaders overcame the structural problems inherent in the Constitution and the ideological restraints often present in American political culture, to establish a partisanly centered means of carrying on public activities.[17] Parties, partisanship, and partisan conflict were no longer unusual, intermittent, or generally seen as objects of great suspicion. But there was more to them than that.

Recently, the editor of a new volume on political parties asked, "have U.S. parties ever been truly strong? What role did their strength enable them to play in the larger political system?"[18] In answer to the first, in the era from the 1830s to the 1890s they were strong, stronger than at any other time in our history. It had become, by the 1830s, increasingly necessary to incorporate individual political effort within centralizing activities and institutions for maximum political effect. The result of that necessity overshadowed all. As Richard P. McCormick has shown, these parties took root in response to the rise of vigorous competition for the presidency which spread across the nation among a large mass electorate.[19] Politics had to be tamed and managed under these conditions. Parties provided the mechanism to do so.

Partisan organizations, partisan commitments, and partisan values shaped and directed the political world in this era as at no other time. Parties became indispensable. They were the main agencies ordering the political system. They carried everything before them in the American political arena, organizing and influencing politics in the most persistent and unyielding ways. They reflected the tensions and divisions of the society, they were integrators and articulators of those tensions. They shaped and structured perceptions, attitudes, and behavior and thereby integrated a complex system. "In general," the editor of the *Albany State Register* wrote in 1850, "great political truths, great principles, important measures, can only triumph through the instrumentality of party."[20]

The antebellum years—particularly from the late 1830s on when the mold had hardened—were a distinctive subperiod within the larger era. They encompassed the defining and institutionalizing part of the larger era with certain very distinct characteristic elements of their own that were later weakened or lost. It was a period when, as Daniel Walker Howe has written, "mass politics was new, political parties were new, and the electorate was not yet jaded."[21] It was a particular kind of partisan golden age—a model of a responsible, and responsive, party system.

The American political order after 1815 reflected the pluralism of the nation at large with its different ethnoreligious groups, economic situations, state and regional foci, incipient sectional tensions, not all fully formed or articulated, but present and intertwined in ways that penetrated the political scene. Despite the many common values and ideas present, different social visions existed in the nation. Ideas, demands, and interests were held differentially throughout the electorate and the rest of the political order. They were operationalized differently. Out of that rose both conflict and the acceptance of conflict as a normal, routine aspect of the political order as well as the development of ways of handling it through the political system. It was an era of bitter political invective growing out of a sharply divisive reality.

Issue alternatives and policy orientations were part of the electoral process. Choices had to be made and fought for. Alternatives had to be framed and presented, and support for each mobilized over a very large landscape. Perception, belief, response were organized and channeled by the political parties. Through an intricate complex of institutions: nominating conventions, campaign newspapers, election rallies, and organized pamphleteering, they drew in hundreds of thousands of males and involved them at every level in the business of politics. Parties articulated conflict and harnessed it as well, they soothed and socialized, made the system a reality and something important to all involved.

Most critically, they bit deeply into the American political process. Americans had been hostile to parties in the late eighteenth and early nineteenth century, and fearful of political warfare. Neither was any longer true. There was antipartyism and individualism to be sure, and yet people came to accept parties and develop partisan commitments and loyalties of tremendous strength, intensity, and vitality because parties expressed their deepest values, beliefs, and preferences. Parties became communities of loyalists with shared values, emotive memories, symbols, and commitments. They were part of the culture of the different social groups in America. Individual and group loyalty and individual and group like-mindedness interacted to form this structure. There was a sense of individual and group commitment to the parties almost impossible to shake.[22]

This was never confined to one group of partisans either. Although slower to develop among many Whigs and much more infused with antiparty attitudes, the party of Henry Clay, William Seward, and Abraham Lincoln reflected the same forces, commitments, and loyalties as did the Democratic party—and never briefly or intermittently. In both parties loyalty was transmitted from generation to generation. Party commitment became in the words of the *American Whig Review*," a life-long ardor, a grand combination of all the loves, passions, interests and opinions . . . Hardly ever . . . [did] men change their religion, or their politics. . . ."[23]

The aura, ambience, and imperatives of political life became so deeply partisan as to make unsurprising the deep voter and officeholder commitments to them. As voters, legislators, and others grew up in, breathed, reacted to, and were affected by this particular environment, they acted in terms of the norms, pressures, and directions of the environment. Candidates for office maximized their identification with their party. They had little existence outside them. Politics articulated group solidarity. Members of each group were affected. It became, as one editor wrote, "a positive duty for every man to become a partisan."[24] People voted not for candidates but for party labels. Party became a particularly salient object in the voting universe and brought with it a remarkable stability in mass voting behavior. Party representatives in office, in legislatures, and Congress could be counted upon to be public, consistent, supporters of a set of partisanly defined policies, demands, and attitudes, and this commitment usually proved stronger than other influences in the political environment for much of the antebellum period.[25]

One of the major components of this system was its almost cement-like electoral stability among the many voters who went to the polls. What emerged in the 1830s and 1840s was an evenly balanced system, in which the two national parties competed effectively with each other, successive elections showing but little change because of the persistent stability of voting choice. Voters did not always go to the polls, although turnout took a quantum jump and was extraordinarily high in this period. About 77 percent of the electorate voted in presidential elections between 1840 and 1860, compared with an average of just under 50 percent between 1824 and 1836.[26] State and congressional elections also had high turnout rates from the late thirties on. When voters did come to the polls, not every one of them voted exactly as they had the election before, but most did—that is, they supported their party's choices regularly in about as stable (not to say rigid) a pattern of behavior as it is possible to have in a variable political world. Their voting choice was generally nonnegotiable.[27]

The strength and intensity of the commitment to parties in pre-Civil War America is clear enough. Behaviorally, we have never had another period quite like the years from the 1830s to the 1890s. Partisan commitment of this intensity survived a long time even amidst great political disruptions such as the realignment of the 1850s and Civil War and Reconstruction years. Certainly, some alterations in voting support and leadership occurred, but for most Americans their commitments and loyalties continued to run in the accustomed channels set in the penetration phase of the party system in the 1830s and 1840s.[28]

But why such intensity, strength, even reverence? Why was popular and elite commitment so strong and parties so important to the mass of voters? One can always look to the primitive, almost tribal, loyalty networks and the much mentioned circus atmosphere of the election campaigns to explain the intense devotion of Americans toward their parties in this era. Politics as popular entertainment: the often exaggerated pageantry and drama of election campaigns, the collective rituals and apparent make-believe in which serious concerns were often packaged in each political season, certainly had something to do with it, but not all. There was much more contributing than simply such contrivances. There was more than unthinking tribal loyalties—or, more pertinently—tribal loyalties were rooted in more than ritual and group memory.

What made the parties powerful were their deep roots in the political nation: the sets of assumptions undergirding the political process, and the many elements constituting that process. Parties represented and organized the political dynamics of the age in ways that people understood, reacted to, and accepted. In the antebellum period parties had two other critical distinguishing characteristics besides their tribal-circus qualities that secured their importance. First, parties framed meaningful choices for the voters, reinforced a sense of real divisiveness in America, played to it, articulated it, and shaped it. There was much at stake in party warfare. Second, parties reflected, in many of their activities, the strong egalitarian tendencies present in the national environment.

Historians have often expressed skepticism, even cynicism, about the way the parties argued and the motives and manipulations of party leaders. Ideology and commitment, they suggest, were subordinated to personal ambition and electoral advantage. The words "unprincipled," "trimmer," "cynical," "manipulator" often appear in historical discourse. The American political system, in this view, confronted few real issues, elections were merely trials for office, not principle, politicians evaded the major problems of the day. Each party was deceptive, incoherent, discordant, and ideologically incompatible, and willing so for the sole pleasure of holding office. One historian has recently summed up his long standing position about them by arguing that "the great parties were in a large sense great hoaxes."[29]

A less extreme view takes parties seriously but still finds them incomplete in crucial ways. A brilliant student of antebellum political parties, Richard P. McCormick, who takes them quite seriously, has recently written that parties performed almost exclusively as electoral machines: establishing the mechanics of political conflict. They, he notes, functioned best in securing agreement on candidates, conducting campaigns, mobilizing their partisans in the electorate, and sustaining and rewarding a large corps of organizers. They were less successful in articulating issues, formulating programs, and enforcing discipline on elected officials."[30]

Both of these perceptions are, at best, partial truths. They are cases where more contemporary ideas about nonideological electoral machine politics seem to have been applied retrospectively to another age, one with quite different political qualities. There is simply not enough in either to embrace the complex interaction among expediency, ambition, ideology, and collective belief systems that shaped party behavior before the Civil War. The fit is not a good one, too much evidence is left out.

Concerns about electability, the need to win a particular election, certainly existed prominently in the minds of political activists in the antebellum years. But such concerns could never be unadorned—and that is the crucial matter. Two counts in particular militate against the cynical view and the larger issues drawn from that view about the nature of parties. First, the cynical view underestimates the realities present in the sharp divisiveness of political rhetoric and political perceptions. Second, it does not sufficiently take into account the presence of limiting boundaries within which the political leaders operated when they framed political appeals and political activities. In that bounded system not everything was permissible and some crucial things were demanded of those who ran the system.

Similarly, the stress on parties as primarily electoral machines, while appropriate on one level, does not confront the other dimensions present nearly enough. There were tensions between the search for victory at the polls and the devotion to the principles each party espoused. But there was more than that. The electoral machine perspective plays down, far too much, the intimate connection between the two sets of elements—electoral and programmatic—shaping party behavior. The imperatives of party recognized, dictated, and celebrated a relationship between the two that cannot be overlooked. Elite maneuvering for partisan advantage always went on. But it did not occur within an anything goes for electoral victory mentality. It could not. Such political maneuvering was always bounded by other matters.

Rhetoric was a weapon of party warfare and an expression of organizing foci in the political world. I do not take elite arguments or their estimates of the political situation or their expressed claims to holding certain values totally at face value. But their rhetoric was politically purposive and not always divorced from realities of belief and commitment. As political leaders worked out the problems of politics, their language took on specific characteristics. Phrases in the flood of campaign speeches, pamphlets, fliers, and the other often vivid paraphernalia of the campaign season were carefully designed to legitimate, point with alarm, argue in favor of, and stress the polar opposites existing between the different parties. Partisan declamations provided clues and signals to the voters. The use and repetition of favorable signals, the reduction of complex policy matters to manageable and easily understood phrases, and the development of negative images of the ideas, policies, personnel, and goals of the other party were all mobilizing techniques designed to reinforce voter attitudes.[31]

But this did not mean that arguments were not without content. Even the most banal speech on the hustings necessarily contained important kernels of belief. Political leaders always had in mind what impact their words would have on the electorate but that did not mean that they could or would say anything. They could not do so unless there was a common discourse and a sense of difference present—strings to be plucked. Political rhetoric was used to mobilize and reinforce voter consciousness and direct voter behavior. It had to take into account, therefore, what elites believed to be voter perceptions and values. The public agenda was there. It needed to be codified and articulated. What leaders said had to characterize the world in understandable and responsive ways. The many mass political subcultures existing in the United States, each with its own perspective, values, and ideas, had to be linked together and to the larger patterns of belief and issues.

The ideological constructs elaborated in this rhetoric were never the same nor did they lack a confrontational bite. Some of what was said in partisan rhetoric was common to each party. In keeping with the republican synthesis, American political language contained many congruent elements. The protection and promotion of the republican experiment were certainly something held in common.[32] This was because of each party's need to establish its legitimacy by appealing to the republican tradition and getting its views aligned with general or consensual views present in the society. But within such congruence divisive confrontation was both possible and present. Republicanism meant different things to different people, its norms could be called on for very different purposes. Within a singular political experiment a plurality of responses was present.

These differences were reflected in the structuring of party arguments. Each party tried to pluck the right strings for its component interest groups. Although coalitionism is the basic nature of American party structures, these were different coalitions, with different sweeps. Each party coalition aggregated society's interests in a selective way.

Different social groups were attracted to each party by each's stance and where their own friends and enemies were locating themselves. Parties had different centers of gravity based on their component groups. There were clearly distinctive political mind sets in America. There was a Democratic mentality and a Whig, later Republican, mentality. Neither party could digest every demand, interest, and pressure within society at a given moment. They could never be all things to all men. "In politics," a writer in one party journal pointed out, "there is a moral chemistry which obtains and vindicates itself as imperatively as natural chemistry does in the laws of the physical universe. We aggregate all bodies which have an affinity to ourselves, and this aggregation will take place whether politicians will it or not." Parties could not build what they often referred to as "unnatural coalitions."[33]

Party rhetoric, therefore, structured around different perspectives which became the center of bitter, sustained conflict. The two receptacles labeled Whigs and Democrats were not empty. Their rhetoric reported who was with them and who was not—clearly. Basically the Whigs wanted to use the federal and state governments to develop and control the social and economic realm. They were cautious in foreign affairs and pushed for a government-orchestrated social stability and controlled economic growth. The Democrats were suspicious of strong government, especially the national, partly for social reasons: their constituents feared government action to restrict immigration or re-shape their lives and values. Partly it was for economic reasons: the Democrats stressed individual action to shape outcomes free from government restriction and control. Parties, therefore, enshrined hereditary animosities between groups, reflected the most up-to-date differences about the society, and provided a way of looking at the world and its problems.[34]

In short, how parties campaigned had an ideological content. They espoused policies not poses. There was a political dynamic that involved the use of such content. Party leaders never forgot that if effective links were to be forged responsive chords had to be struck. As noted, changes in most voters' habits at the polls were glacially slow in the antebellum period. But that did not mean that popular voting behavior was automatic. Stimulation was always an aspect of political warfare. But it had to be the right kind of stimulation. Mass understanding of the electoral necessities in a given situation was not as fully formed as was the leadership's. But like their leaders, the masses had drunk deeply of the imperatives of the partisan political culture dominating their lives. Even as platforms were written and political elites began to articulate political positions, the elements of mass belief and commitment were present, rooted in existing communities. No party leader could ignore for very long, therefore, the things that made their party different from the opposition in the minds of the voters.[35]

The parties' communications networks certainly spelled out a clear attitude about this. They celebrated principles, not men. "In politics, as well as in everything else, men should strictly carry out in practice, what they profess in theory; and it is as much a moral crime . . . to practice deceptions, falsehood and fraud, for political effect, to obtain from the people their votes, contrary to their expectations and belief, as it is to use the same means to defraud individuals of their good name or property." There was little choice with this. "There is a certain limit within which a party, in making its nominations may have regard to availability; but when this principle is made to slight the fundamental principles of the party . . . it can bring nothing but destruction in its train." Democrats "care little—perhaps too little sometimes—for the individual availability of the candidate put forward; but their nominee is placed before the electors as the representative of a clearly defined and fully discussed platform, and every vote that is cast for him is thrown with a full knowledge of the *principles* which lie behind the *man*." We must elect everyone we can, an intense party worker summed up, "at any sacrifice but that of principle." Everyone operated within such defined limits set by the party's traditions, principles, and distinctive outlook.[36]

This rhetorical confrontation allowed the electorate to get a clear sense of identification with their party. Each saw sharp differences between the parties and with good reason. There were such differences. These ideas were received by the masses because they resonated with their own concerns rooted in their own social roles, values, and tensions. I am aware of the research into the class similarities among party leaders and the lack of a democratic distribution of offices. Formisano rightfully argues that "the impulse to dismiss party politics as sound and fury has taken courage, no doubt, from studies of political elites which find that opposing party leaders came from similar social backgrounds."[37] Certain conclusions have been drawn from this research. But what is crucial is that people did see "grounds of differences between the contending parties," that these had policy differences and implications so far as people believed and wanted to believe.[38]

These perceptions and beliefs were not fictions. Too much energy went into formulating and presenting the rhetoric, too much in getting it right. Both parties were too quick to condemn the other for deviation from principle for them not to believe that there was an important political connection forged by battles over principles and differences.[39] Election campaigns served important functions. Part entertainment, they rallied the faithful to the cause, identified friends and enemies, brought everyone into the party camp; part informational, they debated what was right, what was wrong, and provided direct and simple access to the political process. Some of what was said was ritualistic incantation perhaps, but it was understood and reacted to as propounding a set of ideas and connections that were important. Parties meant something. They gave off the unmistakable aura that they were accomplishing what everyone wanted. Party warfare was critical, continuous, and meaningful. The result was that individuals became part of the process, grew devoted to their parties and committed, in intense ways, to the whole system. As one contemporary summed up, party organization had proven "as necessary to the success of principles as truth is to their usefulness and vitality."[40] That belief was an important anchor of the partisan system. Intense party loyalty was rooted in the clash of issues.

There is a second and related matter here. Parties are institutions always in the process of deciding how to act. But how do they decide? How do they frame their platforms, stances, and activities, decide on candidates? Where did power reside within parties? Many historians emphasize elite manipulation, the oligarchic aspect of affairs.[41] It seems implicit in many accounts that when party leaders and political managers are on the scene, they are able to have things pretty much their own way. That, however, is too facile and distorts a more complex reality. Parties need leaders. The leaders dominated the formal process of party activities before the Civil War. But decisions were not made by elite manipulation alone. There was much more complexity to the situation. Antebellum political leaders could never say or do just anything they wanted. Boundaries were set by how the rank and file thought about politics and what they considered to be involved in party battles.

My perspective on this is clear. Who says "who says [political] organization says oligarchy" has not quite finished his sentence.[42] Political cadres organized the channeled politics. Political elites suggested, pushed, and structured values. But they were not alone. Party leaders moved through the complexities of factional politics and, more often than not, successfully, in that they kept the parties together. They articulated political appeals and shaped the grounds of battle effectively and repeatedly. But they did their work in conjunction with other forces: their fellow party members, the mass of party voters. Voters and party workers were not only dependent variables acted upon and responding only to stimuli. They were not only manipulated. There was an inter-active relationship between the two levels whose balance varied over time.

Elites understood and accepted that there was a popular role in politi-cal affairs. It was an era when not only were the people deeply involved, but one in which political leaders were very concerned to deal with that mass involvement. Popular will was a part of politics, to be assessed, understood, and listened to. In pursuing both their expressive and their policy arguing functions, political leaders had to listen carefully, hear, and deal with the opinions and needs of their constituents. They cer-tainly could try to manipulate and direct them. But such actions had to be within set boundaries that they could not be transgressed either ideo-logically or behaviorally. Parties could not take rational electoral calcula-tion beyond certain boundaries. As Giovanni Sartori has written, "party members are not altruists. . . . The power seeking drives of politicians remain constant. . . . [But] even if the party politician is motivated by crude self-interest, his behavior must depart . . . from the motivation . . . Parties are instrumental to collective benefits, to an end that is not merely the private benefit of the contestants."[43]

Everyone had to operate within defined limits set by the party's understandings, traditions, principles, and distinctive outlook. Leaders organized, structured, and helped make coherent the political world. But it was a world that already existed, had many elements to it, including a mass presence, and sets of rules, understandings, and assumptions, what the Albany *Atlas* referred to as "the common law of democracy."[44] Such rules, assumptions, awareness of limits, and what is and is not acceptable, are present in any political system. These may not be well articulated or always clearly spelled out. But the people involved understand them full well. Leaders had to speak and act within these understood boundaries of how decisions were made, how activities went forward. All of these could be ignored only at some peril.

Party leaders were aware of the system's boundaries and spent a great deal of time and effort ensuring that their behavior and what they produced fell within the understood limits of the permissible. There was undoubtedly a great deal of political calculation in all of these pro-cedures, arguments, pleas, and assertions. Pragmatic expediency was part of the leadership's makeup. Some of what they said was cant. But why repeat endlessly how well their behavior squared with democratic expectations and how their opponents' did not unless something else was being touched as well, something basic in regard to assumptions, usages, and traditions? For a group of alleged cynics, party leaders engaged in a tremendous amount of conversation among themselves about propriety, about how to frame ideas to carry the masses with them, about how to win the things that they wanted. As the Whig congressman John Minor Botts put it in 1853, "with me it is not a question of power; it is a question of right and of propriety." In short, party leaders were compelled "to keep true to the same general tack [as the rest of the party] under the necessary penalty of ceasing to be either our leaders, or of us at all."[45]

The extraordinary number of party meetings, conventions, and mass assemblages were all occasions for the rituals and reality of two-way interaction between elites and party supporters. They were held at every level of political life: local, county, district, and state as well as national. The pyramid of representative nominating assemblies, in particular, took on a mystical aura where democratic partisan activities centered. Andrew Jackson referred to convention delegates as being "fresh from the people," perhaps a value judgment, but one that he believed described reality.[46] Others involved in the politics of all parties of the time repeatedly and vigorously agreed with Jackson. Conventions, Andrew Stevenson said, are "the only practicable mode of uniting and giving effect to the popular will." They were useful and central. "Our republican institutions offered nothing so splendid, nothing so well calculated to inspire the American with a firmer belief in the eternity and the justice of democracy, as these voluntary and periodical assemblages of the people."[47]

Their faith had merit to it. The ubiquitous antebellum party conventions did reflect a representative principle and a responsiveness to larger pressures. Those who attended them, and other mass meetings, as well as workers on the hustings, were not all leaders or even aspiring ones. Nor were they all in the pay of some partisanly dominated government agency. Many of them were. But party activities and party meaning reached out beyond such numbers. And the internal dynamics of these meetings generally included careful attention to democratic proprieties. Activities became thoroughly routinized. But policies, arguments, and candidates were rarely simply imposed. They were shepherded through carefully and always within understood boundaries of what was permissible. The delegates were clearly conscious of their representative status. Disagreements abounded and had to be resolved. There were certainly management techniques utilized to accomplish the conventions' goals. And not all of the procedures utilized were always democratic in practice. But many of them were, and all of them helped promote democratic decision-making and party unity, the latter considered a crucial element promoting democratic achievement.

What all of this added up to was a set of institutions, the parties, that reflected much of the egalitarian impulses of their age in the way that they carried on their activities. The political system, as it operated, encompassed not only democratic assumptions and expectations but democratic practices and commitments as well. In so doing the second linchpin of mass commitment to the parties was firmly set in place. In their participation, and in their absorption in a process that seemed bounded by their wishes and demands, the mass of party loyalists found good, strong, and sufficient reasons to commit themselves to parties, believe in them, and remain committed to them, passionately and continuously. Parties were part of their own world, they reflected their own perspectives, and they were guided by their own hands. The political system thus appeared to them to be more responsive and more democratic in this era than it had ever been—expressively both in terms of access to it and in terms of the understanding of how it worked.

Nor was this the end of the interaction. The norms of the political culture established by the 1840s mandated a strong positive linkage between party promises and party performance. The structuring of electoral competition was a prelude to the exercise of power and the enactment of policy. The practice of statecraft was the end result of party warfare. Contemporaries certainly had an instrumentalist view of parties—which was not misplaced.[48] As power was harnessed effectively, a strong tendency existed for party programs to be translated into more or less appropriate government action. Congressional and legislative voting is one good example of the translation. There are many studies indicating how important party labels were in structuring the behavior of the legislative branch of government. Party unity was remarkably high at both national and state levels. This unity had content to it. Voting positions tended to square with rhetorical stances found in the party campaign literature.[49] Nor was this all. There are other examples. We have some studies showing that platforms do count throughout our history, that is, that once in power parties did try to legislate as they had said they would in their campaigning.[50] Certainly in this period they did so. Platforms and campaign rhetoric were considered true guides to subsequent actions. If we are to argue the next step—that there ultimately was little difference between the parties once in office, that argument depends on perceptions. Certainly, Nicholas Biddle in the early 1830s, the Mexicans in 1846, the Irish immigrants of the late forties and early fifties, did not think so, nor did many Southerners, before the late 1850s, think that both parties were the same.

The rhetoric may have been more divisive than the policy reality that followed, but the reality was there, nevertheless. Political elites may not have personally believed in what their parties promised (although a case can be made that they did). But they did believe that it was politically necessary that party promises be kept, not casually discarded after election day. If they were not kept, strong sanctions tended to be invoked. Delinquents were subjected to sharp external and internal party criticism. The close electoral competitiveness between the parties, the intense partisan watchfulness that dominated political activities, made these commitments constant subjects for review, charges, and allegations. As Whig congressman Alexander Duncan of Ohio put it in 1840, "party is the salt of the nation. It establishes a watchfulness and wholesome guardianship over the institutions of our country; it checks and restrains the reckless ambition of those in office and never fails to expose the nonfeascence, misfeascence, or malfeascence of those in power."[51] Such watchfulness and criticism had considerable effect in closely contested areas frequently enough for the sanctions to have had significant force. In sum, in the antebellum political culture of the United States, political organizations were partly independent variables, able to act, shape, and direct. But they were also dependent variables— shaped by the ideas, customs, and practices of the political culture, all of which gave them legitimacy.

Unfortunately, the forms of a democratic and partisan political culture lasted but the realities undergirding them did not. None of what existed here can be explained except as facets of a particular stage of American political development: The emergence of a mass electorate to be managed over a complex, expanding landscape was a central core of antebellum political development. The demands of a pluralist and democratic political culture put these frameworks and processes to work. The parties responded well to that and contributed in this era to the evolution of a democratic and responsive political process. But all of this was time bound to the particular stage of political development. The responsible democratic party-system quality did not survive the impact of the Civil War.

The "party period" continued for almost thirty years after the war's end. Party dominance remained the centerpiece of the political process. But the internal dynamics of that dominance shifted. The war reinforced what had been but also ritualized it out of democratic channels. Forms and procedures remained as they had been. But they were hardened by emotionalism, ritual, and repetitiveness into something more routine and less interactively responsive and democratic than what had been. Political stagnation set in. Platforms became more and more automatic incantations about loyalty to the Union and faith in the G.O.P—or its opponents. Party loyalty became more instinctive and less thoughtful.

Conditions in society changed. The parties reacted slowly to new forces, when they did at all. Other political forms began to emerge: ethnic machines, well-organized interest groups, and independence in voting, for example, as direct results of the parties' failure and their increasing obsolescence.[52]

All of these elements did not lead to decline all at once. But the elements of decay began to appear even as parties continued to dominate the political scene. A new era loomed after 1865, one that would have enormous impact on American politics. By the opening of the twentieth century, the "party period" was gone forever, although it took a long time for that to sink in among those involved. One consequence was apparent almost immediately. The responsive quality of the political system centered on political parties significantly weakened and reappeared only occasionally thereafter. The democratic aspect, the responsiveness, became only an intermittent element in party life.

Nevertheless, while their model age lasted, American political parties had demonstrated some responsive and responsible critical and defining qualities that should not be ignored or underestimated. It had not been a perfect system. People may have persuaded themselves that these elements were present and important. But there was a great deal of truth to that persuasion as well. In the welter of bitter partisan invective and repetitious assertions of the need to behave in certain, responsive ways, were clues to the nature of the political order. Ideas and understandings so widely discussed and accepted bore some relation to facts. They were not all delusions. These understandings and beliefs served some purpose, reflected much reality. They revealed the structure and tone of the political society of the day.

5

"LET THE PEOPLE SEE": REFLECTIONS ON ETHNORELIGIOUS FORCES IN AMERICAN POLITICS (1982)

In a long editorial, "Let the People See," in the *New York Tribune* in 1852, Horace Greeley, the great editor and leader of the Whig party, gloomily evaluated his party's chances at the polls that autumn. He believed that in any workplace, a machine shop, for example, fifteen out of twenty workmen supported Whig economic policies. However, they would not vote for the party. Why not?

> Jones hates the Whigs because Esq. Simpson is a leading Whig, and feels too big to speak to the common people. Marks has been trained to believe that the Whigs were Tories in the Revolution, and starved his father in the Jersey prison ship. . . . Smithers is for a tariff himself, but his father before him was a Democrat, and he isn't going to turn his coat. Smolker doesn't object to anything his Whig shop-mates propose; but he is a foreigner and thinks the Whigs hate foreigners; so he feels bound to go against them. Pilkins is a heretic in religion, and most of the leading Whigs he knows are Orthodox; and he can't stand orthodoxy any how you can fix it.

And so, Greeley concluded, "for one or another of a hundred reasons, *equally frivolous or irrelevant* [emphasis added], votes are piled up against us—not for anything we as [a] party affirm or propose, but because of considerations as foreign from the real issues of the canvass as is the subjugation of Japan."[1]

Greeley's lament reflected his impatience with such politics, and his refusal to believe in the relevance of any political choice not based on economic matters. Political attitudes, assumptions, and values rooted in religion, nationality, history, memory, and prejudice, rather than in a rational, specifically economic, calculus of issues, parties, and candidates, could not be important. Greeley recognized their presence but denied their centrality in the political world even when he continually encountered evidence that he was wrong.[2]

Most social commentators and many involved public figures have traditionally agreed with Greeley. Nathan Glazer has written, for example, that American society is one which "there are no strangers." Despite examples of persistent ethnoreligious tensions even in such advanced Western societies as the United Kingdom and Canada, the United States is "unique" in its refusal "to define itself in ethnic, or religious, or national terms, as our basic founding documents make clear."[3] As long ago as 1940, Judge Sam Rosenman capped this attitude in a resolution presented to the American Jewish Committee. "Differences in religion, race or nationality," he argued, "have no part in an American political campaign. Elections should be determined exclusively on an American basis rather than on the basis of the alleged separate interests of any religious or racial group. No member of any religion or any race or any nationality has any right to vote on any basis other than his belief as to what is best for the United States alone."[4]

Behind such denials has lain a particular conceptual view of the world, one held both by scholars and by the larger public. As Benjamin R. Barber has recently written, we live in a political culture in which

> in almost every case, our idea of the political begins with the *homo economicus*: man conceived as a secularized, privatistic, self-regarding calculator motivated solely by hedonistic interests and conscious of the political only by dint of selfish prudence. Our politics, in the blunt reductionism of Harold Lasswell, is thus defined by the question "who gets what, when, where and how?" Right and left may differ on the answer but they concur on the question. Our radical, no less than our conservative, ideologies consequently tend to be secular, material, privatistic, and commercial. To the extent community plays any role at all, it is community held together by prudential justice but not divine order, by conflict and contract but neither fraternity nor patriotism, by economics rather than religion, and by interest rather than faith.[5]

But are such matters as frivolous and irrelevant as Greeley thought and generations of American historians and other commentators have believed? In the past twenty years, as part of a major scholarly interdisciplinary movement, specifically the interpenetration of history and the social sciences, a group of American scholars, the "new political historians," has sketched an American political landscape dominated by just those forces and influences Greeley and his successors denied as either relevant or central.

The findings grew out of a different kind of historical research, one that focused on first measuring the observed political behavior—usually on election day—of aggregated masses of voters, considering the way they distributed themselves between the parties, and examining the defining elements in each party's coalition. The research focused on "the whole man in his total social environment and a multiplicity of potentially relevant variables whose mix can kaleidoscopically shift over time and place."[6] When done, its discoveries, with their undercurrent of a persistent prejudice so complex and intractable so as to escape melioration, have been disconcerting to both those who wish to think in terms of class conflict and economic confrontation and to those who think in terms of America's ability to escape tribal conflict. Political warfare in the United States was neither sound and fury signifying little nor a persistent great battle between hostile, competing, economically defined classes and groups.

Electoral politics, at least, had a pattern to it. The American people were intensely politicized, highly organized for political warfare: they turned out to the polls in extraordinary numbers, were steady and traditional in their voting habits, and battled fiercely to establish their different visions of the United States. Only occasionally did a powerful force shake them from their habitual patterns of behavior. Different subcultures existed within America with different values, belief systems, and mores, which become politicized under most conditions, certainly in the nineteenth century, to shape the substance and structure of American politics. The particular texture of the political culture was ethnoreligious. There was a wide range of different religions, ethnic groups, denominations, and practices in America. The distinctions among these led to different styles and attitudes which came into politics as specific political ethoses.[7] Groups had been hostile to one another in Europe. They proved to be no less so here. The dead hand of history and the live interaction between groups living close to one another had an impact on the way masses of Americans defined their situation and acted in politics. In short, the ethnoreligious factor in American politics is not confined to recent days, the Moral Majority and the Creationists, or to the slightly more distant question of whether a Catholic should be President. It is, rather, an old, deeply rooted element of our political culture. "At least since the 1820s," Lee Benson has written, "ethnic and religious differences have tended to be relatively the most important sources of political differences in the electorate."[8]

Horace Greeley once described Irish immigrants flooding into New York City as "deplorably clannish, misguided and prone to violence."[9] The first point can be applied to most groups in nineteenth-century America—deplorable or not. People lived closely circumscribed lives in small distinct communities—even within large cities, villages, and intermediate sized towns—with, in David Potter's terms—"strong social and psychological forces holding them together."[10] Within these communities a complex and cohesive web of relationships developed that heightened community solidarity and community isolation from other groups. Most of these communities were ethnoreligious in composition, that factor providing the substantial element of community solidarity. Nineteenth-century American culture was particularly imbued with ethnic awareness and religious consciousness, practices, and behavior. Community institutions fostered that ethnoreligious heritage, as well as a deep sense of separatism from one another. As one commentator wrote in 1857, about German Catholics, they "avowedly desire to keep their people apart from Americans with a view more surely to separate them from Protestants and infidels." The Protestants and infidels felt the same way.[11]

At the center of this political world, for much of our history, have been the parties. They reflected the multicultural bite of American society. Early on, as a community developed a particular political ambience and stance the political aspect of that was associated with a party. People came into constant contact with their friends and enemies through the parties. "Each party represented not a single denomination, but a loosely structured set of denominations sharing a collective central tendency."[12] Each party absorbed and reflected the political ethos of its constituent groups. Each had different epicenters and was perceived to be different from the others. As the editor of the Know-Nothing Almanac put it in 1855, the object of each party was clear. The purpose of the Republicans was "to take care of the colored population"; of the Democrats, "to take care of the Foreigners and the spoils"; and of the American party "to take care of America, the American people, and American interests."[13]

It was not only that parties reflected such differences, however. They led battles, as Allan Lichtman has described them, "across the trenches dividing . . . systems of competing values."[14] One of the crucial things about these tribal groups and one of the major reasons for partisan organizations was the willingness, waiting to be energized, of the different groups to use the government to accomplish their specific ethnoreligious goals. "History shows us that the contest of race and religion is the bitterest of all, that it has ever been attended with the most frightful, terrible results . . . ," the editor of The Democratic Review wrote in 1855, "Government [therefore] ought not to undertake to make, or unmake, religious creeds, for any man. . . ."[15] That was certainly one libertarian strain in the political ethos of the time, but another also existed strongly, one that wanted to correct, repair, and reform any iniquities present in society. The state had a role to reflect and impose specific ethnoreligious tribal values.

In short, Americans did not have proper regard for each other's differences, rather the differences became the occasion for political confrontation as different groups maneuvered for political and social advantage through government action. Arthur Mann reminds us that the early Americans found a case for immigration in "the absorptive power of the host society"—Yankee, evangelical, Protestant—and in "the adaptability of human beings."[16] But this did not work. Acute group conflict existed in America of a very particular and persistent kind. Beneath the trappings of unity a war went on to define America— a war fought by political armies each rooted in a different political ethos. The issues produced in this atmosphere "touched lives directly and moved people deeply."[17] One issue, a bill, a matter of dispute, or some specific policy, be it schools, temperance, banks, or tariffs, meant different things culturally to different Americans. Such evidence strongly underlines the fact that "cultural politics is not a side show that occasionally attracts our attention with odd issues like temperance and sabbatarianism; it is as pervasive and powerful in shaping public life as the impact of economic politics."[18]

II

Paul Kleppner has enriched and clarified our understanding of this process in numerous, important ways. First, to continue an earlier metaphor, he elaborates and delimits many of the contour lines on the political landscape. He deepens our knowledge of the role of ethnocultural forces in shaping American politics, most specifically, by expounding the particular importance of the religious belief/style dimension. Second, he emphasizes more clearly and fully than anyone had ever done before, the role of contextualism in affecting the various determinants of the vote. Third, he sketches the particular way that parties played their roles as constituent integrators of social-group tensions and conflicts, rather than as policymakers or instrumentalist institutions. Each of these things had been said to some extent before. Kleppner, more than anyone before him, takes these ideas much further, makes them much richer, systematizes the material, and thus makes our understanding much more complex.[19]

American politics, from the electoral realignment of the 1850s, through the party stalemate after the Civil War, to the political disruption and realignment in the 1890s, was the product of a vibrant social reality and the political dynamics it unleashed. Voters, Kleppner wrote in his first book, "were more often concerned with matters which impinged on their daily lives directly and which immediately challenged their personally structured value systems than they were with national problems whose direct salience was not clearly perceptible to them."[20] Nineteenth-century American partisanship "was not rooted in economic distinctions. Neither gradations in wealth nor perceived differences in status nor shared orientations toward the work experience were at the core of partisan commitments. Partisan identification mirrored irreconcilably conflicting value conflicts emanating from divergent ethnic and religious subcultures."[21] He particularly hammers on one central theme: the pietist-antipietist split among religious denominations as the major shaping influence determining the character of the political world. The partisan cleavages of the era, he sums up, "involved a value-and-interest conflict between Yankee moralist subculture and white southern subculture . . . [and] a religious-value conflict between pietist and antipietistic subcultures."[22]

There were some interesting limits to this central thrust of American political life. Kleppner is very careful to remind us that ethnoreligious differences "were *relatively* more important as determinants of nineteenth-century social-group cohesiveness and party oppositions than were economic attributes or social status."[23] This is a recognition both that other possibilities existed and that a matter of subtle measurement is involved.[24] Still, Kleppner makes it very clear where his research has brought him.

Kleppner's findings open up another, very large, question as well: that of a contextualism which affected and shaped the patterns of American voting behavior. As Philip Ennis suggests, each generalized defining influence on political behavior "is differentially drawn into political life depending upon the kind of community [present]—its makeup, situation and history."[25] Analyses of mass voting behavior, Kleppner reminds us, "require sensitivity to sociopolitical contexts, specific conditions, and historical experiences—as well as economic, ethnic and religious identifications." What looked like the same general influence had differential impact on voters because of differences in people's outlooks framed by such contextual factors. Being a Baptist, Kleppner suggests, does not have "the same psychological meaning in all contexts; [the] intervening experiences of the group, prevailing political-structural conditions, in social-structural milieux, and variations in party characters" all have "salience" in determining "specific partisan choices."[26] Such variations have to be carefully specified and delimited for our full understanding.

Kleppner also reaffirms the centrality of the political parties in this environment. "For most social groups," he writes, partisanship was "a means of expressing and defending subcultural values," party choice was an act of group solidarity. Each party represented and reflected the shared values of its component groups.[27] Parties were delegates to the national government from their constituent groups. Each party fought for the future of the nation. The character of each was determined by its ethnoreligious clientele. The Republicans, in general, were the home of the absolutist, moralist groups nurtured in the Yankeedom of New England and the pietism of that region's western outposts. The Democrats were different. They were the product of Catholicism, Southernism, antipietist Protestantism, and of certain ethnic groups as well. As one of the Adams clan succinctly put it, they were "Copperheads and curs—their ideas low and Irish."[28] Public policy emerged out of the particular constituent demands of each's membership. Increasingly the GOP appeals were rooted in nationalism, anti-Catholicism, and positive government action to purify America. The Democrats, at least until the 1890s, fought against such in the name of cultural heterogeneity and in favor of freedom from the coercive restraints demanded by Republicans.

Parties were clung to loyally and tenaciously by their members because to many they were something much more than cold, lifeless organizations. "Late nineteenth-century American parties Kleppner argues, "can meaningfully be thought of as political churches . . . parties became the secular analogues of churches."[29] The Republican was, as one preacher at the time put it, "the *party* of God, the *party* of Jesus Christ," battling "against the party of iniquity." It was "the Republican Church." The Democrats, in their way, were the same. It is no wonder that a New York governor could suggest in this atmosphere that a "nonpartisan is an unbeliever."[30] Even third parties, including those usually defined as economic protest groups, in Kleppner's view, did not escape this religious quality and the ethnoreligious structuring of their membership.

Professor Kleppner's work completes a stage in the revision of American political history by the new political historians. His research has taken the basic arguments of that group and made them clearer and fuller than they were. Their substance is out in the open, the landscape well marked and the roadmaps nicely detailed. This is a tribal conception of politics. Despite tendencies toward unity and the presence in our history of a common set of shared assumptions, institutions, and rituals, American social life in the nineteenth century produced situations in which tribal, not national, mores imposed group standards, objectives, and behavior in politics albeit within a national frame of reference.

Tribes were religious, ethnic, and cultural groups that identified themselves as distinct in some form—certainly they did so in politics. The members may have clustered together geographically—they often did—but the important thing about them was their awareness of their common association and of the threatening presence of hostile others close by. It was a complex tribalism, not always easily sorted out but present and predictable nevertheless. Sometimes the interaction among the different tribes inhabiting the American space was visceral, sometimes ideological, sometimes the result of specific policy formulations and pressures. A lot depended on how the different ethoses of each tribe were perceived or activated within the political arena. There were occasional flashes of violence in the confrontation but perhaps it is a testament to the power and importance of the political system that the tribes usually relied on it to handle and resolve their conflicts.[31]

III

All of this is quaint and interesting, but has not that world departed forever? Recently, in the *Yale Review*, James Turner cited Professor Kleppner's research findings as "one of the most spectacular triumphs of historical research in recent years."[32] Our nineteenth-century politics is now subject to "a much more subtle interpretation . . . as a form of cultural conflict and accommodation." But, then he goes on to say, "except for a few political scientists, who cares? Unless history has some meaning for our lives now, what good is it?" Certainly there have been many alterations in the dynamics of American politics. Economic differences and forms of class consciousness have, for example, played a much greater role in affecting popular voting since the 1930s than they did earlier. Still, politicized tribal forces continue influential in both similar and revised guise, perhaps with as much commitment to government interventionism as ever. Such forces can still be appealed to, they can still be mobilized, there are still political responses to ethnoreligious impulses—not all of the time but under the right circumstances because Americans continue to find it appropriate to distinguish people along ethnoreligious lines, and such distinctions penetrate and often permeate political conflicts.

The politics of ethnoreligious differences, of different subgroup value systems, and conflicts among them, are as recent, therefore, as the latest anti-abortion rally, the most recent electoral campaign. Kennedy in 1960, the Goldwater campaign which startlingly revived very ancient divisions indeed, the revival of white ethnicity in the 1970s and of black and religious difficulties, all suggest the persistent quality of these patterns as does the persistence of an interventionist ethic in the American psyche rooted in conceptions of right behavior. We have much scholarly evidence of this. As one recent study of popular voting concluded, "religion continues to exert an impact on party identification over the period [1952–1972] studied. . . . Furthermore, the connection between religion and party identification does not seem to diminish across groups with changes in socioeconomic status or suburbanization."[33] It can be "openly questioned," another scholar argued, "whether the dual processes of acculturation and assimilation have so eroded the culture bases of ethnic groups that distinctive political styles are no longer identifiable. Fundamental value orientations die hard, and unless assimilation runs its full course, distinctive ethnic value orientations will remain to act as guides to distinctive ethnic social and political behavior."[34]

In the everyday realm of political activity similar evidence abounds. According to an Associated Press story in July 1980, Ronald Reagan, in trying to lure Democrats to his side, intended to appeal, in familiar language, to "a community of shared values." His people were said to have targeted white Baptists as a group to be particularly wooed by the party in the campaign.[35] The government's power continues to be involved as well. A libertarian is recently quoted as saying that "government shouldn't be in the business of trying to wipe out sin." But many have believed otherwise in the name of imposing one set of tribal values on others in the society. They continue to do so as the just quoted lament makes clear. Since the presidential election, efforts to, in David Broder's words, "expand the government's efforts to prescribe and regulate individual behavior" have grown. In one story about book censorship in high schools, *Time* magazine again used quite familiar words and concepts. "This is not book burning or book banning," it reported, "but a rational effort to transmit community values."[36]

To be sure, as some observers have argued, contemporary ethnoreligious conflicts do not, at first glance, appear to have the sharp edges of those in the nineteenth century and often take different forms. But while they may be more muted and have altered substances, the role of different ethoses rooted in religious, cultural, ethnic, and locational differences, remains unmistakable. They may take many forms but the rhythms expressed and the motivating impulses are the same. Clearly, while the ethnoreligious/tribal dimension of political cleavages has not always been alone in importance, or even been the most influential cause of voting behavior at every moment, it has persisted longer and formed more of an underlying pattern in our politics than any other. That remains as true in the 1980s as at any other time in our history. There has been a strength and tenacity to it even in a supposedly secularized and technocratic world. Science, increased education, and economic rationalization had been expected to reduce, if not eliminate, "man's attachment to ancient ties of common ancestry, common land and common faith." They may have, to a degree, but really such "ties of race, nationality and religion," the sense of us versus them, retain a great deal of importance in the contemporary world.[37] There remains a deep current of attitudes and feelings running within the American political environment that can still be tapped, that still has influence, and that still operates to shape political life and the role government plays in our society. So strong has this quality remained that Walter Dean Burnham suggests that "the pervasiveness of religious cognitions in American political life is yet another—and very important—comparative peculiarity of this country in the cosmos of advanced industrial societies."[38]

The idea of a potent, persistent, ethnoreligious tribalism bothers many historians and public commentators. Some have been quick to dismiss its importance or its persistence. Professor Carl Degler, president of the Organization of American Historians, recently argued that "surely the American people are more than a collection of diverse nationalities, classes and genders living between Canada and Mexico."[39] Others have sought solace in the presence and strength of cultural pluralism as the dominant force shaping American history. One popular magazine recently defined America as "a mosaic of cooperating cultures, differing in lifestyles and languages within the broad confines of U.S. democracy and nationhood."[40] One actually quoted Horace Greeley as pointing to the "fragility" of such forces. In writing about the Know-Nothing movement in 1855, Greeley said of that movement that "it would seem as devoid of the elements of persistence as an anti-Cholera or anti-Potato rot party, and unlikely long to abide the necessary attrition of real and vital differences of opinion among its members with respect to the great questions of foreign and domestic policy which practically divide the country."[41]

Such comments miss the point. It is true as I have said, that polarization is no longer as important or as clear cut as it once was. But, on the other hand, the realities of American pluralism have never been all that dominant. That pluralism was only one, and not the major, force in the relations along the different subcultures in America. Certainly, within the political structure of nineteenth-century America there was a persistent battle over whether or not Catholics, and some other groups as well, should be allowed here, and if they were under what conditions. The battle went a particular way. Nevertheless all of this suggests the presence and power of certain constraints in the American political system. Given these realities their complexities have to be explored. It remains, in other words, for political historians and analysts to get on with the job of specifying and sorting these out within the general tribal environment present.

IV

Political historians still have much work to do in defining these ethno-religious forces and how they operated. A full research agenda would include much about the political parties. The old and persistent canard that they were nothing more than Tweedledum and Tweedledee—with nothing in the way of principles or issues dividing them—has been laid to rest and replaced by the vibrant confrontations of tribal warfare. But, parties, as confederacies of tribes, were joined together in a bipolar political world due to constraints imposed by the Constitution. That bipolarism levied conditions and restraints on each individual tribal cluster and a continuing emphasis on the common themes that held the clusters together against the other coalition of their enemies. Coalitions impose the necessity of compromising, watering down, looking the other way about divisive matters. The need to find a winning formula dictated careful interacting among different tribes with different priorities. How was all of this done?

Party leaders were at the center of the process of building winning coalitions and keeping groups together. They had to become adept at fitting the different pieces of a complex mosaic together in constructive ways for their purposes. At the same time, they had to be adept at arousing their troops through specific appeals and visions of the world. How much room for maneuver did they have in all of this? How autonomous were they, how free of the influences shaping them? Party leaders had to meet the symbolic needs of their constituents, but how do they mediate and compromise and operate among intense groups as political leaders are supposed to do? Party leaders in this kind of situation were, as Morton Keller refers to them, "part tribal chieftain[s]" and part coalition builders.[42] Professor Kleppner is particularly good in tracing the difficulties, the always present vicissitudes of the party leaders, as they tried to operate within the constraints of the internal dynamics of the party coalition.

If the parties were primarily constituent and shaped only by their social groups, then there is a very big problem indeed. They cannot be generally responsible and instrumentalist in policy making but become, instead, primarily symbolic and myth reinforcing. Professor Kleppner's findings seem to stress the inability of party leaders to escape from their tribal delegate roles even though some tried to do so. His party leaders usually were buffeted by internal pressures and unable to overcome that social situation. They apparently had little maneuvering room or leadership capability. The parties he describes have been characterized by one reviewer as "vessels with neither rudder [nor] crew."[43] The passengers ran the ship.

Professor Jensen has argued that a new kind of party leader emerged in the 1890s, one more cosmopolitan than earlier and less bound by the dictates of the tribes.[44] Still, there is a tension here that has not been completely resolved. Both kinds of party leaders were present, even between 1850 and 1890, and we have not yet fully examined the possible varieties of the leader's behavior and the possibilities under different conditions and within the different parties. The point is that for the moment, the questions of the constraints on and the opportunities for political leaders to operate remains less clear than they should be. The matter needs further research and elucidation before the crucial question as to how American political leaders functioned within the specific kind of political universe they inhabited will be fully understood.

A related and equally important question rising from the tribal nature of parties concerns how, when, and with what effort voters were mobilized to go to the polls on election day. The American scene was a rich cauldron of simmering problems, ideas, behaviors, and events that were all possible political foci and ones that could affect and be affected by the cultural tensions present. But how were they set off, ignited? The significant thing in electoral politics, once the nature of group loyalties has been established, is this triggering matter. We have to elaborate how campaigns are structured and carried out given the resources present to carry on political warfare. What did the parties do here? Was the mobilization the product of the ways parties operated in campaigns? Professor Kleppner's answer defines the direction of affect clearly: "These antagonistic political subcultures did not spring to life in response to partisan rhetoric. Rather, the rhetoric expressed the emotional and psychological perspectives of each party's constituent groups."[45] This implication of generating from within would leave little for parties to do.

But the question of mobilization still remains undeveloped. The stimuli provided by the parties, the importance and nature of campaigns to get out the vote, the reasons voters came out and did what they did, all need further elaboration. Were voters stimulated to be purposive, or automatic and unthinking, or a mixture? Was party the translator and starter engine? What was the nature of the interaction between voters and party? Voting was not simply a given but the product of perceptions and actions that often had to be stimulated or else they would remain immanent, not actual. There is a reservoir of deeply held passions and attitudes about others. It has to be triggered into political action, as Al Smith's candidacy in 1928 and John Kennedy's in 1960, for example, triggered significant increases in religiously defined voting. Such increases were not automatic. The thrust of recent research into voting behavior emphasizes the stimulative effect of the way campaigns are carried on, candidates act, and parties engage themselves. As Alan Lichtman points out, for example, Al Smith met the religious issue unambiguously and directly in 1928.[46] The result was an upsurge of a certain kind of behavior in that election consequent to Smith's behavior. At other times too, specific kinds of campaign activities have produced specific voting responses. Walter Dean Burnham, refers to how these tribal issues emerge "under the right circumstances and *with skilled leadership*" (emphasis added).[47]

Finally, the focus of voter loyalties in a highly tribal but also highly partisan political system needs further elaboration. There is much evidence of the strong, primary political attachment of voters to their parties, first, last, and always, not necessarily only to or generally to their social groups, both in present and in past situations.[48] It is the party that comes to embody their political faith. They call themselves Democrats (or Republicans) first when engaging in political activity—not Catholics, Pietists, or Germans. Does such party loyalty change or affect the interaction among tribal groups and parties? Strategies need to be developed to explore this further since it goes to the heart of how the political system functions and how tribal warfare occurs. In short, once more, questions of the relations among social-tribal tensions, the party system, and voter behavior remain open for further exploration.

All the answers to these questions are affected by the other major factor stressed by Professor Kleppner, the contextual element in American voting behavior. This has profound implications for the study of American politics, past and present. If Americans react to political stimuli, or behave in a variety of wide-ranging ways due to a difference in place, history, experience, and perceptions, then formidable consequences follow. At one level, for example, such contextualism, along with the tribalism already referred to, goes a long way to explaining the relative and persistent failure of class-conscious political movements in American political history.

As Geoffrey Blodgett has written, "class consciousness and economic radicalism were shallow and ephemeral characteristics" in the American electorate.[49] Friedrich Engels, as quoted by Professor Kleppner, expressed the importance of tribal influences as long ago as 1893. "American conditions," he wrote, "involve very great and peculiar difficulties for steady development of a worker's party. . . . [I]mmigration . . . divides the workers into two groups: the native-born and the foreigners, and the latter in turn into (1) the Irish, (2) the Germans, (3) the many small groups, each of which understands only itself: Czechs, Poles, Italians, Scandinavians, etc. And then the Negroes. To form a single party out of these requires quite unusually powerful incentives."[50] But this becomes even more devastating, given the profound difficulty of putting a workers' party together, if "the many small groups" themselves react differentially even to tribal stimuli, let alone economic ones. Czechs, Poles, Italians, etc., each may understand only itself, but the behavior of each in the political world varies in some degree from group norms. The "unusually powerful incentives" suggested by Engels are almost impossible to contemplate or conceive given contextualism in group reactions. We know from the research of several historians that even during a depression of widespread impact, a variety of different responses, not all to the economic pressures present, occurs even within a central tendency.[51]

The larger implication to be drawn from all of this is that the American people have never been able to see anything whole, react uniformly, cleanly, clearly, and directly to specific stimuli. In recent years, much has been made of the fragmentation and particularism in our politics even in the face of national danger.[52] Contextualism is one aspect of that, one that has not always been fully grasped. It suggests not only how heterogeneous we are (observers going back to James Madison have seen that). It also suggests how difficult the shaping of responses, reaction, and action always has been in America. It remains likely to continue as such despite the growing power of the media and other forces whose power and nature might be expected to counteract the contextual element.[53] Research incorporating this idea promises a great deal of additional understanding of such problems throughout American political history.[54]

This last matter underscores one final item. Description of the way people choose to vote and of the nature of the party system that follows is both useful and necessary and leads to another question directly: Given what we have learned from the work of Professor Kleppner and others about tribalism, contextualism, and the nature of political parties, what, then, is the capacity of the political system to perform the necessary functions of governing? The people rule, or more accurately, vote, in our system, but how, why, and for what purpose? It is clear that the nature of the voting system suggests repeated, formidable problems in the shaping of public policy, public understanding of the needs of the polity, and in developing mass support for the political system.

Walter Dean Burnham has described our political system as one rooted in premodern conflicts of a nondevelopmental, noneconomic nature even when problems of development, the distribution of economic resources, and the shaping of economic policy have moved to the center of the national stage. Instead of confronting them, Burnham remarks, we have remained "preoccupied" from the start of our national history and into the present "with problems involving the integration of diverse and often antagonistic subcultures."[55] He further suggests that this misplaced concern and the persistence in our affairs of the dead hand of a history and attitudes long gone, of preoccupation with conflicts rooted in a deep tribal past, open the way for the hegemonic domination of the system by cosmopolitan elites rather than by the people, with the consequent atrophying of the institutions of public policy making and political expression. This is followed by the decline of popular involvement in politics.[56] It is a pessimistic commentary based on his reading of present realities and of what the new political history has discovered about our behavior. More, it is a devastating comment on the capacity of the system (only reinforced by the implications of contextualism discussed above). Burnham's interpretations have not been universally accepted by scholars. Nevertheless, his preoccupation with a system's ability to rule is a necessary one that political historians are only beginning to turn to and consider extensively. It is a next assignment rooted in the implications drawn from the concerns and findings of such new political historians as Professor Kleppner.

V

The visions of the new political history have not swept everything before them. That work, produced over the last generation, remains an important aspect of a longer-range challenge to the traditions of the Progressive historians who so long dominated American historiography with their visions of the onward march of history toward the triumph of the good. That challenge has found great fault with what Christopher Lasch has called the Progressives' "drastic simplification of issues; synthetic contrivance of political and intellectual traditions . . . [and] strident partisanship," and most of all, their commitment to a certain kind of persistent political conflict in the American past.[57]

What will replace the Progressive vision among historians at least, remains unclear at the moment. There are several candidates of unequal strength and merit. As earlier noted, many people remain uncomfortable with the new political history and its findings. They seek to avoid taking into account a certain kind of past rather than trying to confront it and proceed from there. But the finding that politics is often shaped by traditional differences, ancient prejudices and antagonisms, remains an important interpretative finding and one that seems to have much applicability throughout our history from colonial times to the present. The ethnoreligious interpretation articulated by such new political historians as Professor Kleppner, therefore, holds out a most important insight into the American political process, one that has to be incorporated in and taken into account in any and all historical research and understanding. "God has an eternal role to play in the continued unfolding of American history," Senator Robert Byrd recently told his colleagues.[58] But whose God, which of his people, and which of their practices, creeds, and values, continue to be debated and fought over even in the very secular United States of the 1980s. And the role of government power continues to be a major aspect of that battle.

THREE:
PARTIES, SECTIONS,
AND THE UNION

6

"THERE ARE OTHER QUESTIONS BESIDE THAT OF SLAVERY MERELY": THE DEMOCRATIC PARTY AND ANTISLAVERY POLITICS
(1983)

Any attempt either to end slavery in the United States or to prevent its further expansion had to take into account a political system largely dominated by the Democratic party after 1828. Democrats did not always have their own way, but despite significant opposition from the Whigs and occasional defeats, as in 1840 and 1848, they usually controlled the federal government from Andrew Jackson's day to James Buchanan's. The way that the party's hundreds of thousands of supporters reacted to the rise of political movements against slavery was a major factor in the calculus shaping antislavery fortunes after the 1830s.[1]

While recognizing that the Democrats were generally hostile to the antislavery movement in every form, historians have paid particular attention to those in the party who espoused antislavery extension in the 1840s and then moved into the Republican party in the 1850s. The role played by the "Democratic Republicans" in the years leading to the Civil War has been especially well told. With the Barnburner revolt in New York and its transformation into the Free Soil movement in 1848 as the starting point, the Hannibal Hamlins, Francis P. Blairs, Preston Kings, James Doolittles, and Gideon Welleses have all had their actions recorded in the annals of the antislavery political movement.[2] The reasons for their behavior are clearly marked as well. The "Civil War Synthesis" in American political history assigns a persistent, all-encompassing centrality and influence to sectionalism and the slavery-extension issue in antebellum politics.[3] Opposition to the expansion of slavery, Eric Foner writes, became "the central political question of the late 1840s, and the vehicle by which antislavery became, for the first time, a truly mass movement in the North."[4] By the beginning of 1848, another historian has written, sectional antagonisms were heated "to the flash point, and in both major parties sizable free-soil factions stood ready to renounce old allegiances rather than acquiesce in the South's latest demands." Party splits and party collapse followed, all made possible because "traditional issues were fast dropping by the wayside."[5] The Democrats were not immune. "Antislavery sentiment was increasing among their constituents," Aileen Kraditor sums up, and, therefore, they had to take a stand as a matter of political survival.[6]

The focus on the antislavery Democrats is understandable in certain terms: tracing the linear development of American politics toward the emergence of the Republican party and the sectional confrontations of the 1850s is attractive because it is an important matter. The Civil War did occur when the forces opposing slavery's extension won control of the government. Some Democrats, as recently joined converts to the Republican party, did play a role in that triumph. But does such emphasis accurately depict the politics of the time or portray the overall posture and behavior of the Democrats in response to those politics? The answer is clearly "no" to both questions. Too much emphasis on the power of the sectional forces in the politics of the period from the 1830s on, distorts the rich complexity of political reactions to the events of the day.[7]

The scholarship of the past twenty years has sensitized us to the amount of hostility in the North to sectionalism and antislavery movements, a hostility that lasted late into the era of sectional conflict.[8] Many antebellum politicians were not especially responsive to the slavery question. Furthermore, sectional fears and tensions remained largely unfocused into the late 1840s because there existed in the United States a set of nonsectional partisan political divisions. As a result, the response of politicians and voters to the rise of antislavery political movements was inconsistent and complex, never exclusively sectional and clear-cut. And nowhere was this complexity more evident than in the Democratic party's posture toward antislavery politics.

There was antagonism toward independent, antislavery extension, third party movements among Whigs and later among some Republicans as well. Similarly, many Whigs proved hesitant about changing their accustomed ways in politics. Nevertheless, the core of such hesitating responses to the rise of sectional politics clearly lay with the bulk of the Northern Democrats. The number of Democrats who supported the Liberty party or became Free Soilers and later joined Republicans on the slavery issue was but a very small part of the whole Northern constituency of the party. The majority—the mainstream of the party in the North—challenged the rise of antislavery and did not join the movement when it did emerge, even when some of the key leaders of their party defected either temporarily or permanently. They remained loyal during the Van Buren defection in 1848 and stayed on after 1854 and the rise of Republicanism. They soldiered on in their party with its antislavery stance despite the loss of friends and power. As a result, the party's vote in the North remained high right through the election of 1860 (see Table 6.1).

Table 6-1. Democratic Vote, Northern States:
Presidential Elections, 1840–1860

	No.	Percentage
1840	809,485	47.2
1844	927,333	48.8
1848	810,662	40.0
1852	1,153,556	50.2
1856	1,227,106	41.4
1860	1,488,391*	43.8

*Combined Douglas and Breckinridge totals.

Antislavery politics involved different levels of commitment, different intensity, tactics, and even diverse opinions on the legality of slavery's suppression. Mainstream Democrats, for the most part, vigorously resisted all genre of antislavery politics. Democrats marched to a different drummer from the reformers and followed a different political tradition.[9] Throughout the political turmoil of their generation they remained loyal to their old associates and the commitments and traditions of their party.

They never assigned to the antislavery movement a high priority among Democratic issues and concerns. Moreover, Democratic spokesmen attacked antislavery political movements and did their best to ignore, play down, and contain the sectional tensions rising within the country. In so doing, they reflected some of the mainstream political currents of their age. Given their numbers, given what they represented, their advocacy and behavior and the reasons that underlay each, the Democratic posture toward the movement to abolish black slavery is worth tracing, clarifying, defining, and emphasizing. Only then will the antislavery political movement, the Democratic party, and the larger political culture to which they both belonged be fully understandable.

Rhetorically, the Democrats never left anyone in doubt where they stood. Their intense opposition to antislavery and antislavery political movements, in whatever form and degree, was well and fully articulated. As early as 1835, in their *Address to the People of the United States*, the party's battle cry for the upcoming presidential election, they proclaimed that "it has ever been a fundamental article in the Republican creed," that "Congress has as little right to interfere with the domestic relations of *master and apprentice* in Massachusetts, or *master and servant* in Virginia, as they have to meddle with similar social relations in Great Britain, France, or Spain. . . . No man, nor set of men, can interfere or even wish to interfere, with the reserved rights of the States, embracing their domestic institutions and social relations, and call himself a Democratic Republican, or a friend of the Union." Therefore, the official Democratic organ, the Washington *Globe* succinctly summed up, "the whole democracy of the North . . . are opposed, upon constitutional principles, as well as upon views of sound policy, to any attempt of the abolitionists" to accomplish their purposes.[10]

In every one of their national party platforms between 1844 and 1856 the Democrats repeated the same attacks on abolitionism, branding it a threat to the Union and thus detrimental to "the happiness of the people." During the battles over the question of slavery in the territories in the late forties, a Democratic Northern newspaper lamented that too much of Congress's time had been taken up on the question of slavery. Every act that Congress passed on the slavery question, the paper asserted, "will be a violation of the Constitution, and a usurpation of powers that were never delegated by that instrument." The general government simply had no power to do anything about slavery "without violating the Constitution, and he who would sacrifice the constitution deserves to be branded as a traitor."[11]

Such sentiments were cool and reasoned in comparison with the more bitter, hostile expressions of Democratic opposition to antislavery reformers which appeared with increasing frequency. Pamphlets, platforms, and speeches exuded a litany of hostility, condemnation, and abuse persistently from the 1830s onward. Some politicians made distinctions between abolitionism and antislavery extension. Mainstream Democrats did not. David Potter's remark that the Barnburners "shunned abolitionists as if they were diseased" is descriptive of a broader Democratic reaction as well.[12] Abolitionism was "politico-religious fanaticism." It was the evil work of extremists, of the "Hartford Convention and Nullification factions," a "joint plot" of sectional "disturbers." Abolitionist schemes were "mad and fanatical."[13]

Even as sectional agitation increased in the mid-1840s, the Democratic position remained largely unchanged. The behavior of Democratic dissenters and Wilmot Proviso supporters during the Polk administration was "factious and unnecessary" and grounds for withdrawing support from them at election time. The Wilmot Proviso itself, a "miserable hobby," had been "introduced out of time, and of place." Representative John Smith Chipman of Michigan believed that the preservation of the Union "was worth a million times more than the pitiful consideration of a handful of degraded Africans."[14] Free Soilers of 1848, even with their Democratic component, were "disunionists . . . a sectional faction." Martin Van Buren was "the leader of a faction of disorganizers" who would not attract Democrats from their integrity to "pander to his treason." Democratic congressman William H. Bissell argued that the South was misbehaving as well but had been "goaded and harassed by . . . Northern fanatics until they have become as unreasonable, impracticable, insane and reckless as the most fanatical abolitionist." A circular from Tammany Hall in 1850 referred to "the fanatics and demagogues who are waging an unholy crusade. . . . We sincerely deprecate sectional issues and contests." The Democrats' mission in this situation was to "rebuke fanaticism," reassure the South, and "renew old associations."[15]

Finally, when the Republicans emerged in the mid-1850s, they were, in Democratic eyes, no different from their antislavery Whig antecedents. Republicans embodied the "wild spirit of abolitionism" that destroyed everything. They had "but one common aim—the dissolution of the Union." How could it be otherwise, given the nature of their leadership? "The arch-fiend of American politics during the last twenty years has been William H. Seward."[16]

Such constantly repeated expressions were more than a grab bag of miscellaneous quotations. There was a steady, repetitious, consistency from first to last, a continuity to the Democratic assaults on all forms of antislavery, no matter what its nature. Abolitionism, antislaveryism, and Republicanism were enemies of the Democracy and of everything for which the party stood. Antislavery advocacy and political activities were inimical to the country and the things that were important in politics. The repeated raising by antislavery leaders of an issue that was superfluous, dangerous, and outside the pale of reasonable concern could only be laid to a desire to distract voters, fragment parties, and destroy the Union. Antislavery advocates were, therefore, not to be seen as legitimate, but for what they were and to be described in the harshest terms possible.

Rhetoric, of course, is one thing, behavior another. But mainstream Democratic behavior conformed to what Democratic leaders said. Whenever they could, Democrats acted clearly, directly, and hostilely toward antislavery efforts. During the presidential election of 1836 they moved briskly against abolitionist petitions and the demands embodied in them.

They first issued a pamphlet: "Opinions of Martin Van Buren . . . Upon the Powers and Duties of Congress in Reference to the Abolition of Slavery Either in the Slave Holding States or in the District of Columbia." This was followed by Van Buren's promise to veto any bill of Congress abolishing slavery in the District of Columbia.[17] Governor William Marcy of New York sharply assailed the abolitionists' "pernicious schemes" in his annual address to his state legislature in 1835. Other Northern Democratic state legislatures passed resolutions against abolitionism. Those of the Michigan legislature argued that since "domestic slavery of the southern States" was "a subject exclusively within the control of said States, every interference with the subject by the General Government or any other States is an assumption of power not delegated by the Federal Constitution." Although "the freedom of the press, and the freedom of speech, are sacred and inviolable rights guaranteed to the people" there was also an "obligation to preserve them from abuse." Finally, "the formation of societies, and the acts and proceedings of individuals in the non-slaveholding States, having for their object an interference in the rights of the slaveholder, are in direct violation of the obligations of the compact of our Union and destructive to the tranquility and welfare of the country."[18]

All of these activities reassured those sensitive to the dangers posed by abolitionism and helped reinforce the bonds of the Democratic community. Southern Democrats described Van Buren as bringing with him into the presidential race of 1836 "principles congenial to those of the South." What that meant, specifically, was ideological: "his political creed is republican of the old democratic school." At the same time, other Northern Democrats were commended for their assault on the abolitionists. All of this was of a piece. As the Milledgeville (Georgia) *Federal Union* summed up in 1836, "next to Andrew Jackson, Martin Van Buren is the most powerful enemy of the abolitionists; and the safest president for the South."[19]

In Congress as well, Democratic hostility toward antislavery activity was marked and clearly different from Whig reactions. In the House of Representatives during the Tyler administration, congressmen voted on a number of resolutions relating to black rights, antislavery petitions, and the slave trade in the District of Columbia. On these issues, Northern Democrats generally voted against the antislavery position in alliance with Southern colleagues from both parties. Northern Whigs, in contrast, did not. Later in the decade, as sectional tensions increased in the aftermath of the Mexican War and the introduction of the Wilmot Proviso, such partisanly defined differences in behavior on these matters continued. Unlike the Northern Whigs, most Northern Democrats resisted committing themselves to the antislavery side of matters whether on the Wilmot Proviso or on similar issues dealing with the expansion of slavery.[20] Some congressional Democrats succumbed to antislavery voting most of the time, many did part of the time, but in general, their position varied from indifference and hostility to antislavery-extension activities to lukewarm support of the reformers at certain moments. Their position was echoed by Democratic state legislators and delegates to state party conventions even as tensions and pressures increased. A few of them joined the bulk of the Whigs to create majorities in favor of the Wilmot Proviso in several state legislatures, but most of them remained true to their hostile position.[21]

Finally, the behavior of Democratic voters when faced at the polls with the option of voting for antislavery political parties was consistent from 1840 onward. The total vote for antislavery political parties grew from 7000 (0.3% of the national total) for the Liberty party in 1840, to 1.8 million (39.8% of all votes cast) for the Republicans in 1860. But where did the votes for these parties come from? Or, more pertinently, how many came from Democrats?

There was a clear tendency among voters in the pre-Civil War era to vote repeatedly for their own party and not to defect or drop out of the electoral system. Thomas B. Alexander's study of voter constancy in presidential elections between 1836 and 1860 concludes that about 90 percent of the voters for a party in one election supported that same party in a subsequent contest.[22] His figures suggest that the Democrats were hardly a prime source of antislavery political votes. Observers at the time were certainly quite conscious of the difficulty of luring Democrats away from their party homes. William Gienapp quotes one Republican as complaining about how long it took to wean any Democrat into antislavery politics, no matter what his ideological commitments. "When men have formed the habit of acting together & have got their party into power," he wrote, "its policy will be shaped by the majority of the party and the minority however reluctant will continue to act for a long time & till they are led away from their own purposes rather than seek a new alliance."[23] The voting returns confirmed that persistent pattern.

There were occasional deviations, to be sure. They were small in numbers, and many defectors went off only temporarily. Gienapp cites the behavior of those Democrats who deserted the party in opposition to the Kansas-Nebraska bill in 1854. Many of them "quickly returned to the party fold. Their 1854 bolt represented a one-time protest against party policy. Torn between their party identity and a dislike of national party policy, they eliminated the cross pressure they felt, not by abandoning their party, but by gradually adopting new opinions."[24]

Analysis of Democratic voting behavior supports Alexander's and Gienapp's findings. The Liberty party attracted few Democrats. Rather, they drew the bulk of their support from Whig constituencies. A Whig complained to Hamilton Fish in 1844 that "every new faction that springs up . . . subtracts largely from our votes while the rascals on the other side escape without even a blemish." The various "isms," including abolitionism, were "the bastard children of the Great Whig party." In the opinion of at least one Democrat, each "ism" and its Whig supporters were separated from the Democratic party by a kind of "unholy alliance."[25] That judgment about numbers has been borne out by a number of close studies of popular voting returns.

Lee Benson points out that in New York State Democratic popular vote percentages remained relatively constant between 1840 and 1844 in towns where the Liberty party received more than a scattering of the vote, while Whig percentage declines in those towns almost equaled the Liberty percentages. The exception to this general pattern occurred in only one county: Madison—the center of Liberty activity—where Democrats apparently were affected by the pressures there.[26] Benson uses Putnam in Washington County as more representative of the Democratic pattern:

Table 6–2. Vote in Putnam Township in Washington County, New York

	Whigs		Democrats		Others	
	(N)	Percentage	(N)	Percentage	(N)	Percentage
1840	113	80.7	27	19.3	—	—
1844	68	50.4	25	18.5	42	31.1
1850	—	79.1	—	20.9	—	—

He quotes, in summary, Horace Greeley's observation in 1844 that "any third party based on convictions of moral duty must naturally draw ten recruits from the Whig ranks to every one taken from the other side."[27]

Even in the much more wide-ranging Free Soil revolt in 1848, led by the greatest Democrat of them all, Martin Van Buren, mainstream Democrats largely shunned the chance to participate in the milder form of antislavery politics. It was during this election that Democrats unleashed a particularly raucous version of what two historians have called their "nigger yell" against blacks, their defenders, and any politics based on changing the situation of the blacks in the country—even when slavery extension, not abolition, was the issue.[28] The party's call to duty was usually effective. As James Buchanan noted, Pennsylvania Democrats, with few exceptions, were "sound upon the slavery question."[29] Traditional party ties remained very strong in the election of

1848. No more than a small, albeit vigorous, minority of Democrats voted for Free Soil.

The numbers of such voters varied dramatically from Northern state to Northern state. Kevin Sweeney estimates that 83 percent of the Democratic voters in the Massachusetts gubernatorial election in 1847 voted Democratic in 1848; only 17 percent of them voted for the Free Soilers.[30] In the four Midwestern states of Ohio, Indiana, Illinois, and Michigan, Ray Shortridge found that neither the Liberty party nor the Free Soil party drew many Democratic votes. In the latter case he concludes that "only an insignificant number of 1844 Democratic voters turned out for the Free Soil party in 1848 in the Midwest." The major pool of Free Soil voters were either 1844 Whig voters or people who did not vote then.[31] In New Jersey, where there was an insignificant antislavery vote (0.1% for Liberty in 1844, 0.9% for the Free Soilers in 1848), the correlation between the Democratic vote before the rise of the Free Soilers and their vote in the election is so high as to suggest that the number of defectors was very few indeed.[32] Only in New York State, site of the largest Free Soil vote anywhere in 1848, was there a different pattern. Paul Kleppner estimates that 40 percent of the Democratic vote in 1844 went into the Free Soil party four years later, that is, about 95,000 Democrats of the 237,000 who had voted for Polk. In summary, Michael Holt suggests that the Democrats held about 84 percent of their 1844 presidential vote in 1848 in the Northern states.[33] The total defection figure is distorted by the large defection in New York State—a defection that reflected many more things than commitment to antislavery politics. It is also pertinent to note that the majority of party supporters in New York remained loyal to the Democracy as they did in much larger numbers elsewhere. Finally, and tellingly, most Democratic defectors in New York and elsewhere returned to their traditional party base in time for the election of 1852.[34]

All of which confirms the comment in the *Albany Argus* just after the Free Soil election, that "the great body of the democracy could not be seduced from their true party attachments."[35] The Free Soilers saw the Democrats somewhat less favorably while making the same point. The Democratic party, a Free Soil pamphlet of 1848 argued, "is so openly and recklessly committed to the slave power, that it seems like a needless work to offer any proofs of its proslavery character."[36] This mainstream Democratic behavior prompted a Virginia Democrat to comment that "all reflecting men . . . must see, and do see, that the association of the Democratic party is now the only hope of the Union. The fidelity of Northern Democrats to the compromises of the Constitution . . . will defeat all the base sectional maneuvers of fanatics and knaves."[37]

But it is the movement of Democrats into the Republican party that is the crucial indicator of the nature of the Democratic-antislavery political relationship. There have been a number of estimates by historians (based on newspaper and manuscript reports) that suggest that as high as 25 percent of the Northern Republican vote by the election of 1856 was made up of ex-Democrats. These estimates, however, cannot be taken for granted for, as one critic noted, the "judgements may be correct, but they cannot be proved by the manuscript sources" on which they rest.[38] Twenty-five percent of the Republican vote in 1856 is 335,586. Since the Democratic vote in 1852 in the North was just over a million, such a figure suggests that a very high proportion of Democrats, almost 34 percent, became Republicans four years later. However, voting data available do not bear out such an estimate. Two extreme cases suggest the boundaries of the Democratic defection. In 1852, Massachusetts was one of the weakest Democratic states. The party received 44,569 votes there. Dale Baum estimates that, in fact, 25 percent of these 1852 Democratic voters permanently defected to the Republican party in the mid-1850s, that is, about 11,000 votes.[39]

But in the Midwest the pattern was quite different. The rank and file did not come over in large numbers even though the Republican party's leadership contained a significant number of Democratic politicians. One-quarter of the 1856 Republican vote, just over 350,000, was cast in these four states. It consisted largely of Free Soilers, former Whigs, and nonvoters in 1852. Only 11 percent of the region's 1852 Democrats (42,563), voted Republican in 1856, and this was the result of a skewed pattern. In Indiana, 4 percent of the Democratic voters of 1852 moved over to the Republicans. In Ohio the figure was 12 percent; in Illinois none did. In the least populous state, Michigan, 28 percent of the 1852 Democrats moved over.[40]

These returns suggest that an extraordinarily high Democratic defection took place elsewhere in the North (approximately 282,000 of 670,000 voters, or about 42 percent of the total in the northeast outside of Massachusetts). But close scrutiny of the returns does not bear out such a figure. In the largest state, New York, for example, the Democrats won 262,000 votes in 1852, and just under 196,000 four years later. They lost 25 percent of their total vote. But some close county-by-county and township assessment of this drop suggests that it went in three directions, not only to the emerging Republicans. The bulk of the Democratic defectors went to the Know Nothings, but others became non-voters, simply sitting out the election. Moreover, by 1860, many of the 1856 defectors had returned to their original party home.[41]

In the Midwestern states, post-1856 defections from the Democracy were also relatively small. In the region as a whole, 2 percent (8900) of the Democratic voters of 1856 switched to the Republicans in 1860 (almost all of these from Indiana where 5 percent [5900] of the Democratic electorate moved over). These are hardly impressive figures. By 1860, just over 51,000 of the 390,000 voters who had supported the Democratic party in the early 1850s voted Republican in these states. In short, in the Middle Western states, the rank and file movement of Democrats into antislavery political coalitions was very limited from 1848 onward.[42]

What is most to the point is that Democratic defectors in the 1850s left behind a majority of the party's rank and file and a significant portion of its Northern leadership as well. As Shortridge concludes in his study of the Middle West, "the voting choices made by the mass electorate seem to have been remarkably stable. Most Democrats apparently resisted the blandishments of the Republican and nativist politicians and continued to support the Democracy."[43] Even without a full study of all of the permutations of voter behavior during the years of antislavery political activity, it is clear that between 80 percent and 90 percent of Democratic voters in the Northern states were habitual and steadfast in their behavior and remained true to their normal party loyalties. Many were periodically concerned with Southern expansionism. But most of them usually eschewed the sectionalist impulse. The importance of the Democrats who defected should not be minimized, regardless of numbers, in shaping the way the Republicans behaved and in helping them to victory. Nor should we minimize how the core and masses of the party reacted to the attractions of antislavery political movements, even in their least revolutionary guise.

The mainstream Democrats' record on antislavery reform is clear. Less plain is the reason for their behavior. Some historians see the origin of the party's stance rooted in a conscious agreement, worked out as early as the 1820s, between leaders in the North and the South to protect slavery, a position necessary to maintain the party organization, win elections, and hold the reins of national power. Because of Southern sensitivity about slavery, Martin Van Buren's principal concern from 1819 onward was "how best to protect Southern security in the Union." The answer was to keep in office a party "responsive to the South because it was dependent on it for election."[44] Slavery, as a moral issue, would be ignored and antislavery forces would be repressed in the North. Neither was difficult because of the indifference of most Northern Democrats to the fate of the slave.

There was more to this position as well. Many Northern Democrats have been seen as ideologically proslavery. They believed in what they were doing. As a result, the Democrats, when in power, protected and then helped extend slavery into new areas of the continent. In John Quincy Adams's terms, the "South has the Democratic party in its pockets."[45] That section "was in the saddle of national politics" so long as the Democrats ruled. This was "the central fact of American political history to 1860." The Whig, Zachary Taylor, "was the only president between John Quincy Adams and Abraham Lincoln whose politics was not proslavery."[46]

Historian John McFaul dissents from this position. He believes that the Jacksonians were not "a conscious and active agent of the slave power." Party members, he concedes, engaged in strong anti-antislavery rhetoric and their actions often were useful to slavery's defenders. But he believes that the central core of Democratic concerns were not ideological but politically "expedient." The party leaders were political animals indifferent to moral concerns and to slavery and interested primarily in their own electoral survival. They had to maintain a party containing many different interest groups. They believed in mediating among the different groups and did not make moral distinctions among them. Since Southern slaveowners were members of their party, since they were sensitive about antislavery, and since they threatened dire consequences if abolitionist agitation continued, Democratic leaders responded by doing their best to tame that concern. They chose to maintain their organization and preserve the political situation as it was. They acted the way they did because it made political sense, in their view, to do so.[47]

McFaul's corrective emphasis has much to recommend it. The fact that Democratic behavior was proslavery in effect does not mean that party members were proslavery in intent, an important distinction necessary to understand the nature of their behavior. Nor would they even understand such terms of reference. The Democrats' hatred of abolitionism was deep and enduring. But they were not, in their own minds, any more proslavery than pro-Northern in their approach. Their hostility and commitments ran in other channels. They came out of different traditions; they had little comprehension of the central concerns of antislavery advocates. Some nineteenth-century reformers and others involved in politics, as well as many twentieth-century historians, have argued for the centrality of the slavery issue—or at least its importance for much of the antebellum era. Such arguments would have surprised antebellum mainstream Democrats.

There remains more to understand about the relationship of political expediency to the behavior of antebellum Democrats. Too often political expediency has been defined simplistically as the "hunger for spoils."

Among party activists, "the hunger for spoils was basic." They were "opportunistic, materialistic," and "ambitious for worldly success."[48] This is direct enough and a common enough historiographic characterization. But it is distorted and leaves out too much. If, by expediency, we mean conscious political calculations to achieve essentially electoral ends only, this does not cover the whole situation affecting party members. The Democratic leaders were political animals, and it was not out of character for them to act for political reasons, particularly to consider tactical necessities. They tried to manage conflict in a way that ensured electoral success. But party calculations and conscious activities to further specific ends stemmed not only from the leaders' rational assessment of the specific costs to the party and to themselves, especially the dangers to their future electoral success of rousing sectional tensions. Their behavior also stemmed from a wider and deeper commitment to the way their political world operated and what was important in it. One consideration was never favored to the exclusion of the other—both interacted with each other.

There was a powerful political culture developing and taking control of the American scene in the late 1830s.[49] Partisan politics played a central role in that scene as part of the process of national integration and as a focus for achieving power. It was an important aspect of the matrix of people's lives. At its center were the two national political parties. As the Liberty party appeared in the early 1840s, the national parties were defining themselves in sharp, highly differentiated terms from one another. They were reaching out to encompass the entire political world as it then existed. Democrats, as did Whigs, used the party to organize that political world.

Parties did two things extremely well in this political culture. They combined intense emotive loyalties based on deeply rooted family and community norms and tensions growing out of the social differences within the society, with attention to a structure of issue commitments and desires. They organized and agitated for specific policies desired by their members. Both reasons, loyalty and faith, as well as policy and principles, structured political competition in mid-nineteenth-century America in wide ranging and crucial ways. Party loyalties ran deep among Americans. Parties were clung to tenaciously and with an intense loyalty almost impossible to shake, for ideological, social, and symbolic reasons.[50]

Americans lived within highly charged, close-knit, partisan networks. An intricate web of interactive institutions, centered in the communities, functioned constantly—and in a most partisan manner. Parties appealed to their communicants in massive, broad ranging, ways, symbolically rooting out devils and threats surrounding them all, emphasizing issues and interests of concern to their component groups. At the local levels, highly partisan newspapers with no commitment to objectivity led the way; vitriolic pamphlets followed along. Even social organizations, volunteer fire companies, for one, were rooted in community norms and often highly partisan. In every community there were frequent nomination and election rallies as well as partisan meetings on New Orleans Day (the anniversary of Jackson's victory over the British), or over a new piece of significant legislation. Few occasions passed without one of these hectic meetings with large attendance.[51]

Party rhetoric and platforms presented by each party gave strong clues to their positions. Parties were not ambiguous about what they stood for. They forthrightly asserted what they believed. More to the point, they stood for different things quite distinct from each other. In the rousing political debates of the period, each party strongly spelled out its advocacy and its conception of what the other side was up to. Political meetings, with their fiery speeches and extensive activities, served as entertainment and as social gatherings for a community. But their main purpose was to reinforce the communal solidarity and partisanship of the group involved. There was intense and constant reinforcement of one's beliefs, the identification of one's enemies and friends. These were polarizing debates that clarified and made coherent what was at stake and why votes should be cast in particular ways. They reinforced existing commitments.[52] The exposure of the average voter to an unbiased version of the other side's viewpoint was minimal.

Elections had important societal functions in this atmosphere. They provided an opportunity for communities to express themselves, their desires, fears, and problems, and to affirm their communal commitments. Elections usually were intense experiences: the partisan communications networks offered them as the moral equivalent of war, providing opportunities to reaffirm one's devotion and to smite one's enemies. And as time passed in this atmosphere, Americans developed formidable allegiances to the parties because these institutions expressed their deepest values, beliefs, and preferences. Parties were part of the culture of the groups. An individual's values, ideals, and desires were caught up in them. They were communities of loyalists with shared commitments and emotive memories and symbols.[53]

Democrats were particularly committed to politics as organized and practiced in the middle of the nineteenth century. They intensely accepted and strongly advocated the imperatives of the partisan political culture of their time. It is easy to detect hunkerism, lusting after the spoils of office, and traditionally defined expediency as the pivot of

Democratic behavior. There were party hacks, and there was expediency and lusting for office—but within certain boundaries that deserve as much understanding as that of the political opportunism present. As John Van Buren said in a speech in early 1848, there was much at stake in American politics. He had "been brought up to believe" that the fights between Whigs and Democrats "involve some principle." Later, John Dix added, "I consider [the Whigs to be] at an immeasurable distance from us in all that concerns the true interpretation of the Constitution and the proper administration of government."[54]

It is easy to dismiss all of this as cant. But there was more to it than that. Party leaders could not be, nor did they desire to be, exclusively or simply pragmatic in their calculations. Pragmatic expediency was part of their makeup. They constantly had to think through how to build coalitions and how to prevent divisions in their party. But there were boundaries to their expediency. First, Hunkers (those who supposedly thought only about victory at the polls and not principle) were as ideologically committed as anyone else in the party. They, too, were communicants in what one convention delegate referred to as "the Democratic church."[55] They never advocated that the party abandon, or even temporarily suspend, its principles. Rather, they wanted those principles supplemented—not weakened, by careful attention to electoral context and a willingness to shape an appeal in such a way as to improve chances of winning.

Second, boundaries were also set by how the rank and file thought about politics and what they considered to be involved in party battles. The leadership was never alone in shaping party behavior. The Democratic party, despite factional strife was a robust entity. What gave it its robustness was the extent, depth, and intensity of its mass support and the reasons that underlay that support. Elite perceptions of party differences were absorbed at the mass level, given the partisanship of the atmosphere and of its communication and prevailing social institutions. The constituents' understanding of the electoral necessities in a given situation was not as fully formed as was the Democratic leadership's. But, like their leaders, they had drunk deeply of the imperatives of the partisan political culture dominating their lives.[56] No party leader could ignore for very long, therefore, the things that made their party different from the opposition in the minds of the voters. Everyone operated within defined limits set by the party's traditions, principles and distinctive outlook.[57]

The political debates of the antebellum period were marked by the Democratic focus on so much other than antislavery. The dominant influences shaping partisan discourse and belief found little room for such matters. The "old and true measures"—banking, tariffs, foreign affairs, the nature of the federal government's power and responsibilities —were the everyday concerns of Democratis throughout the period.[58] Antislavery, on the other hand, was part of a quite different world with a different set of priorities from those of mainstream Democrats. Their vision of the way politics operated and what was important in politics confined sectionalism/slavery concerns to the periphery. While always present, these issues did not have the force and influence that many historians have assigned to them. Partisan institutions had been defining and shaping political activity and reactions for a generation, certainly for most of the active lives of antebellum Democrats, while sectional concerns had remained unfocused and largely undefined.

It seems clear, then, that any understanding of Democratic reaction to antislavery politics has to take into account the intense imperatives of the existing partisan political culture as they penetrated among all of the members of the Democratic community, top to bottom. The Democratic leadership thought about slavery and antislavery a great deal. There was a great deal of calculation, for instance, in their response to the slavery issue and to antislavery politics—something that has always been recognized by historians. The leadership, socialized in day to day contacts with sensitive Southerners and having to weigh the balance of forces within the party, often talked about the danger of slavery disputes to current politics, ultimately, to the union. They constantly had to maneuver with the Southerners, to work out agreements, to soothe, and to hold hands—to evaluate prevailing pressures.

It is not clear, however, that such a highly conscious weighing of sensitivities and consequences existed among the rank and file mainstream Democrats. To some of the leaders such as Van Buren, necessity led them into political actions that may be overstressed as representative of rank and file Democrats. The latter—the masses of the party— moved in a world where highly specific, conscious calculations about political affairs were less present and where priorities about issues and politics emerged in a different form. They remained loyally committed to the imperatives of the partisan political culture, partly consciously, partly not, partly principled, partly not, partly expedient, partly not. They shared with the leadership a set of assumptions and interacted with them to preserve a particular vision of the political world. In the mass-defined world, antislavery politics of every variety, from abolitionism to Free Soil, to Republicanism, were vaguely understood foreign ideologies to be ignored, rejected, and repudiated.

All of the elements helping define the Democratic reaction were present when issues connected with sectionalism and slavery erupted in the 1830s. It is not surprising that Democrats treated them as something foreign, something they were not used to and did not understand, since they were not part of their normal political discourse.[59] In Democrats' reactions, therefore, partisan commitments and responses and the particular rhetoric that flowed from them, predominated. As some Virginia Democrats put it in 1839, the old battles over the two principles of government, centralism and localism, were still at the center of the political stage. "All the rest is ephemeral and transitory."[60] Echoes of such aspects of the partisan imperative kept coming up again and again. The New York Democrats, for instance, who later led the Free Soil revolt, at first saw the introduction of the Texas issue as a Southern-inspired plot to win party laurels for a particular faction of the party. They were irritated and resistant but understood the issue in a partisan way. "Calhoun has designedly put slavery in the foreground for mischief," one wrote in late 1844. The "Texas humbug" was being used by the South to defeat Van Buren for the party's nomination. Again and again that theme ran through their private correspondence.[61]

Prominent Democrats reacted by reminding the South that Northerners, too, had their own local questions, demands, needs, and difficulties and that if the South made too much of a fuss then even Northern Democrats would have to strike back against excessive Southern attempts to get their own way. Intraparty strife would be regrettable after such a long time of ignoring local concerns in favor of joint fighting on behalf of common Democratic politics.[62] In short, the problem was seen as entwined with Democratic politics. It was the understandable reaction of a group shaped by partisan norms, not sectional ones.[63]

Another aspect of this partisan reaction concerned such Democratic stalwarts as the two New York congressmen: John Dix and Preston King, who were clearly against admitting Texas as a slave state. They, too, thought about it in party terms when it first arose. They looked to their party leaders for advice and guidelines to action.[64] Again, such is not surprising. Behind their behavior was their sensitivity to what they believed were Whig attempts to use sectional rhetoric against the Polk administration. They saw efforts under way to thwart them on matters other than sectional ones. The Wilmot Proviso was "stalking horse for factions and ambitious politicians." It was but a link in a chain of measures "designed to give aid and comfort to the enemy." Its supporters "are not governed in their course by a love of the slave or a horror of the extension of the 'area of slavery' but by an inveterate hatred of the administration." Therefore, Democrats should ignore "this pretended question of free soil."[65]

Echoes of the full range of partisan reasons continued to affect Democrats' discourse throughout the late 1840s. When a severe party disruption occurred between 1845 and 1848, centered on differences over slavery extension, the leadership was fully involved on the battle-lines. But how much were the masses involved in that disruption or affected by it? Most specifically, how committed were party voters to the factions erupting all around them? The New York leader Silas Wright had one answer in a letter to James K. Polk in 1845. "The democratic party of this State is not a unit . . . ," he wrote.

> It is not, however, so much divided as appearances at a distance would indicate, although the division between those who have held prominent places in the party is extensive. It is rather a difference among the officers than the men, the leaders than the members of the party.[66]

This had immediate meaning for the President. Polk's "sound measures . . . will be sustained by the friends of Governor Wright," the New York party leader Azariah Flagg wrote late in 1845, "without regard to the person who may be in his cabinet from this state." This was because "the great mass of the party" supported Polk's program, which contained the old and true measures of the Democratic party. On those he will be supported by both "the friends of Mr. Calhoun & Mr. Wright."[67] Even though the elite split then occurred between the New Yorkers and the President, similar sentiments about mass behavior continued to be expressed. "The masses of the party are disposed to get together," despite the splits over slavery extension and the Wilmot Proviso, even though the leaders were so "embittered against each other" as to make that difficult.[68]

"The principles of Free Soil are the only ones at issue in the contest for President," the editor of the New York Evening Post argued in October 1848. It was reassuring to the Free Soil Democrats to repeat that their principles "are fast gaining the ascendency" and that there was "a great revolution in public opinion" under way.[69] Not so, most of the main-stream Democrats replied. A Democratic meeting in Cuyahoga County, Ohio, in 1848, resolved that despite the fact that they were opposed to slavery, "we cannot throw aside party usages or relinquish regular nominations to join any bolting movement founded on this one prin-ciple." A Midwestern party newspaper thundered that Democrats "are not Mexicans to break up into factions and follow leaders instead of old principles and social party attachments by which these great principles are carried out." Alfred Burr, the editor of the Hartford Times, reminded Gideon Welles that "a large portion of the Democrats of this State do not look upon the [Wilmot] Proviso as a practical or at all important question. They think that Congress should not meddle with Slavery in the territories." Welles had been receiving similar letters for some time and their view of local Democratic attitudes confirmed Burr's estimates. Former Senator John Niles wrote, for example, that although many people attended Free Soil meetings during the campaign of 1848, "a considerable part of them came out of curiosity or some worse motive." Joseph Rayback quotes a New Jersey newspaper as saying that "it is true that Gen. Cass does not advocate the Wilmot Proviso, but he is a democrat. On every cardinal point of the democratic creed he is known to be right and we have no wish to introduce other issues in this election." Another Democrat agreed. "I have so strong a repugnance to see the Whigs . . . elect General Taylor," one wrote, "that I am resolved to give my vote to General Cass." Cass is "with us on all those issues that have divided parties for years past." The correspondent was in favor of Free Soil but not at the expense of the other issues he held dear and sacred.[70]

Such partisan assertions became a familiar, oft-repeated litany. The *Detroit Free Press* argued that while it opposed the extension of slavery, "we opposed the introduction of new issues, and the Proviso is one of them."[71] Even as many Northern Democrats grew restive, irritated, and then, furious, against their Southern colleagues on such matters, their devotion to their common partisan associations continued to be present and potent. They did not believe that the old issues of partisan definition grew obsolete or faded away. These issues remained important. Factiousness and sectional irritation would only allow the Whigs to impose the bank, tariff, and the rest of their odious program. As Silas Burroughs, a New York Democrat, put it at the state convention in 1849, "he did not believe that the great questions of a Bank, a protective tariff, internal improvements by the general government . . . were now settled—that we could dispose of the old platform and make something new." Therefore, another argued, "we can act with democrats, whatever their views in regard to slavery may be, if in other respects sound."[72] Even John Wentworth, leader of the pro-Wilmot Proviso forces among Illinois Democrats, wrote in 1848, "let us Barn Burners strive to lick Taylor first. He must be beaten, & if we have an independent organization in democratic states, he will beat us." And, after the election, Wentworth lamented that "in losing sight of the old issues between the two parties at the elections," those who voted for Free Soil would see too late that they committed an error.[73]

All of this rhetoric and behavior put the issues raised by the antislavery movement into a highly specific perspective. As the *Cleveland*

Plain Dealer put it early in 1847, "we have been in the habit of supposing, and still believe, that there are other questions besides that of slavery merely which should enter into the canvass and election of [the] President of this country."[74] "No one," a resolution of the state convention of Hunker Democrats in new York argued in 1848, "can be regarded as a true democrat who at any time would insist upon the political agitation of a moral abstraction, as of paramount importance, when the direct tendency of such agitation is to create sectional dissensions and divisions and divisions between us and our natural allies in upholding and advancing the great doctrines of the democracy." Another New York politician, Samuel Beardsley, saw the party's divisions based on a "wretched and most frivolous" controversy. The party's position in regard to slavery has always been "entire toleration of opinion in regard to it." Let us, therefore, he concluded, "discard now and forever, the idea of dividing on abstractions which have been brought out for the sole purpose of getting up a quarrel between the democracy of the North and South."[75] In short, the important matters of the time united Democrats. Whatever divided them, they argued, was unimportant and unnecessary, only "passing excitements and controversies."[76] Divisive issues had been raised for political reasons, in order to hurt the Democratic community.

The leaders of the Free Soil revolt came to perceive the basic problem they had in dealing with Democrats. The latter saw the political world as unchanging. They wanted no new issues, no new problems, no changes. Mainstream Democrats did not want to expand the boundaries of political discourse. Democrats continued to believe that there was much more distance between themselves and Whigs, later Republicans, than between Northern and Southern blocs within their own party on issues related to sectionalism. Most Democrats, the Free Soilers wearily concluded, were "passion-blinded partisans who resolve to see nothing but through the mist of an unreasonable prejudice." When parties err, honest citizens should leave them and form third parties. Unfortunately, they found that many of the Democrats they counted on were simply not willing to desert.[77]

This reaction, partisan and static as it was, continued well into the 1850s, despite the escalating sectional crisis. The Democratic congressman, William Bissell of Illinois, complained in 1850 that all of the discussion of slavery extension fomented by the original introduction of the Wilmot Proviso was "embarrassing and retarding the proper business of Congress."[78] Differences between the parties "never die out," Horatio Seymour said in 1855, "Today we are discussing the very questions which divided parties at the very formation of our government." Parties continue to differ "with regard to principles of action."[79] Mainstream Democrats clung to and constantly reaffirmed the importance of the old issues and the general nature of political warfare as they had always known them. There was little weakening of this for most of the period during which antislavery politics established itself. The commitment to what one group called the "pure and holy principles" of the Democratic party remained staunch and continuous. Democrats had to continue together to contend for "the *principles* of our faith." In 1856 the pro-Wilmot Proviso Democratic leader of Illinois "still defined 'Republican' as the 'name generally used to designate a Whig of Know-Nothing and Maine Law proclivities.'"[80]

Even given the great sensitivity among Southerners to the antislavery crusade, so frequently and strongly expressed by some political leaders there, and frequently and strongly noticed by historians since, there were Southern Democrats throughout the period from the 1830s onward who also tried to maintain the party structure. Their reasons included seeing the parties as a means of defending slavery. But their arguments also included many of the same things Northerners espoused —most particularly the importance of the party and its stances in their lives. They too, argued in favor of continuing the existing pattern of politics despite the rise of agitation about slavery. "The Wilmot Proviso is paramount to all Party," a South Carolinian wrote in 1847. But neither his correspondent nor many others agreed. As the resolutions of the Democrats of the 6th Congressional District of George said in 1847, after listing all of the traditional policy positions of the party, "that with . . . every member of the Democratic party, it is a cardinal duty always, and under all circumstances, to maintain the doctrines of his political faith above all other considerations, and that we as a party adhere to, and do hereby declare it as a fundamental rule of our action; that the great principles and measures of the democratic party are entitled to our first, and last, and only allegiance."[81] The Northern Democrats could not have said it better.

These ideas, whether emanating from Northern or Southern Democrats, were always powerfully stated, obviously designed to convince and reinforce mass party opinion. But such advocacy could not achieve its political goals unless it resonated with an already existing mind set among partisan loyalists. As Lee Benson has written, it is easy to dismiss partisan rhetoric as not always stemming from the fervent convictions of those who write and speak the chosen words. But "no one can deny," he continued, that such statements reflect the author's "convictions on what the voters want to hear" and were prepared to believe, given their commitment and loyalties.[82] Some mainstream

Democrats were hostile to slavery, others were indifferent to it, or had guilt feelings concerning it, or thought it was appropriate as a form of social control or economic endeavor and/or were sensitive to its implications. None of this made it a prime political issue for many of them even into the 1850s and the beginnings of the Republican party. If slavery was an evil, it was a distant one. If it was a major political issue, it was not theirs. They did not believe that a new political era rooted in North-South differences had emerged in the mid-1840s.[83]

Historians frequently seek to pinpoint the end of one pattern of behavior and the onset of another. The 1840s are usually marked as a transforming period when sectional antislavery forces rose to a new importance to replace what had been. One historian has suggested, in a useful description, that as sectional forces erupted, old political landmarks disappeared. It was, he writes, "as if the entire state [Ohio] had lost its political memory."[84] But, when it came to the mainstream Democrats, this never happened. They did not ignore slavery and antislavery. They were aware of both. They could not keep the issues raised out of their calculations, especially after 1846. Recognizing them to be part of a crosscutting political cleavage incorporating matters of less value and concern to them and yet of some difficulty, they reacted in familiar terms. They lived in another kind of political complex and wanted little to do with what was being said and demanded about slavery. When a Massachusetts mass meeting of anti-Texan advocates argued that Texas "transcends all the bounds of ordinary political topics," the mainstream Democrats did not and could not agree.[85]

This led to a policy of containment and attempts to play down the slavery issue. More to the point, through it all, Democrats constantly looked for ways out, to return to party unity and the party's real commitments. Their position became that one's position on slavery extension should not be a test of fealty to the Democratic party. You suggest, one wrote Gideon Welles in 1849, that "Democrats & Free Soilers should come together and 'agree to disagree.' That is my doctrine . . . I supported candidates last spring so long as they went with the Democratic party, whether they were Proviso men or not."[86] They should bend over to allay Southern fears and not push except when absolutely necessary. Democrats followed this policy partly out of fear of splitting the party and partly out of impatience with the issue altogether.[87] Thus, they were quick to endorse the compromise measures.

American politics in the pre-Civil War era began by defining where one stood in relation to other groups in the society, in setting priorities as to policy goals, and in building coalitions based on one's stance and commitments. Democrats strongly resisted any transforming of the political outlook, values, assumptions, and practices into something new and different revolving around the slavery-extension issue. It was the Republicans, seeking to wean people to their new coalition, who argued that the political issues of former years were "obsolete." Democrats did not think so.[88] As the editor of the *New York Post* sadly lamented during the Free Soil election, "if the action of the people in the free states were not diverted from their convictions by prejudices, by old and defunct party ties, and by incorrect representations," the Free Soil candidate for the presidency would receive every vote from the Northern states.[89] Perhaps the editor believed party ties to be old and defunct. The mainstream Democrats did not. They did not lose their memory. They continued to react to the political world in their established, traditional ways.

Still, from the early 1840s through the final emergence of the Republican party in the 1850s, some Northern Democrats did throw off their partisan commitments and join the final version of the antislavery political movement. As noted, their numbers were relatively few in relation to the size of the total party constituency.[90] But a question remains: given all that can be demonstrated about the Democrats and their outlook in the era, why should any of them become part of the antislavery political movement at all? Some historians have ventured reasons that combine a certain amount of sensitivity to sectional-slavery issues with some political expediency as well. Eric Foner, for example, has vigorously reiterated the traditional assessment that antislavery pressures grew strong enough in the North to force some Democrats to go along. The growing sectional anger and rising sentiment against slavery extension among their constituents left them no choice. He also argues that Republican ideals interacted with Democratic conceptions of the free individual in a free society to draw Democrats over.[91]

Such pressures and ideals may have affected some of the Democratic defectors. Still, more remains to be said about those who left to join the ranks of antislavery politics. From the beginning, such Democrats did so for a variety of reasons. In the late forties many of them who joined the Free Soil revolt had other motives besides that of slavery extension in general. The reasons some joined the Republicans may have included antislavery sentiment. But the electoral realignment of the 1850s, with its consequent Democratic disruption and Republican ascendency, was also only partially based on the attractions of antislavery politics. It is worth remembering, for example, how much regional and intrastate variation there was in such defections. In Pennsylvania, Roger Peterson found Democratic movement into Republicanism limited to former

New England and New York State residents living in a narrow band of counties close to the New York border. In New York State a similar limited pattern of movement occurred.⁹² In Massachusetts, where the Democrats were always in a hopeless political minority, defection toward any movement that might help them gain something from the Whig majority—such as in a Democratic-Free Soil coalition—served as a motivating force. In a state such as New Jersey, however, where powerful competition between the two parties was highly organized and constant and the primary fact of political life, defections were rare.⁹³ What broke the second party system apart and cost the Democrats a certain number of their supporters and, crucially, their national majority, was a set of local conditions and diverse pressures reflecting the powerful cultural tensions in the society. These were far more important in drawing masses of voters away from the Democratic party than any direct, single-minded commitment against slavery and its expansion. The Know-Nothing movement played a significant role in these developments. Paul Kleppner's careful quantitative study of the national realignment of the 1850s argues that as a result of the electoral disruption, the emerging Republican party inherited the old Whig vote, the Free Soilers, and a "strong majority" of those who first supported the Know Nothings. Yankee stock areas, he writes, because of their "congruence of . . . antisouthern and anti-immigrant . . . attitudes produced a reasonably rapid consolidation of voting support against the Democracy, the party of the South *and* of the Catholic and German Lutheran immigrants." In Cincinnati, William Gienapp found Know Nothingism a crucial factor in detaching many Protestant and Freethinking Germans from their traditional Democratic moorings. In parts of New England, land of a very weak Democracy, Dale Baum argued that Know Nothingism and Republicanism seemed to have been distinct phenomena not readily united. But elsewhere the two movements eventually melded together.⁹⁴

The electoral disruption had another quality. Rather intriguing national variations and complexities were present in it. The same groups in different situations did not always shift in the same magnitude. Kleppner demonstrates, for example, that there were two different realignments in the North: one in New England, the other among the belt of New England expatriates across New York into the Middle West, the latter a very narrow belt of change, the former a very large shift.⁹⁵

What determined this pattern was the different ways members of demographic groups reacted to the newly emerging political agenda. In most places, Yankee Protestants revolted against the Catholic-immigrant, slavocracy menace. Before the realignment, Yankees had been divided along denominational lines, some in the Democratic party, others in the Whig. Now they became more politically cohesive. But other groups did not shift in a unitary way, and still others behaved strangely. Know Nothings detached some Protestant Democrats, including both Yankees and Irish-born Orangemen. The latter "leaned over backward" to become "ardent nativists," out of their hatred of Catholics. Other Know-Nothing support varied demographically. A very few German Catholics may have voted for them out of their hatred of the Irish hierarchy. But usually German Protestants did not (late in the fifties some became Republicans).[96]

Kleppner's description of one group's behavior illuminates the central reasons and the complexities present that led to a specific political result. Differences in religious outlooks, in sociopolitical contexts, and in historical experiences all explain the variations in Dutch Calvinist voting behavior. New York's Old Dutch were moderately Democratic, and slightly more so where they lived close to Yankees. The Old Dutch had experienced the invasion of the Empire State by "restless" New Englanders and had experienced much Yankee disdain against them. They defended their ethnoreligious identity by voting for the Democrats as the anti-Yankee party. However, the changing context of political behavior in which the Democracy became identified as the Catholic party in the 1850s, cross-pressured them, and began to draw them away. The character of New York's Republican party resonated with their own restrained pietism and strong anti-Catholicism and led many of the Old Dutch to become anti-Democratic voters.[97]

Hostility to slavery expansion and to Southern power affected some Democrats, but not necessarily all anti-Democrats, either, as Republican leaders quickly learned. The antislavery revolt in the summer of 1854 did not attract everyone it might. The Republican coalition reached a certain level of support and then its growth slowed or stopped. The slavery issue, as Robert Imholt has argued, "was not sufficient in [New York State] to submerge antipathies" among the opponents to the Democrats and unite them.[98] The critical task for the Republican leadership, therefore, was to win those still outside their coalition, the Know Nothings and others who were deemed attractable because they had in common, a strong anti-Democratic commitment and values similar to those held by Republican supporters.

The genius of the Republican leadership was to recognize the extraordinary diversity and heterogenity of society and increasingly to structure an appeal that could encompass as many varieties of behavior as it did. In the years between 1857 and 1860 this broadening out effort dominated Republican strategy. Opposition to the South was the nexus of the appeal. However, it was not until antislavery politics merged into anti-Southernism and incorporated other things, especially the ethno-cultural tensions erupting in many areas of the North, that a major part of the political transformation drawing some Democrats into new politi-cal patterns occurred. Republican rhetoric became more anti-Southern and more concerned to promote wide scale affective images of their opponents. They stigmatized the Democrats as the party that used foreign-born Catholics (particularly Irish Catholics) and non-British Protestants, antithetical to native-born Protestant cultural groups, to give government power to arrogant Southern slaveholders. The latter, in turn, bullied Northern freemen and debased the American Republic, in part because contemptible Northern Doughfaces were subservient to them.

As Ronald Formisano has written, "despite extravagant claims . . . the Republican crusade . . . did not pursue the broad interests of humanity. Its passion flowed from the desire of most Northern white Protestants to assert their rights and manhood against the threat of domination by white slavocrats, and to protect their values and status from the threat of distintegration from aliens and Catholics."[99] Republi-cans successfully tied together different things. As an 1854 editorial from the *Cattaraugus* [N.Y.] *Whig* put it, "Temperance and Freedom are as inseparably connected as Intemperance and Slavery." And, on the other side, "the foreign element is a natural ally of the slave power."[100]

Ex-Democrats contributed to the Republican victory in the nation in 1860. But they, like other Republicans, traveled many diverse paths to the polls that autumn. The results of that victory were stupendous for the nation—culminating in emancipation five years later. Whatever the result, however, one thing is clear: antislavery was so insignificant in the world view of those Democrats who voted Republican in 1860 that it had little influence upon how they cast their ballots that year. They revolted against what their old party had become on several fronts: not just against slavery though that was a variable for some more than others. Nor should the importance of later events based on the Demo-cratic defeat in 1860 lead to a neglect of the much larger group of mainstream Democrats that the defectors left behind, loyal in their party faith and hostile to antislavery politics, men who continued to represent an older partisan, nonsectional tradition that remained alive.

The Democratic interrelationship with the antislavery political move-ment was not particularly rewarding for either side. From the 1830s onward, Democrats had been part of the attempts to confront slavery. But, clearly, most of them had always been in opposition to those efforts. Some historians have seen the rise of the antislavery political movement as making the Democrats more aware of slavery and more committed against its extension. But there is little sign that Democrats became more sensitive to the matter on moral grounds, and it is also clear that they tried every device to prevent it from becoming an issue of importance in the Northern states. It is true that for tactical reasons they sometimes spoke in ways that many slave owners found inadequate (an objection that slaveholders had occasionally raised even before this). But these rhetorical flourishes were aberrations, brief and tactical. The mainstream Democrats made it very clear throughout the forties and fifties that they knew who their enemies were.

The evil forces in the society, as they saw it, were the sectional, antislavery extension movements culminating in the Republican party. They never lost sight of this fact and continued to battle against political sectionalism and political antislavery as long as they could. The whole Democratic style and substance dictated such behavior. In short, although they were Northerners, they never subscribed to free soil, free labor, and free men as articulated by the Republican party. Their definitions of each of these things differed greatly from the Republican version.

At the same time that Democrats did not lose their souls to the antislavery political movement, they also did not lose many of their faithful in the Northern states as a whole. Those who did desert to the Republican party were an important force there when joined with the Whigs, Know Nothings, and committed antislavery groups. But their role and victory in the 1860s should not blind us to the pattern and stance of the mainstream Democrats—and their importance in the period as well. In his Webb Prize essay, William Gienapp quotes an English traveler's remark that "unflinching adherence to party is principle with . . . [Americans] and to forsake a party is regarded as an act of the greatest dishonor."[101] Democratic behavior confirmed that. One analyst of the antislavery movement argues that the Free Soil party "helped to break 'the thraldom of party' and to increase the likelihood of more successful challenges in the future."[102] There is little evidence of that in terms of numbers. The Democrats' main losses in the 1850s were not due to the shaking of the tree by Free Soilers ten years before, although that affected some of them, but rather, as already noted, from the complex of local, ethnocultural, and other issues that led people to break away from the party in search of something more compatible and responsive to their needs. It was in the 1850s, not the 1840s, that a political revolution erupted, one that drew only partially on the antislavery extension conflicts of the decade before.

Finally, each party's position in regard to antislavery and antislavery politics was shaped by the contours of its Northern support as well as of its Southern and by the political memories of all of its constituents as well. The particular social groups making up each party's constituency had specific ways of looking at the world that led to specific political stances. The strong racism of many Democrats is well documented. But there were other things too. The Democrats originated as, and remained largely, the party of ethnoreligious outsiders and others (including *some* slaveowners) fearful of the power of the federal government to shape and regulate behavior and institutions.[103] Democratic rhetoric was filled, from the 1830s onward, with their memories of the abusive power of the government as wielded by their political opponents against particular immigrant social and religious groups, their values, habits, and lifestyles. Images of Puritan interventionism against their religious opponents filled Democratic pamphlets and editorials. At heart, they argued, Republicans, as the Whigs before them, were centralizing, overbearing, Federalist Tories, intent on destroying the liberties of the American people through the extensive intrusion of government power into the personal lives, conduct, and beliefs of individuals and groups within the Union.

The essential "principle of Republicanism," as seen through the Democratic filter, was "to meddle with everything . . . to force their harsh and uncongenial puritanical creed down the throats of other men and compel them to digest it under pains and penalties." Behind laws regulating or prohibiting the sale and consumption of alcoholic beverages, vigorously debated throughout the fifties, or other legislation governing the language of school instruction, which textbooks to use, who could teach, or the sources of financial support for schools, Democrats saw a Republican determination to foist on all Americans a particular code of behavior and belief. This cultural interventionism posed grave threats, in the Democrats' view, to individual freedom in America. Party spokesmen, therefore, railed against "the evils of political meddling with morals, religion, and the rights of distinct communities." They demanded that the government not be allowed to "invade the territory of the Church" on behalf of only one particular point of view within a highly pluralist nation.[104]

All of this stemmed from, and resonated with, the fears, prejudices, values, and memories of the outsider groups that made up the Democratic party. They feared the uses to which government was to be put on behalf of moral reform. They wanted no part of it, and it led them to look at antislavery movements in a particular way—as an aspect of an engine of oppression directed against certain white people in the society. Much of their behavior followed from that perspective.

Despite their long resistance to the movement, the Democrats lost their electoral majority in the North and in the nation, and then control of the government to forces that ultimately ended slavery in the United States. By then, many of the Democrats who had remained loyal to the party had come to agree that slavery should end.[105] But there is little sign that they were ever delighted by the turn of events.

It was recently said about the Democrats in the 1860s that:

> They were, perhaps, wrong-headed. They were certainly not congenial either to their Republican contemporaries or to late twentieth-century tastes. But their ideology was congruent with many of the political and social rhythms of their day. Certainly, the Democrats provided a reference point, a focus, for a significant number of Americans.[106]

This is equally applicable to them in the antebellum period as well. The prewar Democrats would not have recognized themselves in the company into which some of them had fallen by 1860. However, most retained a good grasp of what they were about and of their feelings toward their Whig, antislavery, and Republican enemies. Despite defeat and the destruction of so much of what they had fought to save, they never lost that grasp, perspective, and set of commitments that kept most of them loyal to the Democracy.

7

THE SOUTHERN NATIONAL DEMOCRATS
1845–1861
(1965)

On Saturday, August 8, 1846, Congressman David Wilmot of Pennsylvania introduced into the House of Representatives his antislavery extension resolution.[1] Although Congress never acted favorably on the Wilmot Proviso directly, its introduction serves as a convenient starting point for the last stage of antebellum political activity. From this beginning, sectional bitterness apparently increasingly influenced American politics as Northerners and Southerners attacked each other's beliefs and institutions—to the final culmination in the Civil War.[2]

Wilmot's Proviso was not introduced into a political vacuum, however, or into a situation in which men were avidly waiting to sectionalize. Two national political parties dominated the American political scene in 1846 with a consequent intensity of partisanship rarely noted in our history. Men who were Whigs or Democrats, even if they came from the same section, took their party principles seriously and bitterly fought each other in pursuit of their desired ends.[3] In Congress, in the period between 1841 and 1846, regardless of the issue, most Whigs voted on one side, most Democrats voted on the other.[4] Although some men did think and act in sectional terms in this period of high national partisanship, they were few in number and out of step with the main currents of American politics.

So strong were the forces of national partisanship that when John C. Calhoun advocated that Southerners unite to defend their section's interests against threatened Northern encroachment he met a great deal of resistance, not only from his Whig enemies but also from his fellow Southern Democrats who, having adhered to their party since the days of Andrew Jackson, refused to give up their political ties to join a sectional coalition.[5] These antisectional unity men, the Southern

National Democrats, played a very significant role in the politics of the post-Wilmot Proviso South. For a long time their political convictions as Democrats outweighed any alleged threats to their section. Party adherence and party program continued to mean much to them. Then, as they were forced by pressures from their surroundings to think about their section's danger, they chose to work for sectional defense through their familiar political institution, the Democratic party. They did so by looking for some formula which would hold together a party to which both Northerners and Southerners could belong. Their attempts to maintain national party unity did not end during any of the well-known sectional convolutions after 1846, but lasted through the Charleston and Baltimore Conventions and the Presidential campaign of 1860 until the election of Abraham Lincoln.

The number of Southern Democrats who adhered to this group before 1861 varied depending on time and circumstances. As we shall see below, occasionally they were numerous enough to embarrass and hamstring the sectionalists. At the end of the period they apparently were relatively few in number. And, in between, many political leaders, including some former Whigs, joined their ranks while others dropped out. At some point a careful state by state survey should ascertain clearly the number of people who held to and acted upon these ideas at any particular point. In this discussion, however, I am not primarily concerned with the number of men involved. Rather what I wish to do first is to recognize and delineate the ideas held by this group of Southern politicians and then to raise some questions about them, given the major patterns of Southern politics in the fifteen years before the Civil War.

Within a short time after the first introduction of the Wilmot Proviso, Representative Isaac Holmes of South Carolina wrote to Howell Cobb of Georgia that he wished "the Southern Representatives would consent to act together without regard to Whig or Democrat. The Wilmot Proviso is paramount to all Party. We are in great danger. The North is resolved to crush Slavery—are we equally in the South resolved at all hazards to defend it?"[6] Other Southern leaders echoed and developed Holmes's point. They asserted that the old issues which had divided parties nationally in the past were dead; in their absence the Northern representatives would be unable to resist antislavery pressures and would, therefore, have to desert their former Southern allies. Thus, the only hope for the South was for a sectional political unity which would override all narrow partisanship.[7] Even as they developed these points, however, the sectionalists sadly noted the negative response of Southern politicians to their call. Writing to John C. Calhoun in 1847, Wilson Lumpkin of Georgia commented that fealty to party had destroyed hopes for Southern unity. He said:

> We have many patriotic enlightened men in Georgia, who feel as we do. . . . But too large a portion of these noble spirits, have not yet abandoned forever party predilections. . . . It will still require further developments to produce the conviction which rests upon my mind of the utter corruption of both the great parties of the country.[8]

Since the 1830s there had been pockets of anti-Calhoun sentiment in many Southern state Democratic parties, so that any movement to which he was involved was viewed suspiciously by many Democrats.[9] This was certainly true of their reaction to the Southern unity movement between 1846 and 1850.[10] But this was not the only or even the major reason why many Southern democrats refused to join with the sectional unifiers. Their reasons were tied up with their own needs and the necessity they saw of maintaining national party ties. Anyone who has read deeply in the literature of the antebellum period cannot but become aware that many politically interested people held an instrumentalist view of political parties. Such institutions served a real purpose to these men in helping them achieve their general welfare—the social, economic, and political goals of themselves and their constituents. And their reactions to the movement for sectional unity quickly revealed this belief. If Southern unity meant giving up the Democratic party they were very much against doing so. In the first place, as the members of the party who drew up the resolutions of district and state party conventions in 1846 and immediately thereafter pointed out, the important issues for Southerners were the old ones over which Whigs and Democrats had traditionally divided: the tariff, the national bank, distribution of the proceeds of public land sales, and internal improvements. Here was what Democrats should be concerned about. They had to effect and maintain the best laws possible on these subjects and, at the same time, prevent the Whigs from enacting legislation contrary to Democratic desires and American interests.[11] Furthermore, in the finest tradition of Jacksonian rhetoric, they pointed out that if the Whigs came to power American liberty itself would be threatened since the Whig party represented the few in American society, the Democratic party the many.[12] The only way in which the legislative wishes of their Southern constituents and the general welfare of all Americans could be achieved was by maintaining the dominance of the national Democratic party in the United States and not by forming a weak sectional coalition.[13]

The National Democrats also played the sectional unifiers' game by asking what was the best way to defend Southern institutions if the latter were threatened by antislavery pressure. The answer, they said, was certainly not in breaking up the old parties and moving toward sectional unity. Rather, it was by working with the Northern friends of the South, who were in the Democratic, not the Whig party, to keep slavery issues out of politics entirely and to help them combat abolitionism in the North. The Athens, Georgia, *Southern Banner*, pointed out that if the slavery-extension issue did break out anew "the principal hope of salvation for this Union . . . will be in the ranks of the NORTHERN DEMOCRACY." And, a short time later the paper asked, if the South should "drive from us men [the Northern Democrats] who are extending to us the hand of conciliation and, by breaking up the present organization of the Democratic party, endanger the bonds of our political union?"[14]

It was not only with rhetoric that the National Democrats sought to uphold their party ties and defeat those who would forsake such national coalitions in the late 1840s. Perhaps the greatest failure of the sectional unifiers came during the attempt to issue the *Southern Address* in 1849. The sectionalists believed that they had made some gains during 1848, the year of the Alabama Platform, and some of them thought that, despite the strong resistance of the Jacksonians and the Whigs, the movement for Southern unity might now succeed.[15] In December 1848 an opportunity presented itself to unite, finally and completely, the South for defense. The House of Representatives passed a resolution proposed by Congressman Daniel Gott, a New York Whig, to abolish the slave trade in the District of Columbia.[16] The reaction of the Southern unifiers was to call a meeting of all Southern congressmen to consider their course of action in the face of this encroachment on their interests. Despite their hope that the meeting would indicate a united, strong Southern resistance to outside threats, the unifiers were once more frustrated. Not all Southern congressmen attended the meeting; many came only to check extreme actions, and there was much bitter argument over the nature of the statement the meeting would issue.[17] And, even after the writers of the document had toned it down to meet moderate objections, many Southerners refused to sign the published *Address*. Of the eighty-seven Southern Democrats in both Houses of Congress in 1849, forty-six signed the *Address*.[18] To many of the others the implied threat in the document to national unity and the overt sectional tactics used were unacceptable.[19]

In this discussion I do not mean to convey a false impression. In the long run the Southern Nationalists were not fighting a winning battle with the sectionalists. But this they did not know and throughout the fifties they continued to resist the increasing sectional political pressure. They advocated the same formula they had pushed since 1846: the necessity of maintaining traditional party ties despite the new issues confronting them. And they were particularly encouraged by the successes they enjoyed in the early fifties.

In the aftermath of the Crisis of 1850 and the failure of the Nashville Convention and the Southern Rights movement, there was a definite move, in both North and South, to reestablish traditional national political divisions and to reinvigorate established issues, such as the tariff.[20] The Southern sectionalists returned to the national party fold by 1852 so that there was a high degree of Southern Democratic unity behind the candidacy of Franklin Pierce where there had been dissension four years before. The Nationalists supported Pierce because he embodied traditional Democratic virtues,[21] but many sectionalists did so out of the felt necessity of returning to party councils in order to reestablish their position in Southern politics.[22] Despite such efforts, however, many of them found themselves either in political eclipse or forced to withdraw from political life completely.[23] Thus, in the period between 1850 and 1854, the National Democrats could see the triumph of their policy in the fact of party reunion. And when the sectional crisis erupted again many of the Democratic stalwarts, experienced in the fires of 1846–1850, strove once again to maintain the Democratic party as a national institution. Both in their speeches and in their actions through 1860, a group of Southern Democrats continued to push their policy despite the increasing intensity and bitterness of sectional pressures below the Mason-Dixon line.

Their rhetoric particularly stressed a theme which they had pointed up before: that the continued success of the Democratic party was the only assured way that the South could protect itself. Unlike the Republicans, the Democrats could win votes in every section of the country and were, therefore, likely to keep control of the government so long as they remained united. It was better after all, Senator Clingman of North Carolina pointed out, to have a candidate who would run in all thirty-three states rather than one who would run in only half of them.[24] Furthermore, the Northern Democrats, despite the antislavery pressure to which they were constantly subjected, continued to uphold the constitutional rights of the South and to resist challenges to the domestic institutions of that section. They were, in Benjamin Perry's phrase, "firm, sound and sanguine" on slavery matters.[25] The South was safe and should continue to work with such allies. As Howell Cobb phrased it, in a speech to a Democratic meeting in 1856, "I care not whether that Democratic orator who has preceded me hails from the North, or the West, or the South, if he stand on this platform, the truthful exponent of Democratic principles, he speaks one voice with me."[26] But if, on the other hand, Southerners gave in to the suspicions of a few of them and forsook their national connection and their Northern allies for sectional organizations they would not be strong enough to maintain their rights and institutions. With the Southern Democrats forsaking them to pursue a new policy the Northern Democrats would be defeated and the Black Republicans, unhampered by opposition at home to their anti-Southern principles, would be able to extend their dangerous activities. The ultimate result of this would either be Southern submission or disunion. But with the national Democratic party intact the South would never have to make this unhappy choice.[27] In other words, as Cobb put it,

> believing as I do . . . that the best interests of the country, if not its very existence depends upon the preservation of the national Democratic party, I will never abandon that organization as long as the banner which floats over it has inscribed upon its fold the principles to which I am in body and mind thoroughly and unfalteringly devoted now and forever.[28]

At the same time, some Democrats continued to look upon their party in more than defensive terms, supporting it for its past achievements as well as for its future promise. In 1860, in the aftermath of the walkout of the Gulf states from the Charleston Convention, Senator Willard Saulsbury of Delaware arose in the Senate and pointed to the achievements of the Democratic party during its long history.

> Under its guiding counsels we have increased from less than five, until we now number thirty millions of people. . . . This true union party has made ours an ocean-bound Republic; great, mighty, prosperous, and free. In peace it has developed our resources and expanded our power; and in war it has successfully maintained our rights and nobly vindicated our national honor. Under its policy, and by its counsels, in peace and in war, the feeble Republic of yesterday has become one of the greatest and mightiest among the nations of the earth.[29]

This continued devotion to the instrument of party was also reflected outside the oratorical realm. For, throughout the swiftly moving events between the introduction of the Kansas-Nebraska bill and the Charleston Convention of 1860, some Southern Democrats acted in terms which went against the national trend of the political scene. Whether it was in opposing the Solid South movement in Georgia in 1855,[30] or pushing recalcitrant colleagues into the national Democratic conventions as James Orr did in South Carolina throughout the fifties,[31] or supporting the two Democratic administrations' policies in Kansas and elsewhere,[32] the National Democrats continued to act within the framework of their national party connections. Occasionally some of them took very unpopular positions in terms of Southern sectionalism, as in the case of their support for Governor Robert J. Walker in Kansas. Despite much Southern bitterness against the latter's actions, the Nationalists pointed out that regardless of claims to the contrary, Walker's policies had been just and in no way suggested that the Buchanan administration had sold out to Northern interests.[33]

The real test for the Southern National Democrats came, of course, when Senator Stephen A. Douglas broke with the national administration over its Kansas policy.[34] Many of the National Democrats could not and would not support the Illinois Senator in his opposition to the Lecompton Constitution and his party defection. On the other hand, others of the partisan group supported Douglas's stand. He had been their choice for President in 1856 and they had favored his territorial policies then. He and his policies had not changed since.[35] More importantly, they saw in their support of Douglas the upholding of the position they had taken for so long. If Douglas was destroyed, they pointed out, so would be the Northern Democratic party and their policy of national political institutions. And, of course, they believed that if that party went so would the South.[36] Thus, despite the bitter controversy that broke out between the Southern sectionalists and the Buchanan administration on one hand, and the Douglas forces on the other, some Southerners made it quite clear that they stood with the Illinois Senator.[37] When Jefferson Davis introduced his resolutions into Congress calling for positive federal measures to protect slavery in the United States—a policy that had become the *sine qua non* of the Southern sectionalists—there was opposition to their passage from some of the Southern Democrats who favored maintaining their traditional policy of nonintervention in the territories.[38] Once again, during these debates paeans to party were heard as well as statements as to the negative effect such resolutions would have on the continued necessary survival of the Democratic party.[39] To one Southern Democrat, Robert Toombs of Georgia, the Davis resolutions would destroy the party at the North. He himself wanted Douglas defeated at Charleston but "I do not want him and his friends crippled or driven off. Where are we to get as many or as good men in the North to supply their places? . . . It is naked folly to turn out a quarter of a million at least of such men on such pretenses."[40] Furthermore, in a return to the past, at least one Southern

National Democrat, Andrew Johnson of Tennessee, demanded that the Senate stop wasting its time in considering such abstractions as the Davis resolutions and instead take up the more important homestead bill.[41]

The year 1860, of course, saw the Democratic party break asunder with the consequent final dashing of the hopes of the Southern nationalists.[42] Yet, many of them fought to the bitter end for their policy. Despite the hysteria of the galleries of Charleston and the pressure applied by the secession of the bulk of the Gulf states delegation, most Southern delegates refused to bolt the convention.[43] In fact, a few men from the Gulf states themselves stayed with the Douglas Democracy.[44] It is also noteworthy that among the bolters themselves there was some hesitancy about the step they were taking. And after their bolt some continued to cast longing glances at the convention and to express hope that the party could and would be reunited.[45]

In the campaign that followed, Douglas received support from many Southern Democrats who, refusing to break with him, fought to the end against Breckinridge, Bell, and Lincoln in the interest of maintaining the party as they had always done. Douglas's vice-presidential candidate, Herschel V. Johnson of Georgia, who had moved from the Southern sectionalists to the National Democrats during the 'fifties, summed up his own reasons for staying with the national Douglas Democracy, and in so doing spoke the sentiments of many others. Johnson commented years later, that,

> I was satisfied with the doctrine of "Non-Intervention" . . . the South had agreed to it. . . . Hence I regarded the action of the bolters as worthy to be characterized as *bad faith* on their part to the Northern Democracy. . . . Moreover the grand old Democratic party was hoary with honors. It had achieved nearly everything for the Union, which illustrated its greatness and made it to command the respect of all nations. I had been educated in sentiments of admiration and reverence for it. I cordially believed in its political creed. But it was now divided. . . . Its fortunes were declining and its glory declining. I could not consent to desert in this dark hour of its extremity . . . even though defeat was my doom. I thought I should be amply compensated for the sacrifice, if in my humble way, I could be instrumental in part, in preserving a portion of it, North and South—in a state of organization, around which its friends might be rallied again in the future for fresh struggles and fresh victories in the cause of the Constitution and the Union.[46]

The election of Abraham Lincoln in 1860 did not end the story of the National Democrats but it clearly marked the defeat of their particular national policy.[47] Although many of them were to be found in the ranks of the antisecession groups through the spring of 1861,[48] events and forces had moved beyond them, and their pleadings no longer seemed relevant in the increasingly sectional situation. Some of them became officials in the new Confederate government, others sank into political oblivion. And in the years after the Civil War their ideas and stances became lost in the image of monolithic Southern political attitudes. And the relative neglect of them has continued to our own day. Twentieth-century historians have noted the existence of much dissent in the antebellum South. The researches of Arthur C. Cole and Chauncey Boucher, in the early part of the twentieth century,[49] and of Charles Sellers, Thomas P. Govan, Horace Montgomery, and others in more recent years, have paid attention to some of the antisectional forces in the antebellum South.[50] And, although we have several inquiries into the nature of antisectional unionism, particularly among the Southern Whigs, as well as some biographies of the more noted Southern Democrats,[51] it would not be too much to assert that this work remains essentially the minor key in the study of pre-Civil War politics. Our principal interest, after all, has focused on the winners: the sectionalists. As we have examined the disruption of the American Democracy, the growth of Southern nationalism, the coming of the Civil War, and the significance of sectionalism in American politics, the men who stood outside these forces are not given the attention paid to those in the mainstream of Southern secessionism.[52]

Finding, recognizing, and giving fuller attention to the Southern antisectionalist Democrats, however, is not the only function of these remarks. Diligent search through a multitude of secondary works will reveal some measure of what I have pointed out. But what will not really be found is an understanding of the political orientation and tactics of these men, or adequate analyses of the men themselves. In the first place, it seems to me to be of the utmost relevance to note the importance that many Southerners attached to political parties as instruments of achieving their desires in the decade and a half before the Civil War. Whether it is because of intellectual denigrations of party politics or because of the persistence of the sectional theme in our modes of analysis, it is clear that many American historians agree implicitly or explicitly with Professor Charles Sydnor's assertion that, in the late 1840s party battles in the Southern states had the hollow sound of stage duels fought with tin swords.[53] And yet the men of the times obviously saw the parties as more than instruments for fighting false duels or for covering up other, more important groupings such as sections. A few men may have used parties primarily as a means of gaining and holding office regardless of principles involved, but it would be a mistake to believe that all or even a majority of those I have identified as National Democrats did so. We might concede that some of the leaders were interested only in personal aggrandisement, but what about the people who elected them to office and kept electing them time after time? Certainly the latter could not all expect to share in the public plunder or the spoils of office. They would have had to be attracted by the issues stressed and the positions taken in order to keep on supporting the Democratic party in the face of the tremendous pressures working to subvert and break down the party, especially in the late 1850s. To quote an acute observer in another field,

> The very fact that issues could be used for opportunistic purposes by some implies that they served substantive purposes for others. Whether these substantive goals were real or fictitious, whether men's reasons for wanting a particular measure were good or bad, intelligent or silly, based on a reasoned calculation or on a neurotic compulsion unrelated to reality is irrelevant. The point is that it would be useless for a politician to make an instrumental use of an issue unless it represented something that a considerable group in the electorate . . . wanted.[54]

The point is that for a complete understanding of American political behavior in the antebellum period we have to examine the persistence of party adherence as well as the crisis of party collapse. When, in the late 1840s, a leading Southern newspaper complained that most Southern politicians were willing to sacrifice the rights of their section on "the shrine of party," elements of its complaint may have been misdirected, but the editor of the paper certainly had caught the essence of what was political reality to many Southern Democrats.[55]

This brings us to the second main concern growing from these circumstances. How could this situation arise? The fifties were a time of increasing sectional division, bitterness, and influences on the American scene which national institutions were unable to resist and therefore broke apart one by one. The push for sectional unity in both halves of the Union converted and convinced the bulk of men. And yet other men, as, for example, these Southern Democrats, held out against those forces and refused to sectionalize. And, as they did, they developed a pattern of ideas, based on national political parties, which they used to challenge the assertions of the sectional unifiers. Their behavior cannot simply be dismissed as unique, quixotic, or irrelevant. Although their numbers dwindled, they always existed on the Southern scene and for a long period they were powerful enough first to frustrate and then to delay the wishes of the sectionalists. Even in the crisis of 1860-1861 they played a substantial role in conjunction with non-Democratic Unionists.[56] We should therefore seek to determine what made these men act and continue to act as they did, what made them different from the sectionalists, and what characterized those among them who gave in to sectional pressures from those who never did. When we turn to recorded analyses of the men, few though there are, we do find a few explanations for their actions. The answer could lie, for example, in differences of wealth, class, and number of slaves between different groups.[57] It may come out of internal political bickering and maneuvering—something which may well explain the rapid movement back and forth between sectional unity and national party adherence of a Senator Robert Hunter, challenged in Virginia by Henry A. Wise, or the party devotion of Pierre Soulé involved as he was in a bitter battle with John Slidell for the control of the Louisiana Democratic party.[58] Perhaps subregional differences within the South or sectional conflicts within the states explain the differences.[59] The answer may lie in differences between individuals: the sectionalists demonstrating one group of personal characteristics, the nationalists another. Perhaps previous party adherence is the answer, for many Whigs had joined the Democratic party in the 1850s.[60] Clearly, here were different men whose existence has been known but who have not been systematically analyzed. We have developed an awareness of the complexities of political behavior, and the methods necessary to perceive correlations between social, economic, and political variables and men's reaction to them: comparative biography as applied by Charles A. Beard, David Donald, and Georgy Mowry;[61] popular voting analysis as undertaken by Lee Benson and Samuel P. Hays;[62] and examining the relationships between constituency and leaders as engaged in by Staughton Lynd and Forrest McDonald.[63] There is an opportunity for us to analyze systematically a group of people who, in the South of the 1850s, played a highly national and traditionally partisan role. As we search out every possible factor affecting these men, from the personal through the constituency and regional levels, and compare them with the same types of characteristics of the sectional Democrats we will expand our knowledge of the total picture of Southern antebellum politics and of the forces at work that produced a Civil War.

8

"THE UNDISGUISED CONNECTION" KNOW NOTHINGS INTO REPUBLICANS: NEW YORK AS A TEST CASE (1985)

The role played by nativism in the formation and character of the Republican party in the 1850s remains a controversial matter. While the potency of the nativist appeal in the decade before the Civil War has been recognized and well established, the extent of its influence and how it fit into the political system have not. The nativist American party played a critical role in the mid-fifties, declined as an organized force late in the decade, and then disappeared from sight. But what happened to its supporters, their ideas, and their particular commitments? Were they absorbed by the triumphant Republicans, did they withdraw from politics, or did they find their way into *both* the parties surviving on the national scene? Certainly, as David Potter has spelled it out, the two issues of nativism and antislavery each had sufficient clout on the political scene "to make a coalition of antislavery men and nativists highly expedient."[1] But only if there were grounds to make such possible, or one of the two central issues affecting political choice declined in importance, or some kind of agreement was reached on the issues central to each group.

A number of scholars who have recently argued for the central and continuing importance of ethnoreligious matters in Northern electoral politics support the first of these possible pathways. As Paul Kleppner puts it in his thorough and authoritative study of mass voting choice in the 1850s, Republicans in the middle belt of states from New York westward absorbed "a strong majority of those who had earlier cast Know Nothing ballots."[2] The Republicans did not win them over automatically, however. Coalition of the two groups opposing the Democratic party was difficult to accomplish and far from automatic unless concessions were made. Despite frequent historical celebration of the

Republican party's early continued success, the creation of a majority and effective party in the mid-fifties was, to quote Kleppner, a "more protracted and agonizing . . . enterprise than has generally been recognized."[3]

As we know, the Republican party had emerged as a potent national force by 1856. But that was not the end of the story—it was not a clear sail from there through the triumph of anti-Southernism and anti-slavery. Far from it. In fact, the Republicans continued to face very serious problems, not easily resolved, that threatened their positioning as the second major party in the country, let alone as the national majority. As a result, Republicans worked to attract the nativists to them by their willingness to structure their commitments, public rhetoric, and behavior so as to appeal to the powerful voting bloc supporting the American party. Both Michael Holt and Ronald Formisano, for example, suggest that in the states they have considered, Republicans made necessary policy concessions to the Americans. Formisano refers to an "alliance between Republicans and Americans" in Michigan rooted in Republican acceptance of certain Know-Nothing policy initiatives. In particular, an electoral registry bill, a core demand of the Americans, became "the party issue of 1859" among Republican leaders. In fact, the Republican Address of 1859 in Michigan, designed to inform voters why they should vote Republican and widely circulated in the state, "devoted most of its attention to the Registry Law." The result was a successful coalition with strong nativist as well as anti-Southern and antislavery tendencies.[4]

On the other hand, other historians dismiss such a relationship as temporary at best and certainly not a central factor either in Republican success or in defining the nature of the Republican party. Glyndon Van Deusen, David Potter, and, most especially, Eric Foner and Richard Sewell readily accept that many nativist supporters went into the Republican party in the late fifties as the independent American organization weakened. But they do not think that such absorption of the Americans had much influence on the host party—or, to put it another way, the Know Nothings having no place else to go, drifted to the Republicans without making many demands of the latter and certainly without influencing the approach to public policy of the Republicans.[5] Thus, while Republicans had difficulties with the prickly nativists, the former prevailed with little cost to their soul and public face. Eric Foner has written in his influential *Free Soil, Free Labor, Free Men* that in New York State the Republican leaders, Weed and Seward, refused "to make concessions to Know-Nothing feeling." If Republican leaders worked with Know Nothings anywhere else, he suggests, the concessions they made for Know-Nothing support were mild compared with what the Americans usually demanded. That was because of the strength of the more traditional issues raised by slavery and sectionalism, which are more likely explanations for the triumph of Republicanism in the late 1850s. "Animus to the foreign born," Foner concludes, "was less appealing, ultimately, to Northern voters than were the forces of antisouthernism and antislavery." In fact, Foner sums up, by the late 1850s, "nativism became more of a liability than an asset for the Republican party."[6]

Strikingly, the historiographic arguments over this relationship echo more distant disagreements found in the historical record. Republican participants in the struggles of the 1850s when they remembered those events later on tended either to deny a particular affinity between themselves and the nativists or to ignore the issue entirely. Horace Greeley, for example, in *Recollections of a Busy Life*, published in 1868, devotes little comment to the Know Nothings, especially after 1856, when the movement "dwindled rapidly, until its members had been fully absorbed into *one or the other* of the great rival parties" (italics added). Nothing at all is said in Weed's memoirs, but the image there is of Know-Nothing weakness in New York after 1855. Finally, Frederick Seward, in his biography of his father, also barely mentions the Know Nothings, touches only lightly on New York State politics in the late 1850s, and does not note any activities bringing Republicans and Know Nothings into any sort of direct relationship.[7]

A different position was taken by Republican journals at the time. They did not ignore the Know Nothings but very much confused the electoral and relationship issues. Despite longtime efforts to forge a community of interest between Republicans and nativists, Greeley's *Tribune*, argued in 1858 that "thousands of voters still warm from Know Nothing lodges swelled the vote of . . . [the] Democracy last Fall." At other times, Greeley and other Republican editors argued that the Know-Nothing vote was split between the Democrats and Republicans, thereby strongly suggesting that there was no particular affinity between Republicans and Know Nothings.[8]

Republicans, of course, had a vested interest in remembering the consolidation as being without cost to them and rooted in antislavery principles. On the other hand, other contemporaries disagree with Republican diffidence and/or confusion on the matter. To the leading Democratic journal in New York State, the opposition to Democracy in New York had grown from the "odds and ends of factions and isms" in 1855 to "a combination of deceased Whigism, Maine Lawism, Abolitionism and Know-Nothingism." They had come together since there was nothing to keep them apart. Republicanism, after all, "has no objection to Know-Nothingism and its distinctive and proscriptive doctrines, if it will superadd to its creed the Anti-Slavery Republican dogmas."[9]

What is, of course, clear from all of this is how much the interrelationship between these two movements has been an object of some persistent interest, how clouded and contentious the overt historical record, and how much the whole remains an issue not yet satisfactorily settled. Yet, there is more than idle historical curiosity at play here. That relationship provides an insight into a problem of some importance in understanding not only the triumph of Republicanism but also something about the nature of the elements and boundaries of social and political conflict in mid-nineteenth-century America.

Recently Dale Baum has trenchantly summed up the current historiographic shape of the problem. Reminding us that perhaps nothing has divided old and new political historians from each other quite so much as the commitment to, or dismissal of, the ethnocultural explanation of human and party behavior, he sets out to measure, with refined quantitative instruments, the critical dimension of the argument—just where did the Know-Nothing voters go in one important state. Baum's conclusion is simple—in Massachusetts, Know-Nothing voters did not drift to the Republicans en masse—a striking challenge to one important aspect of the ethnocultural interpretation of party politics in the 1850s that, ironically, uses the tools of the new political history to clinch the point. "The anti-Catholic, anti-foreign American party," he concludes, "played a very minor role in the transition from a Whig to a Republican majority in Massachusetts."[10]

There remains still, despite Baum's careful work, the question of how far outside Massachusetts his conclusions extends. Inadvertently his rhetoric may leave the impression that his findings are general. Actually he is too careful a historian for that to be true, but a sense of generality may come through to the casual observer. But we need more cases and to be aware of certain additional variables in the total record before we can argue persuasive generalizations. Certainly there is good reason to emphasize once again that a national phenomenon is always the sum total of a wide variety of individual state experiences. The situation in Massachusetts may be unique to itself, or representative only of certain political cultures. Each state was a singular political system with its own specific working out of challenges and political problems. One state's experience is only the beginning of understanding the whole.

Extending our reach should improve our understanding and may change the direction of our analysis. That fact, as well as the historiographic importance of the matter to students of antebellum politics and of the coming of the Civil War, warrants a fresh look, utilizing recently developed quantitative tools of analysis as well as more traditional sources of information. Certainly, in New York State there is a substantial body of evidence, quantitative and otherwise, suggesting another set of conclusions. In New York, as elsewhere in the Northern states, Know-Nothingism and its particular priorities remained potent well into the later fifties. But everywhere at the end of the decade, the separate party embracing nativism was a party in decline. But, according to DeAlva Alexander, for so long the premier political historian of New York State, the Know-Nothing vote did not go completely into the Republican camp. Throughout the late fifties, the Democrats, he argues, picked up many of them as well.[11] True perhaps, but there is much more to be said about what happened.

There are two problems here that rise out of the historiography and the political realities of the time—numbers and influence. First, what actually happened so far as Know-Nothing voters were concerned? How many went over to the Republicans, how many joined the Democrats, how many dropped out entirely? Second, where the Know Nothings and the Republicans came together what did the Republicans have to do to attract the others to them? That is, what price did they have to pay if any? In New York State, at least, the record shows that not only did the Know Nothings go over to the Republicans to form a substantial and crucial component of the final coalition, but that the Republicans paid a price for their acquisition by making themselves attractive to the Know Nothings on the latter's terms and not because Know Nothings were anti-Southern or that nativism had faded as a significant issue. Quite the contrary in fact. Whatever the size of the American party's vote in its decline, Republican leaders were very aware of strong nativist sentiment in the state that had to be handled in some fashion. As Michael Holt sums up, "men did not have to vote Know Nothing to express their resentment against Catholics as long as they regarded the Republican party as more anti-Catholic than the Democratic party—and they did."[12]

But there was more focus than that. In the election returns, party newspapers, and the speeches, letters, and other surviving manuscripts of party leaders are the details of a complex story of recognition and interrelationship based on difficult coalition-building in the pluralist world of mid-nineteenth-century American politics. Unfortunately, however, the working out of that growing relationship in the state has not been studied carefully enough to catch the complexity of what occurred, especially in the critical two years after 1857. The rise of the Republicans to maturity and majority status and the disappearance of the Know Nothings are routinely marked in most studies. But in the years 1857 to 1860 more than routine markings took place. Arduous efforts to cement a relationship were under way. The result was an "undisguised connection" between the two anti-Democratic movements plain enough for all to see and to react to as they thought appropriate, a relationship that incorporated the central tenets of both partisan faiths and established a formidable political movement in the state.[13]

As noted, the New York case may or may not be typical. It is certainly both revelatory of larger themes and a building block toward comprehending the full dimension of the forces at work in late antebellum Northern party politics. The whole was a many sided, many tiered affair involving politics and response at every level. Perceptions were roused, people responded, people saw a need, the electoral calculus dictated much. A look at behind the scenes activities, public rhetoric and perception, legislative behavior, and, finally and critically, popular voting reveals the whole.

II

New York's size and centrality in American politics in the 1850s give it more than ordinary importance in unraveling this problem. By 1860 the people of the state cast almost 15 percent of the national vote for President, and just under 20 percent of the total Republican vote. New York and its voters counted very much in the politics of the day. The state had long been an arena of long standing ethnoreligious conflict as well as sharp antagonisms over slavery and sectionalism. Reflecting this, the resistance to the Democracy divided into two different and hostile coalitions after 1854. Nativism, particularly its anti-Catholic strain, had been a significant and increasingly well-organized political issue for some time. It took new life in 1854, to be joined a year later by the newly emergent Republicans building on the Free-Soil revolt of 1848 and the rush of anti-Nebraska advocates now free from their former party moorings and at large.[14]

The electoral calculus resulting from this division from the mid-fifties on made Republican–Know-Nothing relationships a focus of some importance. In fact, it made the relationship a critical one in the state. Despite common notions and moods, New York's Know Nothings and Republicans had never been able to come together. Each was quite powerful at the polls and each very hostile to the other, reflecting their vigorous competition to become the main anti-Democratic party. In 1855, in fact, the state Republican platform had explicitly condemned the Know Nothings and their "proscriptive and anti-Republican" doctrines. The feeling was as strongly reciprocated. Know Nothings and conservative Whigs remained particularly and virulently hostile to Mr. Republican in the state, William Henry Seward. They remained "vindicative and inappeasible opponents" of him and the Republican movement he led.[15]

From the beginning, the Republicans prospered at the polls in the state but never enough. Know Nothings rivaled, and twice outpaced, the Republicans as the successor to the Whigs as the main opposition party. As a New York Whig noted in 1854, "this election has demonstrated that, by a majority, Roman Catholicism is feared more than American slavery." A year later George Baker noted to Seward that if the Republicans failed in that fall's elections "it will be because the people have read more about the Pope and Bishop Hughes than about Slavery and Equal Rights."[16] In the state elections in 1855 there was a remarkable tripartite split of the popular vote with the Know Nothings beating out the Republicans for second place. (Table 8.1)

Table 8-1. Pattern of Electoral Support,
New York State, 1854–1857

	1854	1855	1856	1857
Democrats	40.5%	34.5	33.4	44.4
Republicans	33.4*	31.3	46.3	40.3
Americans	26.1	34.1	20.8	15.3

*Fusion ticket of Whigs, Free Soilers, and Anti-Nebraska elements.

A loose set of anti-Democratic groups, taking many different forms, going in many different directions, littered the scene. They were not united, they had a majority of voters—all voting for different candidates. New York's Republican leaders were quite pessimistic and confused about the situation in which they found themselves early on. Thurlow Weed believed there were "elements enough" in the state to carry the election "if combined." But divided as they were, another observer noted, "slavery [i.e., the Democrats] must triumph." William Seward saw the antislavery party as having "a mountain to climb" with the path to the top well concealed. Problems of priorities, different issues, and approaches abounded. Old hostilities and previous commitments remained potent. The problem seemed to make accurate the observation of a Democrat that "nobody believes this Republican movement can prove the basis of a permanent party."[17]

The Republicans finally broke through in the presidential election of 1856, when, despite attracting only a minority of the total vote of the state, they won decisively. Know-Nothing leaders watched in dismay as the "delirium" unleashed by the potent Kansas and Sumner situations that year hurt the American cause and attracted American voters "into the arms of the Republican party."[18] Republican leaders, on the other hand, were jubilant, especially at what had happened to the Know Nothings. One correspondent wrote to Seward after the election that "the Know Nothing party, the meanest, paltriest of all mean & paltry parties has been killed dead, dead forever, never to rise again."[19]

But, unfortunately for the Republican party, that was not the end of the story. In the most recent study of the emergence of the Republican party in New York, Hendrik Booraem suggests that by 1856 "the process of founding the Republican party in New York . . . [was] essentially completed" with "a recognized name, a clearly defined set of principles, a stable array of well-known leaders . . . a well-articulated structure . . . [and] an appeal to a majority of the state's voters."[20] That goes too far, I believe. For, despite their decisive victory in 1856, the outlook was still clouded for the new antislavery party in the Empire State. The Know Nothings and nativism continued to roil the surface and contribute to the substance of state politics well into the late fifties. Three vigorous parties remained in the field, each bitterly hostile to the others. At the same time, the potency of the single theme the Republican relied on: opposition to Southern aggression and slavery expansion, remained of uncertain strength and durability in anyone's calculations.

In 1857 disaster struck. Despite all the efforts of the Republican campaign to keep the focus on the Southern aggression issue, Republicans suffered a sharp setback in the state elections. One scholar, Robert Imholt, has calibrated a sharp drop in the amount of time and space even Republican newspapers devoted to the slavery question in 1857 over what they had given the year before. It was a decline that continued steadily throughout the year. As a result, Republican enthusiasm had waned and with that their total popular vote. They lost 6 percent of the state's vote of the year before—and their plurality. The leading Know-Nothing state organ was gleeful about what had happened to the Republicans. "Nothing is truer," the Albany *Statesman*'s editor wrote, "than *that the Republican Party is henceforth to be the party to desert from, not to go to.*"[21]

It was clear that the antislavery anti-Southern issue was, by itself, insufficient in New York State, as things were, to forge a united majority against the Democratic party. With the terrible setback in 1857, the pessimistic mood returned in great force among Republicans. William Seward wrote to George W. Patterson that it was "frightening to see such a result." The Republican Buffalo *Express* went further. "This result shows that there is no Republican party, and that what appeared to be such one year ago was a sort of mirage which was thrown upon the public view by a peculiar condition of the atmosphere and which disappeared when a change of wind came." The Democratic press gleefully talked about the decline of "ephemeral" issues, and the good sense and "sober second thoughts" of the people, both of which had returned Democrats to power.[22]

For whatever set of reasons, the Republican tide had ebbed. Their growth had stopped while the Know Nothings remained in the field as a significant force. The latter received over 15 percent of the vote in 1857, a decisive amount in the closely competitive political environment in the state. The Republican setback might be temporary but no one could be sure. It was not only the raw numbers but the strategic nature of the totals that disturbed Republican leaders. While their party might have more votes than the Know Nothings, it did not have enough and had failed to get all it needed. Two different anti-Democratic movements had hardened into independence, not coalesced into a potent majority.

What could be done? Every political observer in the state knew the answer. The electoral dimension calling for common alliance was clear enough. Only the virulently anti-Democratic Know Nothings could help. And although their total vote has been reduced since 1855, it was essential for the Republicans to have and was worth fighting for. As the editor of the New York *Courier and Enquirer* argued, the potential Republican gains "from this source will very far exceed its recruits from the Democratic ranks." Simply put, the various anti-Democratic parties were supported by a majority of voters in the state but divided as they were, they could not cash in on the fact. Right after the election the editor of the Jamestown *Journal* summed up the task ahead as the necessity "to cement into a harmonious mass . . . all of the Anti-Slavery, Anti-Popery and Anti-Whiskey electors of the State."[23]

The whole situation was ludicrous. There was an obvious need to bring the two great streams of anti-Democracy together. And both Republicans and Know Nothings were sensitive to this. Therefore, to the "two branches of the Opposition party" in the state, the question of unifying the anti-Democratic groups became an important matter. Neither party "can hope to achieve a victory single-handed" against the "bogus Irish Democracy."[24] But how to overcome the Americans' similarly virulent hostility to the Republican coalition? And were there grounds for compatibility between the parties? The Republican leadership, out of necessity, thought so. Everything centered on, as a small-town Republican newspaper put it late in the decade, the fact "that two-thirds or three-quarters of the so-called Americans are Republican in sentiment and would constitute a valuable acquisition to the Republican party admits of no doubt."[25]

The potentialities of the electorate thus determined the actions and reactions of the state's Republican leadership. They began to work to unite with the Know Nothings as the essential element in their success. The party's editors and other politically sensitive observers began to focus on the nature and terms of a move toward the Know Nothings. More and more they admitted in their press that to beat the Democrats "the first step is to cultivate kindly relations between the different camps of the Opposition." We look upon this, the editor of the Syracuse *Journal* wrote, "as a matter of great importance and one which cannot be neglected without detriment." It was their "duty" to do so.[26]

III

New York Republicans certainly had the Know Nothings on their minds. As Eric Foner has written, "nativism posed a formidable dilemma for the Republican organization of New York." No one could ignore the Americans. As Hendrik Booraem notes, "many Republican politicians and voters . . . still had the feeling that anti-Catholicism was as urgent a crusade as antislavery and . . . that there was some obscure link between the two."[27] As a result, clearly, all the elements for a coming together were present: the imperative of the electoral calculus, the sensitivities to that calculus, elite exploration and interaction, and strong perspectives from the press of the state.

But perception did not lead to immediate and clear resolution. One group of Republicans, such as those represented by the *Evening Post*, tended to deprecate the Know Nothings' importance, while others, such as those represented by Greeley's *Tribune*, worried a great deal about it. Still other Republican newspapers varied in their enthusiasm. Some Republicans were not enthusiastic at all. George Patterson argued that "we want nothing to do with any set of men who will not be true to the principles of *Liberty*." But few rejected out of hand any grounds for a compatible interaction between the parties. Some were quite optimistic about the promise opened up by their commonality. One editor airily referred to the "slight differences" between the two anti-Democratic parties that would soon disappear. "There is no disguising the fact," the editor continued, "that the current of events is fast bearing the Republican and American parties in the same channel." Even the most unfriendly papers appealed repeatedly for the Know Nothings to come over to the Republicans on the basis of similarly held anti-Administration hostility. The differences between them were fewer and fewer and of "small consequence" compared with the things they would gain from working together.[28]

The Republicans could never expect to win over all of the Know Nothings. Too many other things—fears, prejudices, other commitments, past memories—remained at issue. The Know-Nothing voters might do several things other than vote Republican—drop out of the electoral process entirely, for one. Since some of them had originally been Democrats, it was not out of the realm of possibility that some of them might go back there as well. Still, there was a Republican potential there. Enough could be pulled over to create a secure Republican majority in the state. But the potential could only be realized by making a direct effort to convince such voters of Republican soundness and congruence with their views. They had to be made to see that among the various pressures working on them, the things that could draw them into the Republican column were the strongest.

As they argued among themselves, Republicans never lost sight of their main commitments against the extension of slavery and the power wielded by the aggressive slavocracy. They would not back down from that nor come to terms with anyone virulently against their central perspective. But that left them a great deal of room to maneuver, especially given their electoral needs.[29] From the beginning of their emergence as a political force, Republicans had occasionally played with other than sectional issues, issues that they believed enlarged their appeal strikingly. They had allied themselves in some places with the Temperance movement, a separate force but one whose instincts were compatible with some of the impulses motivating the Know Nothings. There were other signs of recognition of mutual interests in some activities in the state legislature. There Republicans and Know Nothings joined together on behalf of bills to restrict the New York City Democratic government's control of its internal affairs. There is also evidence of cooperation at the local level at sporadic moments in different places. In 1857, Republicans and Know Nothings in New York City fused together behind a single candidate in each of several judgeship races. All of these activities established, in Louis Scisco's words, "a vague sort of kinship between the parties."[30]

Anyone who reads William Seward's speeches and follows his public career readily discovers how untainted he was by nativism and how hostile he was to the Know-Nothing movement. But, despite his preeminence in Republican councils, that was not the end of the matter. There were many Republicans who were much less fastidious than he was. The Americans and these Republicans believed that they belonged together on the basis of their common attitudes. No one suggested similar compatibility with the Democrats. In fact, it is striking how readily both Republican and American leaders in New York recognized their compatibility, as well as the difficulties they would encounter in coming together. But accepting the first, they made every effort to accomplish the second. The activities that followed never involved the Democrats.

The politically sensitive in the state were aware of all of this. The leaders of New York's Democracy had no difficulty in seeing the outline of what was developing. Politics had degenerated from coherence to chaos. There remained only the Democratic party and the "odds and ends of factions and isms." But that was not the end of it. Despite the "inherent antagonism" among the "many discordant elements" comprising the anti-Democrats, Republicans had "*no objection to Know-Nothingism and its distinctive and proscriptive doctrines, if it will superadd to its creed the Anti-Slavery Republican dogmas.*" From now on, "proscription of all citizens of foreign birth, or of the Catholic religion becomes a part of the Republican creed." They will end by kindling "a fierce religious and sectional war."[31]

There is much public and behind the scenes evidence bearing out Democratic suspicions involving maneuvering among Republicans and Know Nothings to see what could be done. The Americans certainly made their position quite clear. As the editor of the Know-Nothing Ithaca *American Citizen* put it in 1856, "let each party cherish their own distinctive views, if they please, but let us all unite to drive the Goths and Vandals from power and place in the United States."[32] But the roadway was much more rocky than either Democrats or the most optimistic Republicans believed. The Americans were willing to listen but always with a particular ear. They had no intention of abandoning their own particular beliefs and continued to push for their own important program. Nor would they sacrifice either or ignore the places where they expected the Republicans to give in to win their support. Any union organization had to contain "sufficient Americanism in the bases to enable the Americans to feel at home." Unity, with adherence to one's beliefs unweakened, became the twin hallmarks of all that followed. Americans "will not consent to be swallowed up entirely by the Republicans." The different factions of anti-Democrats must "take the live American issues" as their foundation. While tolerating open discussion and interaction with others, they resolved "yet under every political complication whatever, the pure question of Americanism shall take precedence [before] . . . all other ideas."[33]

In the aftermath of the election of 1857, Americans saw even more reason to remain adamant. "When Kansas ceased bleeding—in the newspapers—the Republican party disappeared, as noxious vapor and fogs and mists do when the sun darts his beams upon them." No observer, their leading state journal argued, can "dispute" that the Republican masses "are prepared now to accept every doctrine of the American Party." Therefore, if the Republicans "want the Americans they must take their principles." They were, in short, "strongly opposed to a union, unless it can be firmly based upon the long cherished principles of the American party. . . . Americans never will consent to throw away all their other planks and stand upon the one of opposition to the extension of slavery alone." Nor had they ever hidden what those distinctive ideas were. We "owe our government, our liberty, our prosperity, mainly to our Protestant religion," E. S. Brooks had written. Therefore, "the issue we present here," one group of Americans wrote Daniel Ullmann in 1855, "is 'shall Americans not rule America?' and we will not allow ourselves to be diverted from this issue by any of the other exciting topics of the day, such as slavery."[34]

Given that, the Republicans had a long way to come. Know Nothings were deeply committed to their particular hobby. They did not believe that the Republicans were, however. Know-Nothing attitudes toward the political world and especially the Republican party were very much shaped by the importance of Seward among the latter. There were two highly related sources of this hostility: Know-Nothing suspicion that the Republicans were actively eager to secure foreign votes, even Catholic ones, and, second, going back to his Whig leadership days, Seward's long and intense commitment to just that, intensified by his well-known friendship for New York Catholics including the leaders of the Church. "The main ground of opposition on the part of Americans to Mr. Seward, is based upon his desire to carve a political party out of the Romish church"—a policy he had advocated back "in the 'palmy days'" of the Whig party and which had "laid the foundations of all the difficulties that arose in that organization." Like the Whigs before them, the Republicans were doing all that they could "to propitiate the alien vote." The Democrats' "degrading policy" of pandering to the Irish vote is now followed "by the republicans towards another class of foreigners." In fact, they will try to "outbid" the Democrats for that vote. The goal of "Bishop HUGHES, Senator SEWARD, and the army of priests and devotees who stand behind them" is to prevent Americans from ruling America.[35]

The Republicans' extremism and "fanaticism" on slavery-sectional issues were also frequently mentioned by American sources as well. They were seen not only as wrong and dangerous but also as the wrong issues to stress because they endangered concentration on the important matters before them. Since the Republicans under Seward would not give these up, there was a "fatuity" in the thinking of those Americans "who dream of obtaining any recognition of the justice of their principles from a party, founded, as is the republican party, upon a policy in direct antagonism to the American organization."[36]

Such hostility and differences between the parties remained important and central. Thus the whole episode of cooperation began grudgingly and with much suspicion, but also with some hope as well. While, to Americans, "the Republican party yet adhere[d] to this foreign element" of "political catholicism," that would have to pass and would. Ultimately, "Republicans must and will come to us." Electoral calculations dictated that. Changes in Republican attitudes in 1857 promised some good. As one observer noted in August, "no inconsiderable number of Republican journals begin to weary of the Irish Hunt." The Republicans might be ready to deal.[37] And Americans needed Republican votes as well. They, too, were willing to find means of cooperation.

But this feeling, and the roots of the maneuvering among the parties, went beyond generalized perceptions and the seeking of common attitudes. Among Republicans there was a constant sense that Americans should be placated in any way appropriate. This came out especially strongly early in 1858, in Republican John A. King's term as governor. There was to be an appointment to the state canal commission. One of King's correspondents suggested that "if a qualified American . . . who would not be obnoxious to the republicans, could be found who would accept the office . . . [then] it would be wise to give it to him." Other Republicans were hostile to such a move. George Baker wrote to Seward from Albany that he and a few others were "trying to prevent the Republicans from making any bargains with the Know Nothings." But the question of this appointment—or more precisely—the reappointment of the incumbent in the position. Nathaniel Benton, as Auditor on the commission, emerged as a form of litmus test between the two parties. King was hesitant to reappoint Benton, who had been on the American ticket in 1857. William Henry Seward made clear his opposition to such a move. But through it all the Americans loomed and could not be overlooked by the Republicans. Petitions from Republican members of the state legislature calling on King to reappoint Benton came in. A Sewardite wrote unhappily that "there appears to be a strong disposition . . . to retain the present Auditor." As one correspondent reminded the Governor, the reappointment "would bring a great many into the Republican ranks." It would "strengthen our party."[38]

King saw the point. He was reluctant to reappoint Benton but ultimately the political realities dictated that he had to. He wrote Seward that the Republicans needed American support in the legislature, and some Republicans would behave better there if Benton was reappointed. "As a party," he concluded, "we owe the Americans nothing." But if Benton was appointed, it would "conciliate the better portion of the American party" to join with the Republicans. Even Seward recognized the political realities (even as he continued to hesitate about working with the Americans). He warned Republicans against their refusal to ease up enough so that all opponents of the Democrats could come together. "We put on the skin of the hedge hog & present nothing but bristles . . . always raised against everybody. . . . A common scold is hateful. A party that becomes a common scold is hateful." We must overcome that while keeping the slavery issue to the fore. "I prefer & think it wiser to agree when I can with people on other topics & soon win a hearing for that one."[39]

The end result of all of this was that King reappointed Benton to the position he held (where he served another ten years). That move by the Republican governor was never explained or defended in any way other than as a political attempt to open up a path to the Americans in the hope of drawing electoral support from the latter into the Republican coalition for obvious common purposes against the hated Democrats.

But that was not the end of matters. Beyond Benton, the Republicans did not stop at pious hopes and generalized political calculation or the appointment of one sympathetic American to office. There had to be a better defined, more extensive hook on which to hang the whole attempt to come together. In fact there was one on the scene and it was well recognized. There was an understood *sine qua non* for the working out of an alliance. As in Michigan and elsewhere, the key to the coalition effort was Republican acceptance of a state electoral registry law, a measure that Know Nothings viewed as crucial to reducing the "alien influence" in state elections and something New York Republicans had traditionally opposed.

The voter registry law had a long political history in New York State and had, therefore, a very clear meaning to the politically aware in the state. There had been several attempts, going back as far as the 1830s, to tidy up electoral procedures by compiling lists of legally eligible voters and by imposing restrictions and punishment against illegalities in the electoral process. To later generations, such attempts seem relatively clear cut, reasonable, and nonpartisan. But they were not in the heated world of mid-nineteenth-century New York. From the first the measure had been fought along partisan lines. Its purpose was to harass new immigrants into the country and to impede Democratic victory in the state. The registry proposal was clearly aimed at Irish Catholic immigrants into the United States. To their enemies, the Irish, who were the backbone of Democratic strength in many parts of the state, were a dangerous force, often, it was claimed, illegally participating to determine the outcome of elections.[40]

Early attempts to impose such a law were seen, therefore, as both pandering to paranoid nativist sensibilities and an attempt to improve the electoral fortunes of the Whig party. The fact that the first such law passed in the state in 1840 was confined to the city of New York by the state legislature, only confirmed this perspective. To the politically aware of the day, as the leading historian of electoral reform in that period has written, "voter registration was unmistakably marked [as] a nativist measure."[41] When the measure rose again in the 1850s, Democratic spokesmen were quick to echo this history. Such a law "was odious in practice as it was exceptional in principle" because its object was "not to facilitate voting, and limit it to legal bounds. It is to obstruct it."[42]

The registry issue came alive again due to the immense influx of immigrants in the state during the 1850s. Know Nothings made no secret of their strong commitment to such a bill and their determination to get one. Committed as they were to "the Bible in one hand and the Constitution in the other . . . Protestant institutions and American rulers," they saw real danger from the immigrant wave. "If there is any lesson in history that stands out more distinctly than any other," one Know-Nothing editor wrote, "it is that Romanism is a Political as well as Religious system." Therefore, Catholics, particularly "the Irish rabble," are "driven in swarms to the polls," directed there by their priests. It does not matter to any of them whether they are legally entitled to vote or not. Once there, they "band together naturally; religious superstition, hatred of the Protestants and the commands of their Romish leaders keep them together under all circumstances." They vote as a bloc for one party and distort the outcome of state elections. But there is a solution. Since "a pure and intelligent suffrage is the only safe reliance of a Republic," we must "pass laws to ensure such a suffrage." There is an "imperative necessity" for "a REGISTRY LAW."[43]

In both 1855 and 1856, the American party's state council resolved in favor of the enactment of laws "for the protection of the purity of the ballot box by the state." One passed the state legislature in 1855, only to be vetoed by Whig governor Myron Clark, considered close to Seward. That setback only infuriated the determined Americans. It did not cause them to back down. By 1857 the Americans were making it very clear, as noted, that their *sine qua non* in politics began with electoral purity. "Our creed," the editor of the Albany *Statesman* underlined, includes a registry law, the ability of voters to read the English language, and a probationary period between naturalization and voting "of from two to five years."[44]

The state Republicans were not officially very sympathetic to this demand. Seward had a long history of opposition to the registry. Although he had signed the first registry law while he was governor, he had made no secret of his distaste for the bill. He was also close to Archbishop John Hughes, the strong leader of the Catholic church in New York. All of which was compounded by the feeling among many nativists that Seward had led the Whigs to destruction in 1852 by pandering to the Irish vote.[45] When the issue revived, therefore, the Know-Nothing spokesmen had no difficulty in suspecting that the Republicans would prove to be totally inadequate on the issue. Their "lurking hostility" to the measure had to be carefully watched.[46]

As a result, when ideas of cooperation between the parties surfaced, the Americans did not back down. In fact they retained the initiative on the matter. They made their demands public at every opportunity, constantly asked the embarrassing question of the Republicans—how could anyone argue against a pure ballot—and made it clear that they expected the Republicans to support the bill if they wished to work with the Americans. They capped the point by once more calling for the bill in their 1857 state platform and keeping it center stage thereafter.[47]

What Americans found, in the winter of 1857–58, was that the state Republican party was not as intractable as they suspected. That winter many parts of the state Republican press began to indicate a changing attitude and a growing commitment to the idea. Clearly, "no other law is half so much needed" as this one was. Its "justice . . . cannot be denied." The people throughout the state realize that now. "The great mass of opinion outside of the Democratic party . . . is arrayed in its favor." Echoing the Americans, one Republican editor could not see "what objection there can be in any man's mind to the guarding of the ballot box against fraud and corruption." Even the most zealous of antislavery Republican voices now said that the registry was "a bill we should be glad to see pass." It was based "on good Republican grounds." The antislavery, and formerly anti-Know Nothing, New York *Courier* went particularly far in its endorsement. It announced that a basic part of Republican principles—and therefore a reason for Americans to come over to them, was "the purity of the elective franchise and a reform of all abuses and defects in the administration of the naturalization laws."[48]

In January 1858 Republican governor John A. King called, in his annual message, for the enactment of a registry. This was no accident. In the few letters in the King collection from the period it is clear enough that the registry was on Republican minds because, at a minimum, of its impact on the Americans. As King wrote Seward, "I recognized the great object of the American party by recommending a Registry Law in my message."[49] Most Republican legislators supported it when it came up, arguing that it was "loudly demanded by the popular voice." The measure passed the State Senate and was barely defeated in the Assembly, although receiving a majority of the votes there—much to the chagrin of some Republican journals. Despite its setback, the actions in Albany proved that the registry had become "a Republican measure."[50]

The Republicans' growing commitment overjoyed the Americans. Nobody could "dispute" that "the mass of the Republican party was prepared to accept now every doctrine of the American Party."[51] Events continued to bear this out. The ground had been firmly established and the stances of the parties clarified in the winter of 1857–58. Things built from there. The legislative events were only the beginning of a very hectic year which brought this particular political situation to a climax. Throughout the year movements were under way to bring about a concrete understanding between the Know Nothings and the Republicans in the state on the basis of this measure and others in the same vein.

The year 1858 is remembered for Seward's highly dramatic and intensely sectionalist "irrepressible conflict" speech in Rochester just before election day in October.[52] But there were other political activities that year as well having little to do with the North-South political dimension. Americans and Republicans forged an understanding of another kind, if not a full, formal, alliance, that became part of the political atmosphere in the state. In significant ways they closed the gap that separated them.

There was plenty of background noise to accompany the groping toward an alliance. Newspaper editors in both parties throughout the spring, beat the drums constantly on behalf of a coming together, leaving no uncertainty as to the actual shape of what was expected. The realities of the political calculus dominated the scene. The American papers kept reminding the Republicans of the latter's need for them, the price quoted for that support, and the "unnatural" nature of the division into two parties given their "natural affinity . . . on important points." Republican newspapers throughout the state came up to the mark as well, constantly reiterating their support for the registry bill. Greeley's *Tribune* took the lead, reminding Republicans that when Americans insisted on the registry law, they were "right," and claiming that nine-tenths of the Republicans in the state supported an alliance between the parties based on this law. The whole began to be convincing. As one

New York Know Nothing wrote to Millard Fillmore, despite all of the difficulties of uniting different groups into a common alliance, "still the necessities of the Republicans are such that we will have less difficulties than usual."[53]

There was a clear marking of boundaries in these discussions. With the masses "largely in favor of the union" of the two parties, it was up to the Republicans to conciliate in order to reach an agreement. No one would lose anything of their distinctive commitments in doing so. A union was possible on a basis in which neither party "shall be obliged to sacrifice any principle upon which they have placed any degree of importance." Slavery remained "the paramount issue" to the Republicans in 1858, but proponents of a coalition saw no harm in adding nativism to that nor did they believe that the Americans had to manifest vigorous opposition to slavery in their rhetoric for the two parties to work together. Americans, after all, had come up "a few inches" on the free-soil scale during the year while the Republicans generally favored "a stringent registry law." The Republican state convention should therefore make "a simple, earnest declaration in favor of a Registration of Legal Voters" and declare its "hearty support [for] . . . all constitutional measures calculated to prevent Illegal Voting." Such "would smooth to thousands the pathways into the Republican ranks, while it would alienate none who have hitherto stood with us." On the other hand, if the two parties fail to unite, it "will knock the timbers from the Republicans and insure the victory of the Democracy."[54]

The pressure mounted as the state conventions neared. As the *New York Times* put it, some Republicans believe we can "carry the State without American aid," but "this assumption may be doubted." Any failure to unite "would argue great lack of sagacity." All of which seemed to have significant impact. By August the state chairman of the American party reported that "there seems to be no longer any difference of opinion in the Republican Party as to the necessity of a Registry law." Thurlow Weed's Albany *Evening Journal* seemed to agree, arguing just as the state conventions of both parties were about to open, that the Republican convention had two duties: to reaffirm Republican principles, and then "to unite and conciliate the aid of all who, though agreeing with us upon the main points at issue, have hitherto acted with other organizations. . . ." It hoped for a "tolerant liberality" among all.[55]

Despite the persistence of the efforts, the calls to duty, and the recognition of what was to be gained, there remained many holdouts in both parties, most especially among Republicans who feared the impact of such an alliance on their central purpose and who questioned the need to do what was being pushed all over the state. American leaders told each other that the Republican leadership around Weed and Seward remained hesitant, some Republicans did not favor the registry law, or any alliance with Americans. The Republican journal in Seward's home, the Auburn *Daily Advertiser*, took a strong lead against an alliance based on the registry, referring to the measure's "arbitrary" provisions, warning that there was no chance of coming together "except by lowering the Republican standard," and questioning whether Republican concessions were necessary to attract American voters anyway.[56]

The *Advertiser* was the most straightforward but was not alone in its opposition. All over the state Republicans voiced similar sentiments, if more privately. "This talk about concession and compromise, or a double headed convention, is all wrong and will be likely to result in ill feeling and alienation rather than union and harmony." Some were suggesting that the Republican party needed another plank in its platform "especially dovetailed in for the use of the American order." That was not necessary. In fact, "new issues should be well considered before being adopted." The growing antislavery feeling among New Yorkers was becoming strong enough that no one had to lose any Republican virtue in order to win.[57]

The state committees of both parties agreed to hold their state conventions on the same day, September 8th, at the same place, Syracuse. Both parties, when they met, followed through on all that had preceded their meetings. The conventions appointed committees of conference which consulted, exchanged ideas, and kept up negotiations over two days. Unfortunately for the most optimistic, suspicion and extreme sensitivity, on the American part, and the opposition of many of the powerful in the Republican camp, both took their toll. State level, formal, coordination failed, or, more precisely, just missed. Both parties came out of their conventions with separate tickets and a determination to carry on regardless of the enticements of the other. As one Republican editor reported, "nothing in the platform could be sacrificed for the sake of Union with the Americans." Still, although "there is no union . . . there *can be* a victory." The American leaders were disgusted by the Republican behavior and condemned Republican leaders for their intransigence and stupidity. They resolved to fight on under their independent state ticket to defeat both the Republicans and Democrats and to achieve their principles.[58]

Among the hardest things to accomplish in nineteenth-century politics was to unite members of different political organizations due to the long-standing hostility, perpetual enmity, and intense suspicion between members of different political faiths. So it proved here. But the prevailing sentiment in both parties was regret. Failure was too bad in the eyes of many. "A failure to unite upon a common ticket disappoints public expectation," one Republican lamented. "We think the masses of the Republican party throughout the State will feel a regret that a more successful effort to conciliate the liberal portion of the American Party was not made. We *may* be already strong enough to carry the State single handed; yet the result of last fall's contest ought to teach a lesson to those who are disposed to repel all advances toward honorable alliance. We would not abate one jot of Republican principle, but we want *men* to help fight our battles."[59]

But that was neither all of nor the end of the matter. The Republican state platform contained two planks that had not appeared in their statewide campaign documents before. Both were similar in wording and tone to items in the American state platform. The first of these resolved,

> That some stringent and effective measure to prevent fraudulent voting is imperatively required, and we urge upon our next Legislature the necessity and the duty of enacting such safeguards for the elective franchise as will render illegal voting thenceforth impossible.

The second added,

> *Resolved*, that the principle involved in our present State Constitution of requiring some time to intervene between the act of naturalization and the consequent exercise of the right of suffrage is sound and just, and we recommend such extension of that intervening time as will preclude the future naturalization of voters under the auspices of partisan committees with the view of using the votes so procured in a pending election.[60]

Both of these were highly recognizable signals in the language and context of the contemporary politics of the state. No one could have any doubt what the Republicans meant or to whom they were appealing. Nor was that the last thing the Republicans did that year. A strong Republican spirit of cooperation, which overcame much of the setback of Syracuse, carried over into the fall campaign. What followed that fall, and in its aftermath that winter, demonstrated, at the very least, Republican sensitivity to the Americans and persistent attempts to win the latter over regardless of the nonexistence of formal party unification. As the New York *Tribune* put it right after the state conventions, the "folly" of ignoring American sensibilities must not be repeated. "Let the Republicans take the initiative in tendering the olive branch."[61] It was not, and they did. Republican newspapers in the state did not hesitate to underscore what was occurring. Our resolutions, one editor reported, "are eminently Republican with strong tendencies toward Americanism." The new planks added "to accommodate the American sentiment" are "clearly right in principle." It was clear that a "strong" desire favoring fusion continued to "pervade the Republican ranks."[62]

These themes dominated Republican campaigning thereafter. Above all, cooperation was the goal and the stress. Throughout the canvassing season, Republican newspapers vigorously reiterated to the faithful the need to work together. When it came to American supporters, we should, one editor wrote, "treat them as brethren, not as adversaries."[63] Those Republican newspapers that had not supported formal fusion previously kept up the drumfire as well, pointing out that if Americans truly wanted a registry they could not support the Democrats, they had to support the Republicans. After all, the Republicans had in fact come over to the American position on that. "In arranging these matters between Republicans and Americans, we go," one editor wrote, "for mutual liberality and concession. Whenever the Republicans cannot prevail by their own strength, they should strike hands with all who agree with them in hating the Cincinnati platform." Familiarly, he added that in so doing, no one advocates "the least surrender of principles by either party. Thus, while Republicans remained true to their principles, "they did not fail to make all proper advances to the reasonable portion of the American party. This they did by freely recognizing that great abuses were practiced upon the ballot box in connection with the system of naturalization. . . . If the American party claims credit for having stimulated the Republicans to advance to this point, be it so." The end result has to be reasonable action by reasonable men for common ends. "The American who, because the Republican party will only give him a Registry law and a regulation making necessary a year's residence after naturalization prior to voting, refuses to cooperate with that party, puts himself in the same category of impracticables as the Abolitionist who refuses to give his vote to Republicans who stand pledged to fight slavery in the Territories because, forsooth, they will not fight it in the States." The whole was as clear as could be. The questions dividing Americans and Republicans having been "settled . . . they should unite."[64]

Beyond exhortation, concrete measures also eventuated. Thurlow Weed held meetings with the Know Nothing leadership at the start of the campaign. And Americans and Republicans came together organizationally at the local level throughout the election season. There were agreements on joint local and congressional tickets worked out in joint county and district conventions; conference committees met repeatedly, common campaigns were carried on, and in one county even the adoption of the full American local platform by Republicans. Where two tickets were nominated in the same district one side or the other withdrew its ticket by election day. Where there was hesitancy to do so, condemnation was quick.[65]

So strong had these efforts become in the campaign of 1858 that the more rigid antislavery Republicans demanded something as well. As one wrote to Weed, he felt beset. The Republican newspaper in Buffalo "takes the only objectionable resolution [the registry] . . . and makes it the 'corner stone' of the republican platform." Late in the campaign Seward made two strong antislavery speeches, the first the Irrepressible Conflict. As Glyndon Van Deusen recounts, Seward told several of his correspondents that both were made in order "to rally the Republican voters in the rural regions of the state who had been made uneasy by the way in which the urban elements of the party were trying to propitiate Know-Nothingism." Seward recognized a clear reality.[66]

Previous acknowledgments of these efforts have either downplayed them or not seen how extensively they resulted in payoffs: coalescence and agreement between the leaders of two anti-Democratic parties. By election day the editor of a Republican journal on Long Island could sum up that "the fusion . . . is very general and perfect. Americans and Republicans have dropped minor differences and joined hands to defeat a common enemy." Robert Imholt estimates that the two parties united on a single candidate in 19 of 33 Congressional tickets and in more than 80 or 128 Assembly Districts that year. These "American Republicans" were quite successful in a very revealing election outcome.[67]

The Democrats were quick to pick up what was happening even if historians have not been, attacking violently, throughout the campaign, the Republicans' new anti-foreign, nativist commitments.[68] They were not wrong. These efforts were crucial indicators of the seriousness of the situation and the role the Americans were playing in Republican development in New York. What was going on here was an acknowledgment of Know Nothing power and of the potency in the larger arena of their particular nativist hobbies as well as a willingness by Republican leaders to deal with that electoral and social reality.

Republican acceptance of the registry in New York and the call for delay in naturalized citizens' voting rights were more than the mild concessions that some historians have suggested them to be. Know Nothings demanded these, and they expected the Republicans to follow through on them despite the prospects of virulent Democratic attacks on the Republicans as a result and the uneasiness the latter felt about the reactions of German voters. Not having read a number of later historians, Republicans were unaware that this was not the way they were supposed to behave. Even if they had read those worthies they still went ahead for two reasons: 1) the importance of electoral calculation; 2) the realization that they were not doing anything that outraged many Republicans but, rather, struck a strong chord of compatibility rooted in common nativist impulses. After all, cooperation is rarely possible without such compatibility even given the power of electoral calculations. Certainly Americans and Republicans differed over issues —but mostly about priorities.

Nor was nativism subordinated in this relationship. Know Nothings, like the Republicans, had a sense of political reality. They knew that they could not get everything they wanted nor did they expect to. But they got a great deal. Nativism was added more directly to the Republican arsenal and brought more fully to the voters—particularly the Know Nothings'—attention. Antislavery was neither forgotten nor downplayed. Nativists accepted that as long as their particular hobby was also given space and prominence. After all, "What American of principle can vote for the Democratic ticket?"[69]

Republican victory at the polls in November did not slow the informal alliance—and with good reason. After the election the same forces pushing for an alliance continued to operate. Acute Republican observers noted the pessimistic side of the election returns. Despite their victory at the state level, the party's margins had fallen precipitously from 1856. In the governor's race two years before they had won more than 60,000 more votes than the Democrats. Now their margin was less than 20,000. Furthermore, the Americans had held on to more than 10 percent of the vote in a very close and competitive situation between the two main parties: (Republicans: 45.6% of the vote, Democrats, 42.3%). The omens for 1860, in Glyndon Van Deusen's words, "were not auspicious." The American party, as a potent independent organization, might be considered "dead" by some, but their voters could neither be ignored nor repudiated. They were still necessary for Republican victory.[70]

What to do? That was clear. More than a "conciliatory" attempt "to allay the irritation" of the Americans against the Republicans over the Fall's failures was needed. The registry law remained an American demand and a Republican commitment. If the Republican party followed through on it then the Americans would have to come over to them "if they prove true to themselves and the principles which they inscribed upon their banner at the last election." Thus, the enactment of a registry law was "most explicitly and emphatically demanded." The members of the Republican party "are committed to this policy." So long as they "have a majority in both branches [of the legislature] and have declared in favor of the measure in their political creed . . . people confidentially look for its early and certain accomplishment." Not to do so "would be acting in bad faith." We trust, one editor concluded, that "they may not be disappointed."[71]

They were not. In January 1859 the newly elected Republican governor, Edwin D. Morgan, in his annual message called for the passage of the registry bill as "one of the highest duties of the State." Republican newspapers generally supported the call. The Governor's message mentions many things, one editor wrote, "best of all, is a law for the Registration of Voters." Morgan had acted "in conformity with the popular desire." Clearly "a good, fair, and impartial registry law is absolutely necessary if our electors are to express at all the popular will." It is "a Republican measure and those who attempt to ignore it must repudiate the party which has adopted it in its creed." Even the hostile Albany *Evening Journal* "acquiesced in the propriety of trying the experiment." Many knew that the Democrats would attack viciously on the matter, seeking to drive a wedge between the Republicans and their German supporters. But the Republicans "cannot afford to disappoint and alienate their friends. The Syracuse pledge stares them in the face, and what is more, the undeniable fact that nine-tenths of their party desire a Registry, and insist on its enactment." By all means, then, "let us have a Registry."[72]

Four bills were offered in the legislature with the Republican members in caucus agreeing to support one of them. They knew what they were about. "We will pass a Registry Law this winter, not so stringent perhaps as some would wish, but sufficient for practical purposes."[73] It passed the State Assembly on March 16th decisively and the Senate a month later. Although somewhat weaker than many thought it should be, both Republicans and Americans strongly supported the bill throughout, with the American statewide organ calling the one passed more "perfect and stringent" than an earlier one.[74]

The way the bills went through the legislature underscored Republican hopes and claims. In the two houses, as the bills worked their way from committee onto the floor, Republican support for "this most righteous and necessary measure" stood out.[75] As had been the case in 1858 as well, the large bulk of the party's representatives went right down the line with their American colleagues in support of the bill, consistently resisting weakening amendments and helping to get the law through successfully. In both years there were some Republican assemblymen who either were absent on critical votes or who occasionally opposed the way the Americans stood on some amendment or in attempts at delay. Thus in 1858, in the first attempt, of 61 Republicans in the Assembly, fifty-four had voting records fully congruent with the American members on the measure. Four of the others voted against the registry on the final vote. In the State Senate the bill passed with the unanimous support of the sixteen Republicans and two Americans. (It was opposed by all of the Democrats.)[76]

A year later the bill passed both houses with all but unanimous Republican support in the State Senate. In the other house, of 90 Republican assemblymen, seventy-four voted for the bill's final passage, with most of them also having stood together on all of the preliminary votes as well. Fifteen Republicans were absent on the final vote (the other was the Speaker), several had also been absent at other moments. Whether strategic or not, the absences made no difference at the end.

The Republicans had gone on record in favor of the bill. More critically, the many political consequences of what they had done were quickly picked up. To one Republican editor, the law was "the best measure of the session. We give the Americans who have been most decided in advocating this measure, credit in this instance for having done the state a great service." And it was the Republican legislators who came through. They were "responsible for the measure," the *Buffalo Express* argued on April 16th. To the Democrats, the law had another quality, naturalized citizens has been "proscribed by the Republican-American coalition." That certainly was what Republican leaders hoped would be believed in American precincts throughout the state. They could quite effectively argue that they had done their duty on behalf of the registry.[77]

The Americans responded warmly. "It is a source of congratulation . . . that at least one of their cardinal principles has demanded public attention and has become a law." The Republicans, too, would benefit. Their adoption of the registry "had the double effect of calling out the honest men of their own party and of drawing votes from the American party."[78] Of course, such political scorekeeping after an event was not unusual. What is brought out by it in this case is the extent that the parties had successfully cooperated in a common purpose. Of course, there is something of the doughnut or the hole perspective present here. Which did one see? Critics could and did argue that Republican absences in the Assembly had prevented the bill from getting the constitutionally necessary 65 votes needed for passage in 1858, while internal Republican opposition somewhat weakened the bill that passed the following year. Certainly individual defections were irritating and occasionally important, but on the other hand, as noted, the large bulk of the Republican party had gone all the way with their American colleagues. Further, and equally important politically, the Democratic record also stood out in stark contrast to Republican behavior. The full contingent of the Democratic party in the legislative had opposed the registry.

There is another aspect of some weight in all of this: the Republican adoption of the registry, Republican play for the American sentiment in the state, and Republican willingness to work in common cause were not hidden from sight at all. The nativist commitments of the Republicans were well broadcast throughout the campaigning season of 1858 and during the following year as well. Republican newspapers continually spoke of the situation and proved strongly committed to a public display of what they were about and of the political relationship they were constructing. Political platforms and broadsides, reports of speeches, and above all, the newspaper editorials containing these sentiments were widely circulated. Other matters were similarly discussed. No Know Nothing in search of knowledge and assurance nor any historian seeking to discover the public nature of the relationship need look very far to find what was under way.

There is, of course, no direct way of relating this publicity to some kind of cause and effect equation. My point here is more modest. That so far as the substance of political confrontation and division penetrated the voters of New York State—and there is evidence to suggest that it did—opportunities to comprehend the common alliance were many and ever present. That, in short, completed the traditional structure of electoral politics in nineteenth-century America: from consideration of electoral calculus to elite definition of what needed to be done, to the broadcasting and penetration of these perspectives among the voters. Only response remained.

But was there ever a formal deal between the two parties? Historians' understanding as to what constitutes a formal understanding—a deal— is not very precise. Certainly many of the comments published in this period contain rhetoric suggestive of an understanding that went beyond a wink and a nod. Democrats saw an arrangement quite clearly: the Republicans, they claimed, had made "concessions to the biggoted [sic] and oppressive doctrines of Know-Nothingism"; The registry was the scheme "with which the Republican hook was baited."[79] But we can go beyond the Democrats in assessing the situation. Evidence exists for some kind of formal understanding, even if no smoking pistol exists. "It is well known," one American paper noted in 1858, "that a few Republican leaders . . . have made overtures to the American Party for the purpose of forming a union upon a state ticket."[80] Nor was the effort confined to Americans: For the "particular object" of passing the Registry, one Republican noted, "more than for any other, was the present legislature sent there [to Albany]." So strong has public sentiment been in favor of a registry that "the Republican Party, by its State Convention, stands Pledged to the measure." Because of that pledge, "thousands of Americans voted with us. Indeed, all regarded it as a fixed fact that the law was to pass if Republicans and Americans had the power to pass it." And during the legislative debate over the registry in 1859, one Republican, Assemblyman Wickham Crocker of Steuben County, argued that his party "had always opposed a Registry law, and only adopted it as a plank in the last State platform, as a holocaust offering to the rotten defunct faction of Know Nothingism." Not very friendly and quite revealing. Certainly court convictions have been realized with less.[81]

At least two things seem clear in New York State after 1857. First, the Republican establishment had come over to the registry even though some of them remained ambivalent about the matter. The Know Nothings clearly gained. When the registry finally passed in 1859 it was an imperfect bill in the eyes of many, but one that was important nonetheless. But the Republicans gained as well: their tactics paid off electorally. Thus, both parties won something from their interaction. The relationship that developed, however, revolved around the question not of whether the Know Nothings dominated the Republicans, but how electorally useful they were and how much influence in shaping Republican behavior realization of that fact gave them.

The second point concerns the aftereffects of the relationship developed in 1858–59. After the spring of 1859 the vigorous activity between the two parties quieted a great deal. The Americans remained on the scene for a time as an independent organization, but a very divided one with many of their leaders now filtering into the Republican party. Some American leaders continued to be skeptical of the Republicans and wary of their sectional commitments. They still found the Republicans wanting. As one American put it, "we cannot consent to abandon Americanism for the privilege of advocating the peculiar dogmas of modern Republicanism." Nor did some Americans believe that the Republicans had really changed: "The foreign element" in that party, "although not as strong" as in the Democratic party, remains "distasteful" to the Americans. Nor had the Republicans been forthcoming enough. Since there was no "diversity of sentiment" between Americans and Republicans, the problem was the hostility of Republican leaders (meaning Seward). If that attitude changed "the two parties like kindred drops, would speedily mingle." As it stood, American "sympathies are with the Republicans," but that did not guarantee union.[82]

The American holdouts did not nominate separate tickets in the strange state election of 1859. Instead, they threw their support to different nominees from each of the other two parties. Finding Republicans still to be too quick to "truckle to the wishes of German Catholics," and the Democrats completely a lost cause, they believed that the Americans had to remain independent. Thus, echoing a familiar litany, although it would be nice if the "now divided opposition to the Democracy" became "concentrated, united and invincible," that was not the best way to achieve American aims.[83] Rather, they opted to show their importance through playing a balance of power role.

But most Americans, in fact, refused to accept the hesitations or the tactic of trying to establish an electoral balance of power between Republicans and Democrats. How could they establish such when they did not hold "one sentiment in common with the bogus Democracy"? And how much more could be demanded of the Republicans? Nothing more could be expected. No party could give all to another group with which it was coalescing. Americans had already received "sufficient and satisfactory" things from the Republicans. "The Registry law, and the reappointment of [N. S.] Benton to the Auditorship were all concessions by the Republican party." It was also repeatedly pointed out that the Republicans had nominated "at least two straightout Americans" on their ticket. As a result, "the union of Americans and Republicans, in the body of this State, has been substantially consummated, without any humiliating sacrifices or concessions of principle on either side." The Republicans now support the registry and admit that "it is a concession to justice and necessity."[84]

Given all of this, Daniel Ullmann, the state's first American standard-bearer back in 1854, now advocated joining the Republicans finally and officially. As always, the Democrats remained unacceptable. "Americans have less affinity with [them] . . . than with any other party." On the other hand, the Republican willingness to treat the Americans as their "political brethren" sealed the situation. The latter continued to be exhorted by their newspapers to treat the Americans with "deference." They should not be "insanely repelled."[85]

The result was a widespread seepage of independent American activity. It was reported that twenty-two of the thirty newspapers that had supported the American ticket the year before now, in 1859, supported the Republican candidates. Local coalitions between the two groups were also the order of the day as they had been the year before. And, on election day, although they still made some difference in the outcome, the American vote withered. In 1858 they had drawn 11.2 percent of the popular vote in the state in a highly competitive race. In 1859 their identifiable vote fell to just under 5 percent of the total cast.[86] They were still bothersome but their total numbers were leading them farther and farther down the road to impotence.

IV

The goal of all of this activity was success at the polls for the Republican party. Whatever the party elites thought and did to meet a perceived need, communicate their plans, and appeal to their targeted voters reflected only one part of the electoral calculus of the time. Did the Republicans in these years give off the right aura so as to allow elite preferences to be translated into popular mass acceptance among Know-Nothing voters? Had they convinced the Know-Nothing voters, imbedded as they were in their own commitments and particular hobbies? Only election day would tell.

Throughout the period newspapers of both parties constantly made claims and charges about what was happening to the Know-Nothing vote in the face of the numerical decline of the American party's support after 1855. In 1857 Democratic statewide strength was attributed to onetime Democrats among the Know Nothings returning to their former party loyalties. A year later there was confusion. Democratic papers claimed "the general absorption of the Americans with the Republicans." Republican newspapers in anti-Know-Nothing areas claimed the Americans had gone to the Democrats. In pro-American Republican areas the fruits of union attempts were made known: One American returned to the Democrats for every five who came over to the Republicans, one newspaper reported in 1858. The Republican party, the editor went on, is "the only safe and genial home for old-fashioned Whigs, as they mostly are." The record is filled with similar statements about the flow of the vote. But anyone reading all of these would be hard put to draw conclusions.[87] We can, however, peer beyond the confusing claims and counterclaims.

The pool of voters in New York State was between one-half and three-quarters of a million in these years, with between 440,000 and 680,000 votes actually cast in a given election. There were statewide elections every year in New York, forming a rich source for analysis. In 1856 and 1858, governorships were contested, in 1857 and 1859, other high state offices were at risk. Political confrontation remained very hot and constant so that turnout in these contests remained high. In 1856, 89 percent of New York's voters went to the polls, 64.1 percent went the following year. In 1858, turnout jumped to 77 percent of those eligible. (It was to reach 91.3% in 1860.) (Table 8.2)[88]

Table 8-2. Anatomy of the Popular Vote, New York State, 1856-1860

Year	Number of Eligible Votes	Number of Votes Cast	Turnout %	Republicans	Americans	Democrats
1856	669,438	594,347	88.8	276,004	124,604	195,878
1857	686,554	440,022	64.1	177,425	66,882	195,482
1858	703,607	545,529	77.5	247,868	61,137	230,329
1859	720,786	503,063	69.7	251,139	24,813*	227,304
1860	737,902	673,469	91.3	362,646		312,510+

There are slight discrepancies in the total votes cast due to different sources, etc.
+Combined Opposition vote for Douglas.
*Subtracting difference in R column between American supported and nonsupported candidates.

In the first of these elections, in 1856, the New York Republicans attracted over 275,000 votes to them in the presidential race (46.3% of the total); the Know Nothings won 125,000 and the Democrats just under 200,000. Two years later, in the last election in which the Know Nothings ran separate candidates, Republican support remained steady at 248,000 votes, Know Nothings stood at 61,000, and the Democrats won 230,000 votes. By 1860 the Republican total exceeded 350,000, the Democrats 300,000. (Table 8.2) Where did Republican support and particularly this growth come from? Where did the Know-Nothing vote go? How much of the change was rooted in the natural growth of the electorate, how much in conversions of voters from other parties into the Republican coalition?

We can begin to understand what happened by some general surveying of the political landscape of the state. The five premier Know-Nothing counties in New York in 1854-55 by 1857 were all dominated by the Republicans. Republicans had gained significantly in each as the Know-Nothing vote fell. But more still was needed given the continuing strength of the Americans. (Table 8.3) In 1857 the Americans pulled more than 25 percent of the popular vote in eight counties, all in the Hudson River Valley. In these they were often the second party in strength; in one, Sullivan, they led all parties in their share of the popular vote that year. In another eleven counties, mostly in far western New York, they still drew over 20 percent of the vote in 1857. It was in these counties that they lost significantly between 1857 and 1858, losing better than 8 percent of the total vote in some. They lost elsewhere as well, but by smaller percentages. Between 1857 and 1858 the

Table 8-3. Republican Growth in
Five Leading American Counties

	Republican Vote	
	1855	1857
Cattaraugus	48.4%	56.7
Chatauqua	42.1	58.6
Erie	19.6	28.1
Genessee	47.6	53.5
Warren	21.3	43.0

American statewide vote dropped from 15.2 percent to 11.1 percent, the Republican vote gained 5.4 percent in the same year. In the eight largest American counties in 1857, the latter lost an average of 6.3 percent of their vote, the Republicans gained just over 6.5 percent between the two years. In the ten counties of sharpest American loss between the two years, of the total vote the Republicans gained an average of 6.4 percent to the Americans' loss of an average of 9.0 percent.

The gross outlines of the pattern of voter choice and movement among the parties can be illustrated by looking at individual counties more closely. In Broome County in south central New York there had been a steady pattern of American decline and Republican gain from 1854 on, and the appearance of some relationship between the two. By 1857 the Americans still held on to just over 10 percent of the vote in Broome with the Republicans enjoying a very precarious majority in the county, the kind of situation prompting an opening to the Americans. A year later the situation had changed in the Republicans' favor and continued into 1859 as well. (Table 8.4) In Sullivan County in southeastern New York, a similar pattern is noticeable but with different chronological boundaries. The Republicans were always the minority

Table 8-4. Broome County, Popular Vote, 1854-1857

	1854	1855	1856	1857	1858	1859
Americans	20.5%	17.9	11.6	10.5	5.6	1.7
Republicans	42.7	47.9	58.7	50.0	54.1	54.5
Democrats	36.8	34.2	29.7	39.5	39.4	43.8

Sullivan County, Popular Vote, 1854-1859

	1854	1855	1856	1857	1858	1859
Americans	23.1	50.0	39.0	41.2	32.4	10.3
Republicans	25.9	17.2	29.9	19.8	27.8	46.4
Democrats	51.0	32.8	31.1	39.0	39.8	43.3

party in Sullivan but they continually sought to build up strength there to buttress their statewide totals. (Table 8.4) Again there seems to be a relation between American loss and Republican gain.

The shifts of voters in these counties (and elsewhere) occurred at different moments and in different patterns. But what sticks out in these particular cases (and in others as well) is the apparent relationship between Republican and Know-Nothing voting, especially after 1857. There is stability in the Democratic totals between 1857 and 1858 but an apparent reciprocal relationship between American and Republican totals in these two years.

These impressions, which orient us in a general way, can be further firmed up. First, a quick look at what happened to the voting patterns in a number of strong American towns in 1854–55 illuminates the situation. In 1854 Americans were the dominant party in each of them. (Table 8.5) By 1860 all but one of these were decisively Republican in voting behavior, with the Republican share of the popular vote ranging from 61.4 percent in Clarkson (up from 42% Republican in 1855), to 50.3 percent in Hancock (up from 15% Republican the year before). Only Ellicotville was a Democratic town, and there the Republicans won just under 49 percent of the vote in 1860 compared with the Fusion ticket's 14.9 percent in 1854.

We can now, having worked out the boundaries and direction of the vote, add one final dimension of concrete analysis to the whole. Some of the changes in party support, as the Republicans claimed in 1857, were due to differential turnout in some years. But much was also due to the interplay among the supporters of the different parties generally and the nonvoters. The nature of this relationship can be worked out with some precision. Historians have made use of a number of techniques to decode political behavior. Ecological regression estimates of voting transitions, for one example, has proven to be useful in segregating out

Table 8-5. Voting Results, 1854, Six Strong American Towns

	Democrats	Americans	Fusion
New Scotland (Albany) 1st election district	16	112(62.9%)	50
Friendship (Allegany)	50	219(63.3)	77
Ellicotville (Cattaraugus)	53	193(66.8)	43
Hancock (Delaware) 2nd election district	95	147(54.4)	28
Clarkson (Monroe)	120	141(38.4)	106
Schroepell (Oswego) 1st election district	68	233(54.8)	124

different proportions of a voting coalition derived from previous voting blocs. Despite some problems with the technique over extended time periods, it can suggest boundaries and directions effectively. As Dale Baum did for Massachusetts in the 1850s, and others have done elsewhere, I have also used this statistical tool to estimate the source of each party's support and to trace the path American voters took after 1856 to find compatible political homes.[89]

Professor Gienapp's analysis clearly indicates that until 1856 the New York Know Nothings had drawn their support as a separate party from former Whigs, some Democrats, and previous nonvoters. (Thus, in 1854 the American vote in New York State consisted of about one-third of the Whig party's support in 1853, a significant group of people who had not voted the year before, and small proportions of the previous year's supporters of the two Democratic tickets.) As the Republicans appeared in 1855, and gained strength in 1856, there began a steady seepage of Know-Nothing voters to them. Significantly, however, some Know Nothings moved into the Democracy as well in the middle fifties. The movement of those who supported the Know Nothings in 1854 and 1856 reveals the pattern. In 1855, the first year there was a Republican ticket, for example, its vote came largely from former Whigs with much smaller numbers drawn from the previous year's nonvoters, Democratic supporters, and 1854 American voters. (Table 8.6) It should also be noted that in 1855 more 1854 Americans went to the Democrats than to the Republicans, suggesting that the Know Nothings had been a temporary party of protest to some of its supporters the year before. This latter point is not surprising given the many reasons—including of a non-nativist nature—that attracted voters to the Americans at mid-decade.

Table 8–6. Percentage of 1854 American Voters
Subsequently Voting Republican

1855	20%
1856	37%
1860	57%

Over one-third of Daniel Ullmann's support for governor in 1854 went to Frémont in 1856. (About 10% went to Buchanan.) But such original Know-Nothing voters comprised only about 17 percent of the total Republican vote in the state in 1856—significant, but not dominant. Furthermore, the Republicans did not enjoy any particular advantage in attracting such voters. In fact, the whole pattern to that point suggests an extraordinary electoral volatility, of much movement back and forth as voters sought compatible permanent homes for themselves in the midst of vast and still confusing political changes. (Table 8.6)

It is the period after the election of 1857 that is crucial for our analysis as both Republicans and Know Nothings, considering their futures, eyed each other's attractive and other qualities. After 1857 the residue of American voters contained the true nativist diehards as well as some old Whig conservatives such as Washington Hunt. Their hostility to Seward and the Republicans remained powerful and caused many to hesitate. What did they do? By election day 1858 the political realities had been fully explored and the possible voting outcomes canvassed and clearly established. One Democratic paper argued three days before the election that the previous months had taken their toll. German Republicans were abandoning that party because of "the undisguised connection" between Republicans and Know Nothings. That may have been. But on election day the Republican state ticket won by about 18,000 votes, a sharp comeback from the year before although still well below their high point of 1856.

The reason for this comeback was clear to the same Democratic newspaper. The Republicans had won because of "the general absorption of the Americans with the Republicans."[90] The electoral reality was more complicated, however. In the 1858 elections the number of 1856 Know-Nothing voters who moved in that year behind the Republican ticket was relatively low (11%) but it was double the number that had moved the year before. About 56 percent of the triumphant Republican voting coalition of 1858 consisted of people who had voted Republican the year before, about 17 percent of it Democratic voters in 1857, and 20 percent of it American voters from the year before. (Table 8.7)

It was in the next year that the dam began to break. What had been a trickle became much more. What had been ambiguous, clarified substantially. As long as the American party remained in the field their voters moved around quite a bit in relation to the other parties. Their varied antecedents in a time of strong party associations and deep distrust of Sewardism among many former Democrats and Whigs combined to prevent any kind of single-minded direct and one-sided thrust

Table 8-7. Percentage of 1856 American Voters
Subsequently Voting Republican

1857	5%
1858	11%
1859	24%
1860	48%

to the Republicans by them as a group. But in 1859 the tempo of movement quickened and the relationship became more firmly established. Some 24 percent of the 1856 American vote now were in the Republican electoral bloc. A year later the Americans were gone as a separate party, and the gubernatorial race that year was to all intents and purposes a two-party affair. Faced by the intense Republican campaign, the decline of their own party, and then the defeat of Seward (in 1860), one can see an intensifying movement of Know Nothings to the Republicans. Fifty-seven percent of the 1854 Know Nothings and 48 percent of the 1856 Americans had found their way to the Republicans and voted for Lincoln.[91]

As noted earlier, the Republicans never attracted all of the Know Nothings to them. That was impossible and politically naive to expect it. Too many cross pressures affected Know-Nothing voters. In the sorting out that occurred, some of the Know Nothings, their anti-Seward hostility strong to the end, dropped out entirely, others returned to or moved to the Democrats, where many had begun. But the Republicans gained a great many of these as well. Their efforts paid off in significant ways. Thus, by 1860 former Americans comprised a substantial portion of the Republican party. The Republicans received much help from former American voters each year and without them they would not have finally won the state. The Republicans' victory margin in 1860 was just over 50,000 votes. Forty-eight percent of the American vote of 1856 was just under 60,000 votes. Thus, Americans were an important part of the Republican coalition. The other important point is that what is suggested here is that without the efforts the party made after 1857 to draw Americans to them, what William Gienapp has called the Republicans' "blatant solicitation of nativist support," the Americans would have had opportunities to find new homes elsewhere or to drop out entirely.[92]

V

The events of 1858–59 could not have been totally satisfying to the Know Nothings of New York. The imperatives of Republican party politics had prevented any kind of sweeping victory for Know-Nothing sensibilities. But to many of the movement's leadership and rank and file, what had been accomplished was enough to clarify their future stand. The Republicans were quite sensitized to nativist fears and demands and could be counted on to advance them (as the 1860s and later would prove) within the constraints of political reality. Republicans had to think locally and pay attention to national affairs filtered into state politics with its electoral calculations, dealing, and maneuvers. Thus, the John Brown raid in 1859 had ultimate meaning to someone like Greeley as a blow against the slave power, but it was a problem as well due to its local effects. The raid, he wrote, will hurt the Republican cause in New York. Reaction against it "will elect the Brooks-American half" of the Democratic ticket. Weed continued to worry about Seward's friendly relations with Bishop Hughes. On the other hand, the Republicans were also going to do well since "all of the better portion of the American party have joined their ranks, and are now supporting their candidates."[93] In the aftermath of the election of 1859 the long battle seemed over. The result "proves as plain as words can be spoken, that a large portion of the American voters, are republican in sentiment, and have voted with that party."[94] Many American party supporters were satisfied of Republican good intentions (a perspective perhaps strengthened a year later when Seward did not receive the Republican nomination). Certainly, many Know-Nothing newspapers came to this position by 1860.

As a result of that and the outcome of the election in 1859, although superficially something of an American triumph, "the American Party, so long a disturbing element" in New York politics, "is dissolved." There is "nothing before us but a straight fight for the campaign of 1860." Still, in all of this, the Americans remained as a center of great concern. Their ranks had dwindled but they had, "to a certain degree," achieved their goals. The Republican party of Chatauqua County was reported as now "strongly American in its leanings."[95]

The abolitionist sentiment was definitely secondary there, having precipitously weakened since the fading of the Kansas excitement. Governor Edwin Morgan, early in 1860, called on the legislature to strengthen the registry law further. By the campaign of 1860 the Americans were still talking about their continuing policy "to Americanize" the Republicans in order to "put down what each regarded as a common enemy." But by 1860 the political context had changed. The few organized American remnants now were joining in a fusion ticket with the Democrats against Lincoln. They, not the Republicans, were now "the incongruous fragments of parties" in the state. The Republicans worried about the fusion's potential to harm and harass them. But the fate of the large mass of the Americans was sealed according to the optimists. The Republicans had done what they would.[96]

What, then, are we dealing with here? First, the Republicans' recognition of a situation and a real effort on their part, despite controversy; and, second, a gratifying response from the Americans. This occurred not because the Republicans adopted all of what the Know Nothings wanted—the political culture recognized that to be impossible—but because they did enough to create around themselves an attractive atmosphere—as parties do—that said to the Know Nothings—we are your friends, we are with you, we will work together. Not everything will be done, it cannot be in this type of coalition, but it will be a start and an important milestone. Know Nothings had, in their turn, every reason to be satisfied.

As a result, these Know Nothings, a majority of the whole, could and did fit comfortably enough into the Republican coalition. The important thing was that American leaders believed the Republicans had gone as far as they could go. Thus, Democratic defeat "requires a union of all the practical elements of opposition—a union that shall be based upon enduring principles." Even though there were holdouts, to all intents and purposes, at the top a relationship had matured—one housed within the Republican party—but one in which the Know Nothings decorated many of the rooms. As a result, in distinct difference from Baum's description of voter paths and party building in Massachusetts, "the anti-Catholic, anti-foreign American party played a very" major role in the transition in New York from Whiggery to Republicanism. By mid-1859, "there is yet a few hundred True *Americans*" left in Wayne County —the rest were largely Republicans.[97]

Several conclusions derive directly from this analysis. First, at a primary level, we have clarified a relationship in a major state between the Republicans and Know Nothings. We have added to the data base toward dealing with that question in more general terms. In these election statistics, party rhetoric, and description of behind-the-scenes maneuvering lies the story of difficult coalition-building in the pluralist world of mid-nineteenth-century American politics. There were many loose ends and a certain lack of symmetry in some instances, but generally the direction and outcome remain clear. In New York State, Republican leaders, pressured by the electoral calculus, and the demands from their supporters, overcame their own hostility to forge a specific opening to the Know-Nothings. The latter, often grudgingly, and never unanimously, responded positively. By 1860 enough Know-Nothing support had come into Republican ranks to accomplish the latter's purposes of forging sufficient electoral strength to become the normal majority party in the state, year in and year out.

Second, the New York case has its unique aspects. But as William Gienapp has effectively shown, what happened in the Empire State occurred (with some differences of scope and activity) elsewhere in other Northern states as well.[98] There were state-to-state differences in the pattern, but that is not surprising given the wide variation in the political experiences of the different states. There is, therefore, another issue here to be marked as well: the extraordinary variation in political situations from place to place within the United States.[99]

But beyond that there is a third, critical, matter, namely, the larger issue of the nature of social conflict in the antebellum United States. The experience of electoral realignment and party coalition-building everywhere was partially embedded in the existence of a powerful nativist political sensibility and organized movement which, more than being ignored, had to be confronted and negotiated with in some fashion. Such realization illuminates a number of important and larger themes present in late antebellum politics and opens the way toward comprehending the full dimension of the forces shaping the political world on the eve of the Civil War.

The eventual coalition of the Republicans with the Know Nothings did not produce a single voice, with everyone cheering solely for the irrepressible conflict. Politics did not operate that way, certainly not in the political environment existing in the late 1850s. Positions and ideas and commitments to particular outlooks and policies counted. Historians who do not pay attention to the difficulties of melding these separate perspectives together and who ignore the persistence of Know-Nothing nativist strength late in the decade succumb to the Civil War synthesis —acceptance of the idea that sectional feeling swept all else aside relatively easily and the Republican party emerged triumphant with relatively little influence within it of nativist sentiment.[100] But the Know Nothings continued to have great support and commitments not rooted in the sectional confrontation. Therefore they demanded an ideological price from those who would deal with them. The Republicans bargained and met much of it, which they would not have done unless the two groups shared strong areas of agreement and common ground. Republicans and Northern Know-Nothings hated the slave power, but they also hated the Irish immigrant—both for the last named's excessive use of political power and foreign intrusion in what was seen as the right way for America to develop.[101]

9

THE SURGE OF REPUBLICAN POWER: PARTISAN ANTIPATHY, AMERICAN SOCIAL CONFLICT, AND THE COMING OF THE CIVIL WAR (1982)

The secession of eleven Southern states between December 1860 and the spring of 1861 remains the central, traumatic moment in the American historical experience. Recognizing its importance, historians have expended efforts over more than a century detailing and explaining why secession became the chosen course and why it occurred when it did.[1] This historiographic enthusiasm has yet to wane, and studies of the dynamics of secession continue to appear. In recent years, in fact, after a period of decline, there has been a resurgence of interest in the subject. In the last decade Don Fehrenbacher, Kenneth Stampp, William Barney, Steven Channing, the late David Potter, Michael Johnson, David Donald, Mills Thornton, Peyton McCrary, Eric Foner, Michael Holt, and Thomas P. Alexander have all made significant efforts to decipher the complex problem posed by the failure of the constitutional experiment at the beginning of the 1860s.[2]

The list of these recent works is impressively long; their findings are useful and important. They have encompassed explorations of both long-range, underlying causes and immediate considerations affecting specific behavior at critical moments. They have paid a great deal of attention to the internal political and social dynamics of Southern society in seeking to uncover and evaluate the raw materials that led to secession. They have applied new ways of looking at and organizing the available evidence: modernization theory, the imperative of republican ideology, the strains of nationalism and of center-periphery tensions. Finally, and most particularly, a number of historians have fully explored the nature and dynamics of elite and mass political behavior. As a result of all this, researchers have illuminated many dark corners of Northern and Southern society, of antislavery and proslavery movements, and of the American political process generally.[3]

Despite the reach and depth of this work and what has been learned, the story of what brought on the secession crisis remains unfinished. Agreement on causation is still elusive. How the various elements came together to provoke a specific reaction continues to be debated. Disagreements about individual and group motivations and the importance and power of the different forces at play are unabated. Some writers emphasize the threat of internal conflict among Southerners themselves, a threat energized by Republican growth and power as "the operative tension in the secession crisis." Secession in this view "was necessary because of the internal divisions within the South, divisions which focused on the degree to which the slaveholding minority could have its way in a government based ultimately on manhood suffrage."[4] Other students, however, stress other Southern fears, such as the threat to slavery or the region's inability to expand into new territories. Still other historians articulate their belief in the inevitability of conflict between two distinctly different societies following different courses. One section, they claim, was committed to traditional, pre-bourgeois social and economic patterns; the other section was a vigorous, rapidly modernizing place, the epitome of nineteenth-century bourgeois development. Their profound differences came to a point when they locked horns over Northern "modernizing" attempts to integrate "the 'premodern' South" into its conception of "a national political and economic system."[5]

There are rich varieties of such historiographic themes with many nuances and differences among them in what Don Fehrenbacher refers to as "the accumulated complexity of the literature on the causes of the Civil War."[6] But what is clear about them is that what happened has neither been fully told nor comprehended in a way that everyone can accept. Nor is there even agreement about where to focus research efforts. The situation has been compared by Willie Lee Rose with being caught in "an entangling morass" whenever we try to account for the causes of the Civil War. "Most of the scholars who have tried to cut boldly through it," she continues, "have had only temporary success. The facts and the variables have proved impossible to account for under any single theory up until now."[7] This traumatic episode remains open and alive to additional historical exploration. Its roots and course, the long-range process and the immediate triggering mechanism, must be considered yet again if we are to understand it fully and accurately.

This last point is particularly highlighted by the recent intrusion into American historiography of a powerful, significant, and new way of understanding politics and the political system in the generation ending in secession, a way that cannot be ignored when we consider what happened in the United States in 1860–1861. Perhaps nothing has been more jarring to students of antebellum politics than the recent findings of those dubbed "new political historians" about the nature of social and political conflict in the decades before the Civil War. According to these historians, far from being intimately, persistently, and directly related to slavery and the sectional crisis, mass political conflicts in the 1840s and 1850s were primarily rooted in a complex interaction of social and political perceptions and religious, national, and racial prejudices and divisions, all brought together under the heading of ethnocultural conflict. As Paul Kleppner sums up the findings, "Nineteenth-century American partisanship was not rooted in economic distinctions. Neither gradations of wealth nor perceived differences in status nor shared orientations toward the work experience were at the core of partisan commitments. Partisan identification mirrored irreconcilably conflicting values emanating from divergent ethnic and religious subcultures." The hostility of Protestants toward Catholics, of pietistic toward ritualistic Protestants, of Anglo-Saxons toward Celts, Germans, and Dutch and other ethnocultural conflicts had more to do with American electoral politics than did arguments over tariffs, territorial expansion, sectionalism, slavery, and executive power. Each political party was deeply involved in this conflict. Party coalitions were based on different grouping of ethnocultural tribes.[8]

Particularly relevant to the process culminating in secession, these ethnocultural variables structured the critical voter realignment of the mid-1850s. Between 1854 and 1856, one of the sharpest turnovers in American politics occurred, resulting in the disappearance of the national Whig party, the ultimate weakening and decline of the Democratic party, and the creation and rise to dominance of a sectionally focused Republican coalition. The Democrats fell from the heights of their sweeping presidential victory in 1852 to a minority position by the presidential election of 1856. Receiving only 45.3 percent of the popular vote that year, they lost control of all but a handful of Northern states and their hold on the few states they had won was seriously threatened thereafter. A massive voter reaction to a perceived alien threat to American culture triggered this political upheaval. As Ronald Formisano argues, the rise of the Republicans was primarily due to a long-standing "political evangelicalism" which revived in 1854 and which was further "politicized and broadened by anti-Popery, nativism, temperance zeal and other Protestant moralisms" into a major political revolution that brought down the Democratic party in the northern states.[9]

This ethnocultural element in the realignment politics of the fifties has been well established; however, its recognized importance has raised a serious problem of analysis and interpretation. What do ethnocultural political divisions have to do with secession and the coming of the Civil War—the culminating cataclysm of a decade in which the electoral realignment occurred? "It hardly seems too much . . . to demand of any new sweeping interpretation of the nation's political history," Rose suggests, "that it give a serviceable account of the causes of the Civil War."[10] But how can we possibly integrate the findings of the new political history into an explanation of sectional rupture? "The frenzy of revolution was in the people" at the moment of secession, a Southerner recalled twenty years later, but what, if any, was the role of ethnocultural conflict in fomenting that frenzy?[11] Confrontations between Protestants and Catholics and between Yankees and Irish, for all their importance in mass voting behavior in the 1850s, seem a long way from a conflict erupting from the clash of different sectional cultures or systems or in response to such immediate matters as the Wilmot Proviso, free-soilism, Kansas, "bleeding" Sumner, John Brown, and the demands of William Lowndes Yancey and his secessionist cohorts. And yet these events, slavery, and the defense of the slave system were ultimately to cause the breakup of the Union.

Most recent students of secession found little place in their explanations for the findings of the new political historians. Some deal with them to a degree, but with obvious difficulty. Others reject these findings out of hand. One reason is the general failure of the new political historians to find ways to subsume Southern political life within the ethnocultural explanation of antebellum politics. Holt points out, for instance, that "for Dixie, evangelicalism and ritualism, pietism and liturgicalism have definite limitations as analytical concepts. The prophets of the ethnocultural interpretation, indeed, have largely ignored the South no matter what period they are writing about."[12]

Those who completely reject the findings of the new political history take comfort in such an admission. A few of them even go so far as to regard with disdain the idea that the kinds of ethnocultural conflict described could have had much, if any, role to play in the momentous events of 1860–1861. Too much else was present of a different quality, the focus on slavery too clear-cut, the ethnocultural interpretation not readily assimilable into most explanations in any convincing way. "I tend to think," Rose writes in summary, that "no theory based primarily on cultural voting patterns in the North is going to explain the coming of the Civil War." She concludes by warning historians away "from the treacherous shores of the new determinism that the ethnoculturalists have located through a narrow examination of voter behavior."[13]

Echoing Rose's sentiments, Fehrenbacher, in the most recent attempt to deal with the secession crisis directly, simply ignores the findings of the new political history except for a passing reference at the outset of his book. He finds such efforts to employ new conceptual frameworks to change our focus as "often synthetic and modish . . . reflecting the latest fashions in behavioral science theory and terminology but adding little to the substance of explanation."[14] These are harsh words indeed, which Fehrenbacher follows up with resort to more traditional approaches and explanations. His focus is on the Southern secessionists and their fears of what Northern Republican voters would demand all right, but what shaped so much of the behavior of those voters, according to the new political historians, does not appear. It is the Kansas-Nebraska bill and debate, not ethnocultural divisions, insists Fehrenbacher, that "more than anything else determined the character of the third party system in its early years."[15]

Finally, one or two historians have suggested, ironically one hopes, that the new political historians would be happy if they could say that the Civil War never happened, because there is nothing in their description of American social conflict or any theories that come out of it that could help to explain divisions based upon a sectional confrontation. The explanation offered by the new political historians, Eric Foner concludes, "has no need for the Civil War. Unfortunately, the Civil War did take place. But the new interpretation leaves a yawning gap between political processes and the outbreak of war."[16]

But this cannot be the end of the story. Secession, a specific political act, cannot be separated from the political world of the time with its everyday concerns, routines, norms, and conflicts. There is, of course, particular irony in noting this, since one area of agreement among almost all students of the secession crisis is that it was the Republican victory at the polls in 1860 that "precipitated the secession of the seven states of the lower South."[17] Why? Because "all the passions of the sectional conflict became concentrated." Fehrenbacher argues, "like the sun's rays by a magnifying glass, on one moment of decision that could come only once in history—that is, the first election of a Republican president."[18] The trigger that ultimately produced separation lay there.

It was the way the political world was developing that threatened the South and drove its leaders to do what they did. But what was it about the Republicans that caused such an action? Fehrenbacher refers to the "expected consequences" of Republican rule, "vague but terrible."[19] In his study of antebellum Alabama society and politics, Mills Thornton describes Alabamians acting, in their "terror," against "frightening" circumstances.[20] What made such vague consequences so terrible, so many good people so terrified? That remains unclear. In dealing with it, however, it seems rash indeed not to consider what we have learned recently about the roots of so much of American political conflict in the

1850s and the political context in which the leaders, both Northern and Southern, had to operate. The findings about the importance of ethno-cultural conflict in shaping political behavior in the pre-Civil War decade unearthed by Lee Benson, Ronald Formisano, Michael Holt, Roger Peterson, Paul Kleppner, Robert Swierenga, Frederick Luebke, and George Daniels, among others, are clear-cut and persuasive. And no one who reads the political idiom of the 1850s can ignore the extensive concern with religious and, more broadly, ethnocultural issues to be found there. As William McLaughlin has remarked, American political rhetoric has often been infused with the metaphors of religious and cultural values. "There has scarcely been an election in American history since 1796 which was not conducted as a fight between good and evil for the power to steer the ship of state toward the millennial harbor."[21]

Moral commitments were particularly strong in the 1850s. Spiritual values, religious metaphors, and ethnic awareness abounded in everyday life. Differences between dissimilar groups in the country had height-ened as well. The political realignment in that decade had sharpened and reenergized both. Both permeated the fabric of the American political system and the lives of most Americans. Its full ramifications and meaning may not have been explored or its intensity fully measured, but ethnocultural conflict was obviously not irrelevant, artificial, or temporary in the politics of that time. To articulate its importance does not narrow historical vision simply to voting behavior. The work of the new political historians strongly underlines how much ethnocultural differences and conflicts incorporated a broad conspectus of the political and social processes in the United States generally. We can no more dismiss such conflict than we can the importance of sectional confronta-tion in explaining America's collapse into internal war.

It is time, in sum, to begin integrating the factors unearthed by students of the new political history into our understanding of the breakup of the Union. Such attempts will not in themselves end the search for the causes of secession and civil war. No one can be that optimistic. But the efforts may at least add important elements to that search. At most they may create a better grasp of the complexities of political choice. And by incorporating those findings we will not omit from our calculations an important aspect of American political history in the 1850s.

Unfortunately, few of the new political historians themselves have tried to deal directly with the coming of the Civil War. Their focus has remained on the mid-fifties, primarily on the electoral realignment and the resulting emergence of a third political party system based on how different social groups voted. They usually separate these electoral confrontations from the problem of the Union's collapse.[22] It is true that in an intelligent development of the Republican critique of the South, Formisano has shown how a number of apparently diverse and unrelated ideas were brought together. He argues that "nativism, anti-Catholicism, anti-Southernism, anti-slavery and racism did not flow through the political universe in neatly separate streams. . . . Rather, one must understand how racial, ethnic, religious, economic, sectional, and other groups were interwoven symbolically and how issues such as Popery, Slavery, Party, and Rum permeated one another with emotional resonance."[23] Michigan Republicans, he points out, integrated attacks on Catholics with attacks on the slave power into a crusade for white freedom. That crusade united Republicans behind an anti-slavery extension, anti-Democratic program. They saw a relationship between the ethnocultural matters and the expansion of slavery.

Formisano's attempts are critical because he relates the two dominant confrontations of mid-nineteenth-century American politics to each other. But, despite his important effort, the surface of the problem has barely been scratched, particularly in understanding the sectional crisis itself. He tells us what made the Republicans act as they did. But the key to any examination of the crisis of disruption is to explain the behavior of the rest of the political community as well, most centrally and particularly that of the Southern secessionists. Why did they act when they did? Why not earlier, in 1850 or 1854? Why not right after John Brown's raid in 1859, as some of them then desired? Any analysis of the crisis must focus on the specific perceptions at the time of the men who committed the overt acts rejecting continuation of the Union. The leaders of the secession movement and those who followed them particularly reflected the fears engendered by the Republican victory. To them, at that moment, Thornton writes, "the Southern future held only horror." Among them "monstrous fears" were feeding on "monstrous realities."[24] Were such inflamed social and political perceptions shaped by the ethnocultural pressures present? If so, why and how, specifically?

It is not that Southerners were affected directly in their elections by their own ethnoculturally structured divisions. There is little evidence of that, and the subject needs more investigation. Rather, it is what Southerners saw in Northern political warfare, highly structured by the ethnocultural cleavages present, that counted to them. To quote Fehrenbacher once more, Southern "fear of Republican rule was to no small degree a fear of the unknown."[25] But there was much more to it than that. Secessionists knew some things about the Republicans all too well. Perception and reality intertwined among the secessionists in a particular way. Secession "was intended by Southern political leaders to be a preemptive strike against the threat of a revolutionary takeover."[26] That takeover was based, in their minds, on the plans of the new power group in the nation, the nationally victorious Republican party. When the Southern states seceded, they made a strong statement about power. They were frightened by the new political configuration within the nation. It was what they saw in the rise of the Republicans, capped by Abraham Lincoln's election, that led them to take the actions they did.

Fehrenbacher refers to "the surge of Republican power" as "what Southerners feared most." It was difficult, he continues, for Southerners to view Republicans as "merely a political opposition."[27] But why not? Secessionists certainly saw the Republicans as more threatening toward slavery than any previous political opposition. There was some realism in that. John Rozett emphasizes that the "Republican party did represent to a predominant degree those who, at the very least, had a distaste for the ill treatment of the black man . . . [and that] the South did have something to fear from the election of Abraham Lincoln." Republicans, he concludes, "did adopt a position of limited equality and of moral judgement which the South could neither accept nor tolerate."[28]

Republicans, however, had been going out of their way to play down such commitments and to calm fears thus provoked. They presented several different sides of their nature to the electorate generally and to suspicious Southerners in particular. Historians have recognized this well enough. Republicans, in one description, "presented themselves as conservatives," while at the same time they "espoused revolutionary doctrines."[29] But which was reality? Why believe one thing about them and not the other? On one level their future course and policies on slavery matters could not be clear to contemporary observers, yet for the secessionists they were very clear. Southerners did not believe either Republican denials of plans against the South or that party's articulated conservatism. They picked out and emphasized the most dangerous, threatening aspect of the Republican argument. They could not simply play it safe, for that would not convince the electorate they had to sway to their side. Republicans could say what they wanted, but Southerners had certain evidence about the nature and intentions of the Republicans which cut through the confusion and ambiguity. The facts that Southerners had and the way they viewed them crystallized and clarified their fears and oriented them in a particular way in the frightening political world they inhabited.

To understand the perceptual prism through which secessionists viewed their enemies, it is necessary first to comprehend the role, importance, and outlook of the larger community of which many of them were part. What framed political discourse and action, for all of the sectional tensions present, was an older and still powerful stream of political idiom and belief. There was a continuity to a particular kind of political confrontation in America from the 1830s onward that shaped the way events were seen at the moment of crisis. The political memories of Southern secessionists contained crucial influences that interacted with their concerns about slavery and the Union to deepen and intensify their fears.

The secessionist prism was partisan. Southern perceptions were intertwined with their long-standing commitments to a particular political party. The most critical of all subcultures in the antebellum period were the political parties. This fact is the second major finding of the new political historians. They argue that parties helped to organize a vibrant, intense politics, one of great feeling, rhetorical exaggeration, and deep commitment.[30] Yet parties tend to disappear more than they should from discussions of secession. There is strong evidence that they retained their important structuring effect throughout the 1840s and 1850s despite the rise of sectional tensions. In his presidential address to the Southern Historical Association, Thomas Alexander forcefully reminded his audience that "the attachment of the individual voter to party in nineteenth century America was affective, even religious." Given that, "secession was a step so drastic and so contrary to the fervor of American nationalism that it could never have been made persuasive to a majority of voters on the basis of arguments that individuals could readily associate with their own well being. Only through the vehicle of the Democratic party was secession possible."[31]

Alexander's partisan religious metaphor is useful and accurate. Nineteenth-century Americans worshiped at what some labeled "the shrine of party" right through the secession crisis.[32] Even in a day of rising sectional differences and confrontations, such worship—that is, intense partisan commitments and adherence—still ran deep. Almost half the Northern voters remained good and loyal Democrats in 1860 despite the role that Republicans cut out for themselves as the party of Northern white freedom. Party battles remained savage in the North as well. In the South, too, there is much evidence of the continued importance of partisan traditions and behavior.[33] Furthermore, the major actors in the crisis of 1860–1861 and most of the other participants as well had been politically socialized during the time that the Jacksonian party system had matured and sunk its roots deeply into the American soil. All of these actors had been affected by the powerful force of the partisan imperative that ran profoundly and intensely through the minds and hearts of most concerned Americans.

Political parties brought together in disciplined ranks groups of like-minded individuals, their unity rooted in their common enemies, fears, desires, and attitudes. People caught up in partisan politics were schooled in certain unyielding truths. Parties were always at war with their opponents. Their perceptions of each other and their ideological commitments found expression in a divisive and rousing rhetoric. Like religious converts, the party faithful were forcefully called to their duty and reminded of the dangers they faced if they wavered in their faith and lost the battle. Stump speeches, newspaper editorials, and election pamphlets were the weapons of this warfare. The warfare varied in intensity but it was persistent and always close to the surface of political consciousness. By 1860, both the Democrats and the Republicans had fully developed and articulated clear perspectives about the policies and behavior of their adversaries. These perspectives were highly integrated. They involved all components of current politics stemming from the electoral realignment and its consequences, from antislavery agitation to nativism. Powerfully asserted, they penetrated deeply into both partisan communities. Both elites and masses subscribed to the tenets of their partisan communities. Republicans talked about free soil, free labor, and a crusade for white freedom.[34] But it was what the Democrats talked about in return that was central to the secession episode.

It was, as Alexander notes, the Southern Democrats who dominated the movement to leave the Union. They formed its "cutting edge."[35] Its leadership and much of its voting support came primarily from Democratic ranks. One study estimates that two-thirds of the popular vote for secessionist candidates in 1860–1861 came from Democrats.[36] What drove them were the specifics of Democratic perception and commitment. Thus the integrated and national Democratic ideology of the 1850s and the framework of party loyalty and partisan belief played critical roles in shaping the perceptions that led Southern Democrats to take the actions they did in 1860–1861. The Democratic assault throughout the 1850s furnished Southerners with a perspective on their immediate political situation. This perspective provided for the faithful an image of Republicans that guided Democrats in their reaction to the rise of the Republican party, the election of Lincoln, and most specifically to the crisis that followed. In their speeches the leadership constantly invoked traditional partisan usages and symbolism to explain what was at issue. In their political exchanges and in their particular understanding of the Republican threat, Southerners demonstrated their absorption of the national Democratic ideology as it had developed. Those partisan components, incorporating the transcendent substance of political warfare, defined for them what was at issue and what, consequently, had to be done.

Southerners gave as much evidence of the Democratic heritage as anyone who lived outside the slave states. Their system of ideas, particularly concerning the Republican threat, resonated with their Democratic ideology. Most observers are so used to seeing Southern Democrats pulling away from Northern Democrats in the late 1850s that they forget that—despite real and crucial differences over candidates, tactics, and specific policies—there remained agreement over the perceptions of the danger the nation was in and the reasons for that danger. Despite disagreements between them, both sectional Democratic factions shared an integrated vision, a common ideology.

The roots of that ideology lay in the cultural patterns informing American political life. Conflict between different religious, ethnic, and national groups, framed in many different ways, had existed for a long time in the United States.[37] Since the 1830s it had taken partisan form. The resulting battles implanted deep commitments and produced sharp partisan memories even as a generation passed and new issues arose. The political battles of the 1850s had reinvigorated the confrontations and reawakened these memories, always close to the surface. The critical part about the resulting political arguments—encased as they were in the realities and demands of the American political system with its democratic impulse and vigor, its reductionist rhetoric, and its deeply held commitments—was that they grew into confrontations of world systems held by quite different cultural blocs. Evidence taken from specific and often minor episodes—the visit of a papal nuncio, the burning of a convent, or the rantings of a demented prostitute—was marshaled and blown into an image of vast conflict.

To Democrats of the late 1850s, ethnocultural conflicts had specific political meaning. Because of the electoral realignment of the mid-fifties, a dangerous spirit permeated American politics, a spirit that endangered the freedom of all Americans and ultimately the Union itself. The "practice of dragging politics into the pulpit" was "rapidly becoming one of the crying evils of the age," they argued. "Religious prejudices are invoked [in] the political arena. . . . The clergy are to be appealed to to take the rostrum. Churches are to be turned into party conventions." The result was clear to see. "As the pulpit has grown political, the stump has waxed pious." Americans now lived in an age "in which it is attempted to legislate not with an eye to the rights, the comforts, the wonts—the well being of *good* citizens" but only with attention paid to how "the wicked, erring will turn the blessings of Providence to bad account." Such behavior was profoundly dangerous to the Union because "persecution is an inseparable concomitant of sectarian power."[38]

The source of this was clear to Democratic spokesmen. It came from New England and particularly from the Puritanism that still abounded there. As the editor of a Texas paper put it in 1856, "The people of the New England States have been as remarkable in their history, for the violence of their fanaticism and proclivity to superstition and intolerance on all subjects connected with religion as they have been for their intelligence, energy and enterprise on all other subjects."[39] The Democrats particularly feared the sectarian interventionism of the New England divine in the affairs of the nation, the region's self-defined crusade to change and uplift people and bring them into conformity with the ideals of the region, indiscriminately, determinedly, and without regard for the desires of those affected.

The descendants of the colonial Puritans, a Tennessee editor suggested during the secession crisis, "retain the salient points which characterized their ancestors, and destroyed the harmony of the earliest settlers of the colonies. The Puritans of today, like the Puritans of 1700, conceive themselves to be better and holier than others, and entitled— by divine right as it were—to govern and control the actions and dicate the opinions" of their fellowmen. New England is "always putting itself forward as the accuser and maligner of its brethren, the marplot and busybody of the confederacy, always crying over its grievances and always arraigning the other states for pretended usurpations. . . . They are unhappy unless they can persecute, either some unprotected class of their own people, or their colleagues in the confederacy." They "first established religious liberty on this continent by hanging and burning all who did not maintain their plan of salvation." An intolerance "social, religious and political leavens the masses there today, the same as when it burnt old women for witches, banished the Quakers, tore down Catholic convents, or gathered together a blue light Hartford Convention." New Englanders arrogantly believed they had a monopoly on truth and exhibited "a fanatical zeal for unscriptural reforms, accompanied by a Pharisaical spirit, which says to brethren heretofore cordially acknowledged, 'Stand back, we are holier than you.'"[40]

But things went further. The importance of all of this rhetoric to Democrats was what such attitudes led New Englanders to do. In a "soil in which every absurdity seems to be indigenous, and is favorable to the growth of every foreign delusion," including sabbatarianism, temperance, abolitionism, "and the other isms imported from Europe," there was devotion to a single purpose: cultural imperialism.[41] New Englanders were so imbued with the fanaticism of religious restrictionism and cultural superiority that they believed they had a "mission" to impose their own values everywhere in the Union. "They persuaded themselves that they had a prescriptive right to impose their politics, their habits, manners and dogmas on the sister States and aspired to convert the whole people of the United States to Yankeedom." The Puritans had demonstrated such commitment again and again throughout American history. They were always at war to shape the future of the nation. They wanted it fundamentally Anglo-Saxon, Protestant, and pietist or Puritan, and not a mixture of diverse ethnic and religious groups which held different values. They proceeded, therefore, "as a central power, dictating to colonies and provinces."[42]

To the Democrats none of this had ever been abstract. The threat by New England was real and frightening. That region abounded with reformers, "people [who] imagine that nothing exists that may not be improved . . . and that they are divinely commissioned agents to accomplish this favorable change." Some of the threat Southern Democrats perceived was obviously rooted in differences over slavery, but it involved more than that. In a region where "sectarian hatred outranks even sectional animosity," the persistent "mutual jealousies of New England and the South do not primarily grow out of slavery. They are deeper, and will always be the chief obstacle in the way of full absolute reunion. They are founded in differences of manner, habits and social life, and different notions about politics, morals and religion."[43] Nor was it simply a matter of anti-Catholicism or hatred among different nationality groups. As the Democrats articulated it, this was a war between two cultures, not necessarily sectional in makeup, but in which sectional and regional distinctions played a major role, "of races, representing not difference in blood, but mind and its development, and different types of civilization. It is the old conflict of the Cavalier and the Roundhead, the Liberalist and the Puritan."[44] Whose country is this? was the question asked. The Democrats had one answer, their opponents another.

The threat to a pluralist nation posed by the Puritans, though always present, had not been that serious in the 1830s and 1840s, although the political battlefield was well marked from the start. Democratic denunciations of their Whig opponents in the 1830s and 1840s often contained attacks on extremism, cultural interventionism, and the great potential for nasty behavior inherent among the Whig descendants of Tory federalism. Fears were always close to the surface. In March 1850 one New York Democrat succinctly summed up the concern and its cogency. "I fear," James K. Paulding wrote, that "it will not be long before we of the North become the tools of the descendants of the old Puritans, who had not the most remote idea of the principles of civil liberty, and no conception of religious toleration, but the most unrelenting intolerance. The despotism of parsons," he continued, "is taking the place of that of kings. . . . Our freedom is in great danger of becoming sacrificed to the texts of Scripture, and fanatical dogmas."[45]

Still, the Whigs were a nationwide party, never as completely dominated by New England as the Republicans were to become later. Nor had the Whigs, though a robust and competitive party, usually been as potent a political threat. Before the mid-1850s, despite often very close elections, the Democratic party usually dominated the politics of the Union, especially through its control of Congress. (Between 1840 and 1854 they held a majority of the seats in both House and Senate in five of the seven Congresses.) But matters became more dangerous in the early 1850s as two factors threatened, in Democratic eyes, to tip an always present but largely subterranean and controllable conflict of cultural values over into open warfare.

First, the coming of the immigrants in great numbers in the 1840s and 1850s strongly revived rarely quiescent Puritanism and gave it new vigor, direction, and expectations. Second, Puritan extremism had become institutionalized into a dominant position within a narrowly sectional Republican party. Although there had been a Know-Nothing interlude first, embodying much of the spirit of New England cultural imperialism, the Democrats were convinced that many of the Know Nothings in the North and their ideas were absorbed, as the fifties passed, by the Republicans. The Democrats' "common enemy, composed of Free Soilers, Abolitionists, Maine-Lawites, Free-Negroes and Spirit Rappers," became embodied in the Republican party in "solid phalanx."[46]

It is nothing new to suggest that Southerners viewed the Republicans as meddlesome interventionists willing to crusade persistently against the institution of slavery.[47] But what should not be underestimated was the way Northern and Southern Democrats in the 1850s rooted such meddlesomeness in ethnocultural conflicts which were, in their view, the centerpieces of the Republican advance. As one editor put it, "Abolition is but a small part of their programme and probably the least noxious of their measures." Republican rapprochement with nativist movements in the mid-fifties and acceptance, as the Democrats believed, of the program and goals of the latter had made the larger threat clear. The coming of the immigrant, the Democrats suggested, had caused New England Puritans to revert "to the intolerant fanaticism which marked their early colonial history." The "prevailing leaven [of] Puritanism, the spirit which is almost as deadly hostile to the civil equality of religions at this hour, as when it burned the witches at Salem and whipped Quakers at the cart-tail," had once more become hyperactive and oppressive.[48] And the Republican party was its vehicle. "The principle of republicanism," as seen through the Democratic filter, was "to meddle with everything—to meddle with the domestic institutions of other States, and to meddle with family arrangements in their own states—to force their harsh and uncongenial puritanical creed down the throats of other men, and compel them to digest it under pains and penalties." The Republicans "assail with equal virulence the institutions of the North and those of the South." They "are equally inimical to, and equally to be dreaded by, the North and the South." Their newspapers "boldly" avow "that it is the mission of the Republican party to overthrow Democracy, Catholicism and Slavery."[49]

The Republican party "now proposes to take up arms against one of the religious denominations of the country" and "array political parties according to the churches to which their adherents belong, or with which they sympathize." The Republican party, in short, "is a machine to put fanatics into office and preachers into politics." During the presidential election of 1856, Democrats charged that "places of prayer were converted into Republican club rooms, and religious conference meetings into political gatherings, where partisan efforts in favor of the Republican ticket were pressed as a religious duty." The party subsidized the "religious and benevolent press, it smuggles its agents into the pulpit. Most of the professedly religious newspapers and very many of the pulpits of the country preached Republicanism and the duty of voting for Frémont, as a pressing religious obligation." Republicans made "merchandise of the various departments of philanthropy,'" prostituting "all causes, however sacred they should be against the invasion of politics, to . . . sectional, plundering and treasonable schemes." The Republicans' virulent attack on ethnocultural diversity and their refusal to tolerate "the existence of any institution not according to the puritanical philosophy of New England" added a new, potent, and dangerous dimension to a generalized and usually abstract fear. Democrats had "to combat" not only "the Black Republicans as a political organization," but also "the powerful influence of frenzied religious bigotry" as well.[50]

But there was a second and much more threatening danger: the willingness of the Republican party to use state power to impose the peculiar standards of Puritanism on everyone else. The use of government for such purpose had been a hallmark of early Puritanism, later taken up and advocated by Whigs, but it was now brought to a high pitch by the Republicans. The coercive tradition in American pietism may have been ambiguous as William McLaughlin has suggested, but it did not seem so to the Democrats in the 1850s with their deep fears of Puritanism and intense commitment against government interventionism.[51]

The Republicans, Democrats argued, were fostering an aggressive and uncompromising program of coercive, cultural legislation designed to order and direct individual behavior within the Union. Where Republicans ruled in the Northern states, restrictive and regulatory laws had quickly been passed because the party believed "men must be legislated into sober habits." They "put the seven deadly sins into a National Platform."[52] Schools came first. As David Nasaw writes, school reformers "were convinced that the only antidote to the diseases of Irish heritage, Catholicism, and poverty was enforced disciplinary training in the common school classrooms." They tried to persuade the newcomers of this, then they "substituted force for persuasion" through state legislation.[53]

More followed. Republicans were "pledged to coercive temperance" and sought "to compass its objects by summary seizures, confiscations and extraordinary punishments upon foregone presumptions of guilt, such as are forbidden by the Bill of Rights." Their commitment to the "temperance swindle" to limit the production and consumption of alcoholic beverages was the "legitimate off-spring" of their "spiritual despotism" as were "the Sunday laws, as well as the antislavery agitation and laws to bring the white man to the level of the black."[54]

The "Republican party majority, usurping the prerogatives of God and conscience, decree that all men must conform to their particular puritanical observance of the Sabbath. . . . Sunday is rendered to them a day of sadness and gloom, instead of a day of rejoicing and happiness. The puritanical and straight laced notions imported here from one portion of Europe are forced down the throats of a population from a different part of Europe, who never believed in them[,] and they are compelled to yield obedience to a holy Protestant inquisition."[55] Such social laws will "reduce all sociability to the condition of a Puritan graveyard." Temperance legislation, moves to Americanize school instruction, and other types of social restrictions such as sabbatarian laws were all designed to impress, by whatever means possible, the inexorable values and beliefs of the Puritans on the immigrants and ultimately on all other Americans. To these causes has been brought "the aid of intemperate action . . . changing into an involuntary and compulsory system [one] which had begun on the principle of moral suasion and an appeal to the better nature of man. . . . Eastern demagogues began to court it as a valuable political adjunct to abolitionism."[56]

The result was predictable. "Whether it shall be a scheme for regulating eating or drinking or the industry of the country, the result will be an effort to govern the World too much." Congress "has heretofore confined itself to punishing the violation of those laws in which it had jurisdiction: counterfeiting, mail robbery, smuggling, etc. Under what clause it finds jurisdiction over the relation of the sexes has never been told." But these "'busy-bodies-in-other-men's matters'" were determined to engineer a Christian society of a particular kind and quality, one in which there would be no room for the kind of values, practices, and beliefs held by a majority of those within the Democratic coalition.[57]

The Democrats obviously had a different view of such issues. First they denied the political relevance of the matters the Puritan-Republicans wanted to discuss. "We never had much faith in promoting the cause of moral reform in any of its different aspects, by linking it with the action of political parties. . . . These parties will give the people better and more intelligent rulers, and a more wholesome administration of affairs, when left to make selections with reference to legitimate political questions." They condemned "the fatuity of . . . dragging into the political arena and subjecting to the vicissitudes of party, the cause of moral reform." The Maine Law and related matters were local questions. They did not "belong in general politics." Concern over such moral legislation was "at war with the real principles of our government as always understood and expounded by the Democratic creed." In sum, "we do not wish to see the Federal government legislating on the marriages or morals of domestic life, and still less on the religion of the people."[58]

Democrats expressed a more general condemnation as well. "Intemperance is an evil," the editor of the *Democratic Review* wrote in 1852, "but for a free government to violate, for any cause, the plainest, most vital and fundamental principles of civil liberty, is also an evil, and one with which the first may not be at all compared." The "heresies of coercive temperance laws, know-nothingism and sectional organizations have their origin in one common error—a desire to interfere with the actions, consciences, and affairs of others." But "the moment . . . democratic principles, that men are to be let alone unless they invade the rights of others, and States allowed to govern themselves—are departed from, we know not what vagaries and inconsistencies communities may run." Clearly "the clergy, in all time, and in all countries, have never interfered in politics or in government without inflicting serious evils or lasting disadvantages upon the people." Let us then, they demanded, "have faith in Democracy! The founders of our government declared that it mattered little if error was left free by government, so long as truth was left free to combat it." Therefore "we will be wise if we learn in time to beware of that political priesthood which . . . commences by arrogating to itself divine attributes, and claiming to speak in the name of God, and ends in the moral and mental degradation and enslavement of its victims."[59]

Many aspects of Republican behavior in their initial national election campaign in 1856 first reinforced and then confirmed Democratic fears. In his massive study of the formation of the Republican party, William Gienapp recounts how quickly Democrats detected the leading role played by Puritan ministers in shaping the direction Republicanism took in 1856 and then in fighting for their party's victory. "We had all the fanatical methodist & Baptist preachers against us hurling their anathemas at us from their pulpits on Sunday and from the stump on week days," one Democrat angrily reported. Another noted that "preachers of all the Presbyterian denominations were out fiercely and fanatically against us."[60]

Gienapp concludes that "the Protestant clergy's support" for the Republican ticket "was both vocal and unusual." Ministers "entered the Frémont campaign with great enthusiasm and more than a little self-righteousness. . . . Political sermons became standard fare throughout the summer of 1856, reaching a climax on the Sunday before election day, when, one Massachusetts Democrat sneered, the fanatical clergy 'appealed to their deluded followers to vote . . . as would enable them to give an acceptable account at the Day of Judgment!'"[61]

The message of such activities, the rhetoric that accompanied them and the aura given off, was clear to Democrats. The Republican party had become proudly and manifestly the repository of all Puritan values in politics. But, even more than that, the ethnocultural fires of the mid-fifties had proved to be potent beyond belief: life-long Democrats of the deepest faith were deserting the party over the matter. The fusion of former Whigs, Free Soilers, renegade Democrats, and Know Nothings into the new Republican coalition had transformed the Democrats' enemies into a powerful and threatening political force. Despite their sectarian and geographic narrowness, the Republicans posed a political threat of an enormous magnitude, one unknown before. The widespread Republican victories in the Northern states from 1854 onward underlined the potency of the threat. The swing against the Democrats in many parts of the North was large and decisive. The elections to the Thirty-fourth Congress in 1854 were particularly disastrous. The Democrats lost seventy of their ninety-two House seats, one of the greatest turnovers in American political history. They lost such masses of voters in many localities that they seemed to be reduced to an incompetitive rump in key areas. They recovered themselves somewhat after that, as the realignment sorted itself out, but at much lower levels of popular support north of Maryland and the Ohio Valley than they had heretofore enjoyed. In the presidential election of 1856 they held onto national power, but the Republican electoral totals in the North were the dramatic story of that contest.[62]

The force of the numbers was clear. The Republicans were surging to power. Although the Democrats remained electorally competitive in the Northern states, the center of power had shifted significantly. The Democrats were now the minority party outside the South. That fact had a clear meaning for all Democrats to see and digest. From now on, a Republican national victory was very likely. That point, as well as the Republican rhetoric and values that underlay their growth in the Northern states, threw a devastating scare into the Democrats, including the Southern wing of the party, which had its own particular hobbies to worry about.

In this situation, Democratic rhetoric pinpointing the source of threat grew more agitated and extreme. Their fear was intense. The Republicans were dominated by a seventeenth-century kind of religious fanaticism. And that party of fanatics intended to use the government when it gained control to impose its values by legislation and executive action. Puritan government would be an activist one determined to impose and deny. Republicans were willing to "combat . . . against the people and institutions of half of the States of the Union—stigmatizing them as tainted members of our political family, whose social system is to be stamped with the marks of public reprobation. But let us not stop here. Let us also combine against the political rights and religious freedom of that large class in the Northern States, who were born on European soil."[63]

The Republican commitments, building on the raw materials long present in the political environment and the tendencies among so many of their supporters, had clearly crystallized in the 1854–1856 period in the midst of a turbulent electoral realignment. They might have pulled back slightly since, but not because of any change in their ideological outlook. More likely, any toning down in their appeal was only for tactical reasons. To both Northern and Southern Democrats, the men who made policy for and dominated the Republicans—that is, that party's power elite—were the ones to be feared, not the simple Republican voters of, say, Wisconsin or Missouri. Even after the Republicans worked to belie their radicalism on the slavery issue, as they did so energetically in 1859 and 1860, they could not hide the legislative proposals and goals of their party which strongly indicated their commitment to interventionism. Occasionally their real attitudes came through tellingly, as with the Republican-led anti-immigrant assault in Massachusetts in 1859, which involved the use of law and the manipulation of the political process to deny deserving immigrants their political rights and access to power.[64] That was real Republicanism speaking. No matter what they said, the Republicans intended to destroy by every means possible the values, institutions, and behavior hostile to their conception of right, from Sunday carousing to tippling in taverns and in private to the holding of slaves. They would let nothing stand in their way. They would use whatever power and means available to them to establish their own view over everyone else. They were defined by their commitment to "the evils of political meddling with morals, religion and the right of distinct communities" and of allowing the government to "invade the territory of the Church" on behalf of one cultural viewpoint within a highly pluralistic nation.[65] They had become a powerful, unyielding monolith, exerting their cultural domination over the rest of the country. Their purifying goals were religious, social, and economic. Where would it all end? In the noncompromising cultural imperialism so often threatened by fanatical New England divines. Puritanism and Republicanism were synonyms. Republicans could not deny it no matter what they said.

This the Democrats argued and firmly believed. Their image of Republicans as manipulators of cultural prejudices convinced them that there was real danger. Certainly, their private communications and the ambience they exuded to both friendly and unfriendly colleagues were little different from their public pronouncements.[66] Their angry and anguished rhetoric in reaction revealed and codified a set of contrasting beliefs, which fueled the political process and drove it toward dangerous shoals. The Democrats simplified the Republican approach, as was normal in partisan rhetoric. They ignored the tensions among reformers involved in coercive reform and came up with a frightening spectacle. An apocalyptic partisan temper invigorated by a specific aspect of Republican character did its work well. Throughout the period of the electoral realignment and into the secession crisis itself, the partisan confrontation escalated mightily. The noise was bitter and fearsome. As Democrats digested what they heard, they came to fear that the ascension of the Republicans to power would culminate in a drive to restrict and revise the very nature of the Union.

"The Civil War was, at base, a struggle for the future of the nation," Eric Foner has written.[67] Yes, it was. But what was involved in that struggle, and what were the possibilities for the future? The Northern attack on the Celtic-Catholic threat, though not at first directly related to slavery, came to be seen by Northern and Southern Democrats as part of a much larger and quite potent cultural interventionism that knew no bounds in its interfering ways. A common ideology linking all

Democrats together still affected the Southern Democratic response to the onrushing Republicans. By 1860–1861 they had both internalized a generation of Democratic ideology and perceived an intense increase in the threat the now-triumphant Republicans posed to them. Southern Democrats shared the common partisan image of their enemy and then gave their perception a specific twist and reading of their own, which ultimately caused them to question the value of the Union—unlike their Northern colleagues.

All of what was being discussed obviously and repeatedly intertwined with the role and importance of slavery in Southern society and the fears of many Southerners about its place and safety within the Union. Nothing could have interacted more tellingly. How could the Democrats, Southerners in particular, not believe that the Republicans would not force all of the social changes they were convinced that the latter wanted? The history of partisan cultural confrontation since 1854, as the Democrats understood it, proved to them that their opponents would let nothing stand in the way in reshaping America in their own image, whatever their protestations in 1860 about being conservative on such matters. Republicans could not be negotiated with, a Louisiana editor summed up, because they were intransigent extremists intent only on "promulgating the teachings of their accursed fanaticism."[68] A Republican victory would lead to a total war of cultural imperialism. As Maryland congressman James A. Stewart connected the problems in 1856, "If the Federal Government has the right to dissolve [the relation between master and slave] . . . then it may also declare, that within its territory the marriage contract shall be considered dissolved—prescribe a plurality of wives—enact all the absurdities characterizing fanaticism —may establish Mormonism, Maine-Lawism, spiritualism, witchcraft, a religious test—indeed all the whole code of blue laws. If this Government has the power in one case, and it is left to its discretion, in what will it draw a line of distinction?"[69] The Republican philosophy, in short, threatened a policy of total destruction. The South's future rested on the continuing triumph of pluralist perspectives within the Union; that is, the dominance of traditional Democratic principles. Otherwise slavery was doomed by the same forces that sought to throttle Catholicism and Celtic life-styles.

Clearly, Southerners were not reacting to these ethnocultural matters and issues *per se*. What is central is that Democrats, including the Southern wing, saw few differences between conflicts over slavery extension and conflicts originating in the coming of the immigrant and Catholic. Ethnocultural matters informed the debate about other things. Slavery was part of the larger matter of cultural hegemony. Neither was trivial; one may have been primary; both were related. The Southern Democrats (and their Northern counterparts) translated all of this into much more cosmic matters. They moved it to another level: one of a war between cultures. This posed a dangerous problem for the South and for Southern slavery. As the editor of one Democratic newspaper put it, "We have found the root of the evil of sectional agitation in the attempt of the moral government to usurp the legitimate jurisdiction of the political government."[70] For forty years, Democrats believed they had been fighting for individual freedom against restriction and coercion. But in the 1850s they were in grave danger of losing the battle. This changed everything, especially for the southerners.

The South was vulnerable to the Republican threat, Southern Democrats argued from the mid-fifties on. Republicans were fanatics unable to forgo their commitment to regulate and reform. They might speak conservatively about slavery when it suited them and claim to recognize the South's constitutional rights, but how could they be trusted or believed? They would be unable to help themselves once in power. The same power used to defeat drunken Irish Catholics could be used to destroy slavery. Slavery, and every other part of the South's values, could never be safe given the character of the Republican party—whatever its reassurances. The Republican conception of a restrictive-coercive government would be as dangerous to slavery as it was proving to be to freewheeling social habits and religious nonconformity. The Republican commitment to a certain approach to society, social values, politics, and the way government operated threatened all. The South was prepared to believe the worst: not only that the Republicans were antislavery but that they would act as well as agitate. Central to everything, the Republicans could and would act.

After the rise of ethnocultural issues, therefore, no Southerner could blink his eyes at alleged threats to slavery or ignore the clear evidence that there was no hope at all for any peculiar values, ideas, or institutions if the Republicans won. Years of partisan warfare told all that was at stake. There was an aura, a sense of purpose, and a commitment to act emanating from the Republicans. Partisan and sectional ideologies converged and sharpened as they interacted in the fifties. Both ethnocultural and slavery-sectional issues defined the Republicans. Both were part of the same parcel, the plans of a small group of regional fanatics to dominate the Union and their willingness to use state coercion not simply in the name of power but in the name of values rooted in a particular and narrow religious perspective.

This was the message that the Democrats offered again and again without respite during the fifties, in the campaign of 1860, and in the months of agony before the Lincoln administration came to power. As Mills Thornton remarks, "Politicians played constantly upon the fear that institutions were conspiring to limit autonomy, and thus to reduce the populace to subservience." They were always looking for something which would be "a symbolic summary" of popular fears.[71] Much of that "symbolic summary" cited here emanated from Northern Democrats. But it is almost impossible to find distinctions between the visions of that group and their Southern colleagues—except about the value of the Union. They both understood the Republican threat in the same way. Their understanding was shaped by and conveyed in static, unchanging images, no matter how dynamic the situation was in which all of them were caught. On both sides of the Mason-Dixon line, Democratic spokesmen hammered away at the many faces of cultural interventionism and imperialism. Democratic newspapers and party spokesmen, North and South, maintained without stint the doom-laden, terribly threatening image of the Republicans.

South Carolina's secession convention voted her out of the Union on December 20, 1860. The last secession convention, North Carolina's, completed its work in late May 1861. There is a rich, full story in the details of the meetings held and the political campaigns that shaped them. Avery O. Craven, Allan Nevins, David Potter, and Don S. Fehrenbacher have each told it very well in recent years.[72] The secession process was dramatic, intense, complex, and often contradictory. Whatever its details, however, at the heart of the actions taken lay the intellectual baggage the delegates brought with them to their meetings. So most historians have stressed, and so it has been stressed here. Clearly the secessionists already had pictures in their minds of what the danger was to themselves and their society thanks to the Republican victory. Those pictures, their perceptions of the enemy, were the motivations behind their subsequent behavior. They were no longer free agents able to consider calmly and likely to have their minds changed by what happened in debates. Matters had gone too far; their perceptual commitments had become too deeply imbedded for that.

It does not wholly matter whether the Democratic-secessionist vision was correct. There was enough evidence around to draw the conclusion they did.[73] Where specific elements of proof were missing, the ideological commitments supplied them and afforded the necessary connecting links. Rhetoric and commitment reinforced, explained, codified, and ultimately helped create perceptions that led to action. To Northern and Southern Democrats infused with this idiom over a decade of battle for the soul of the nation, the evils associated with the Republicans were not separated into distinct compartments labeled economic differences, slavery, or psychological perceptions. The demonology of secessionist political rhetoric was imbued with and the behavior of Southern secessionists was affected by the kinds of ethnocultural perspectives the new political historians have emphasized.

Secessionists constantly made the connection between "black" Republicanism and other peculiar "isms" associated with the electoral revolt of the mid-fifties. All of these were united and integrated, and to Southerners especially they were devastating. As secessionists read the political world now unfolding, Republican rule would lead to an unacceptably restrictive society with a dominant, snooping, interfering government forcing conformity to a narrow set of behavioral norms. Cultural divisions and anxieties of this kind were often expressed in the American past even when they were masked as sectional antagonisms, that is, as different concepts of correct behavior and values. But these had been somewhat controlled when the question of values remained outside the purview of the issues discussed and of the powers and responsibility of government. They lurked there but could be managed. The rise of the cultural imperialists in the fifties changed this. Southern Democratic leaders saw the danger as well as did their Northern brethren. The long adherence to partisan Democratic values and assumptions provided them with a perspective that fortified and intensified the fears constantly stimulated since 1854 over the future of their institutions, values, and chosen behavior. With Lincoln, the interventionist Republican, about to assume office they acted.

NOTES

1. The Civil War Synthesis in American Political History

1. The primary evocation of the sectional theme is found in Frederick Jackson Turner, *The Significance of Sections in American History* (New York, 1932). The persistence of the concept is illustrated in the titles and contents of the two books in the "History of the South" series on this period: Charles Sydnor, *The Development of Southern Sectionalism, 1819–1848* (Baton Rouge, 1948), and Avery O. Craven, *The Growth of Southern Nationalism, 1848–1861* (Austin, 1953).

2. Both Charles Sellers and Thomas P. Govan have called attention to the presence of nonsectional ideas and influences in Southern politics in the 1840s and 1850s. See Charles Grier Sellers, Jr., "Who Were the Southern Whigs?", *American Historical Review* LIX (1954), 335–37; Thomas P. Govan, "Americans Below the Potomac," in Charles Grier Sellers, Jr. (ed.), *The Southerner as American* (Chapel Hill, 1960), 19–39.

3. We have, for example, books on the secession movements in the individual states of the South and which usually begin in the 1840s or 1850 at the latest. See, for instance, Henry T. Shanks, *The Secession Movement in Virginia, 1847–1861* (Richmond, 1934); J. Carlyle Sitterson, *The Secession Movement in North Carolina* (Chapel Hill, 1939); Dorothy Dodd, "The Secession Movement in Florida, 1850–1861," *Florida Historical Quarterly* XII (1933), 3–24, 45–66. Others in this same tenor include Ulrich B. Phillips, *The Course of the South to Secession* (New York, 1939), and Craven, *Southern Nationalism.*

4. "But the antislavery crusade had already gained such momentum that no Northern man could take a public stand in favor of annexation . . . [of Texas]." Charles Wiltse, *John C. Calhoun, Sectionalist, 1840–1850* (Indianapolis, 1951).

5. Charles Wiltse, *The New Nation, 1800–1845* (New York, 1961), 187; George Rawlings Poage, *Henry Clay and the Whig Party* (Chapel Hill, 1936), 151. There is a less certain discussion of this problem in John Garraty, *Silas Wright* (New York, 1949), 327–28.

6. Lee Benson, *The Concept of Jacksonian Democracy: New York As a Test Case* (Princeton, 1961).

7. Benson's methodology is discussed throughout the book and also in his article, "Research Problems in American Political Historiography," in Mirra Komarovsky (ed.), *Common Frontiers of the Social Sciences* (Glencoe, 1957), 113–83.

8. Benson, *Concept*, 260.

9. *Ibid.*, 267.

10. *Ibid.*, chap. XIV.

11. F. J. Turner, for example, suggested that on fundamental issues Congress demonstrated "a persistent sectional pattern." Turner, *Significance of Sections*, 40, 198. And in his *The United States, 1830-1850: The Nation and Its Sections* (New York, 1935), Turner consistently used congressional votes to demonstrate the growth of political sectionalism.

12. Craven, *Growth of Southern Nationalism*, chap. I.

13. Joel H. Silbey, "Congressional Voting Behavior and the Southern-Western Alliance, 1841-1852" (Ph.D. dissertation, State University of Iowa, 1963).

14. Part of the evidence for these conclusions was presented as a paper, "The Response to Recovery: Congressional Voting Behavior, 1841-1845," before the Mississippi Valley Historical Association at Detroit in April 1961.

15. For example, when the House of Representatives voted on the group of issues involving expansion into Oregon and Texas, 82.3 percent of the Democrats voted in favor of expansion while 74.5 percent of the Whigs voted against such expansion. In the Senate the Whigs were 100 percent united against expansion while 78.1 percent of the Democrats supported a more expansionist policy than did the Whigs. Each party contained members, of course, from both sections of the Union. Furthermore, the dissenters from the party positions exhibited here were not sectional blocs, but, in general, scattered individuals reacting to local or personal considerations.

In connection with nationwide support for expansion, see also John Hope Franklin, "The Southern Expansionists of 1846," *Journal of Southern History* XXV (1959), 323-38.

16. John C. Calhoun tried for years to organize the Southern congressmen into a unified bloc to resist Northern pressures. However, his efforts were always opposed by some other Southerners, both Whigs and Democrats, who did not see any reason to organize or vote sectionally and who preferred to maintain their national partisan commitments. Examples of this feeling can be seen in the resolutions of the Democrats of the Sixth Congressional District of Georgia, in the Washington *Union*, June 17, 1847; the resolutions of the Alabama State Democratic Convention, February 1848, in *ibid.*, Feb. 25, 1848; Howell Cobb et al., "To Our Constituents," Feb. 26, 1849, in Robert Brooks (ed.), "Howell Cobb Papers," *Georgia Historical Quarterly*, V (1921), 51 ff.

Calhoun's organ, the *Charleston Mercury*, finally admitted that "the antipathies of Whig and Democrat are too strong in Washington, and their exercise forms too much the habit of men's lives there. . . ." for there to be sectional unity. See issue of Jan. 22, 1849.

17. In the Thirty-first Congress, 95.2 percent of the Southerners in the House voted together on issues rising out of the slavery-extension debate and then they turned around and split fairly evenly (45.6 percent, 11.4 percent, 43.0 percent) into three positions on issues of internal improvements. In the succeeding sessions of Congress such sectional divisions remained the rule on the issues considered.

18. Gerald Wolff, "A Scalogram Analysis of the Kansas-Nebraska Act" (unpublished manuscript lent by author).

19. The background of this election is well covered in Roy F. Nichols, *The Disruption of American Democracy* (New York, 1947).

20. See, for example, Emerson D. Fite, *The Presidential Campaign of 1860* (New York, 1911); James G. Randall and David Donald, *The Civil War and Reconstruction* (2nd ed.; Boston, 1961), 129–32.

21. See, for example, Lawrence S. Thompson and Frank X. Braun, "The Forty-Eighters in Politics," in Adolf E. Zucker, *The Forty-Eighters* (New York, 1950), 120; Ray Allen Billington, *Westward Expansion* (2nd ed.; New York, 1960), 611; William E. Dodd, "The Fight for the Northwest, 1860," *American Historical Review* XVI (1911), 774–88.

22. Donnal V. Smith, "The Influence of the Foreign Born of the Northwest in the Election of 1860," *Mississippi Valley Historical Review* XIX (1932), 193.

23. George H. Daniels, "Immigrant Vote in the 1860 Election: The Case of Iowa," *Mid-America* XLIV (1962), 146–62.

24. *Ibid.*, 155–57.

25. Other issues such as a Massachusetts voting law, which would have made it more difficult for aliens to exercise the franchise, reinforced this feeling during the election of 1860. See *ibid.*, 156–57.

26. *Ibid.*, 156.

27. *Ibid.*, 157.

28. Robert P. Swierenga, "The Ethnic Leader and Immigrant Voting" (unpublished manuscript lent by author).

29. Leon Litwack, *North of Slavery: The Negro in the Free States, 1790–1860* (Chicago, 1961); Larry Gara, *Liberty Line: The Legend of the Underground Railroad* (Lexington, 1961).

30. C. Vann Woodward, "The Antislavery Myth," *American Scholar* XXXI (1962), 312–28.

31. *Ibid.*, 316–18.

32. Milton B. Powell, "The Abolitionist Controversy in the Methodist Episcopal Church, 1840–1864" (Ph.D. diss., State University of Iowa, 1963).

33. Daniels, "Immigrant Vote," 158.

34. Swierenga, "Ethnic Leader," 24.

2. "Delegates Fresh from the People"

1. The standard surveys of quantitative work in political history deal with research into Congress and other legislative bodies. See, most recently, Allan G. Bogue, "The New Political History in the 1970s," in Michael G. Kammen (ed.), *The Past Before Us: Contemporary Historical Writing in the United States* (Ithaca, 1980), 231–51. Quotation from Kammen, "Introduction: The Historian's Vocation and the State of the Discipline in the United States," in *ibid.*, 35.

2. Andrew Jackson to James Gunn, Feb. 23, 1835, in *Niles' Register*, Apr. 4, 1835, 84. Aage Clausen. *How Congressmen Decide: A Policy Focus* (New York, 1973), 6.

3. Bogue, "American Historians and Legislative Behavior," in Lee Benson et al., *American Political Behavior: Historical Essays and Readings* (New York, 1974), 102.

4. Silbey, *The Shrine of Party: Congressional Voting Behavior, 1841–1852* (Pittsburgh, 1967); Thomas B. Alexander, *Sectional Stress and Party Strength: A Study of Roll-Call Patterns in the United States House of Representatives, 1836–1860* (Nashville, 1967); H. James Henderson, *Party Politics in the Continental Congress* (New York, 1974); James W. Hilty, "Voting Alignments in the United States Senate, 1933–1944," (unpub. Ph.D. diss., University of Missouri, 1973); Gary W. Reichard, *The Reaffirmation of Republicanism: Eisenhower and the 93rd Congress* (Knoxville, 1975).

5. As, for example, in Gary M. Fink and Hilty, "Prologue: The Senate Voting

Record of Harry S. Truman," *Journal of Interdisciplinary History* IV (1973), 207–35; Lawrence H. Curry, Jr., "Southern Senators and Their Roll-Call Votes in Congress, 1941–1944" (unpub. Ph.D., diss., Duke University, 1971).

6. John L. Shover, "Populism in the 1930s: The Battle for the AAA," *Agricultural History* XXXVIII (1965), 17–24; Walter LaFeber, *The Panama Canal: The Crisis in Historical Perspective* (New York, 1978).

7. Despite its episodic quality, when one considers the total corpus of work since 1967 in systematic fashion, the chronological reach of the roll-call studies of Congress is, at least, awesome. All of this work and that done on state legislatures is listed and classified in Silbey, "Congressional and State Legislative Roll-Call Studies By American Historians," *Legislative Studies Quarterly* VI (1981), 597–607.

Historians have not been the only scholars to do roll-call analyses of the American legislative process. Political scientists have also contributed a great number of roll-call studies. Most of their work has focused on the period since 1945, although an increasing number of them are engaging in longitudinal analyses that are stretching back to the New Deal era, with an occasional foray even further back in time. The contributions of these studies to historical research has been important and continuing. Historians have borrowed methods, ideas, and concepts from them. Increasingly this relationship has been an interactive one, with historians' findings being incorporated and used by political scientists. The best statement of the current state of political science research in this field is in Nelson W. Polsby, "Legislatures," in Fred Greenstein and Polsby (eds.), *Handbook of Political Science* (Boston, 1975), V, 257–319.

8. Ballard Campbell, "The State Legislatures in American History: A Review Essay," *Historical Methods Newsletter* IX (1976), 185. Rodney O. Davis, "Partisanship in Jacksonian State Politics: Party Divisions in the Illinois Legislature, 1834–1841," in Robert Swierenga, *Quantification in History* (New York, 1970), 149–62; Herbert Ershkowitz and William G. Shade, "Consensus or Conflict? Political Behavior in the State Legislatures during the Jacksonian Era," *Journal of American History* LVIII (1971), 591–621; Peter Levine, *The Behavior of State Legislative Parties in the Jacksonian Era, New Jersey, 1829–1844* (Rutherford, N.J., 1977); Erling Erickson, *Banking in Frontier Iowa, 1836–1865* (Ames, Iowa, 1971); Campbell, *Representative Democracy: Public Policy and Midwest Legislatures in the Late Nineteenth Century* (Cambridge, Mass., 1980); J. Morgan Kousser, "Making Separate Equal: Integration of Black and White School Funds in Kentucky," *Journal of Interdisciplinary History* X (1980), 399–428. There is a complete listing of all of these studies in Silbey, "Congressional and State Legislative Roll-Call Studies."

9. Donald R. Matthews, *The Social Background of Political Decision-Makers* (New York, 1954). Alexander and Richard Beringer, *Anatomy of the Confederate Congress: A Study of the Influence of Member Characteristics on Legislative Voting Behavior, 1861–1865* (Nashville, 1971); Jackson T. Main, *The Upper House in Revolutionary America, 1763–1788* (Madison, 1967).

10. Stephen K. Bailey, *Congress Makes a Law: The Story Behind the Employment Act of 1946* (New York, 1950); Richard Fenno, *Congressmen in Committees* (Boston, 1969); Randall B. Ripley, "The Party Whip Organization in the House," *American Political Science Review*, LVII (1964), 561–64.

11. Bogue, "Some Dimensions of Power in the Thirty-seventh Senate," in William O. Aydelotte et al., *The Dimensions of Quantitative Research in History* (Princeton, 1972), 285–318; Robert Zemsky, *Merchants, Farmers and River Gods*

(Boston, 1971); Margaret Thompson, "'The Spider Web': Congress and Lobbying in the Age of Grant" (unpub. Ph.D. diss., University of Wisconsin, 1979).

12. Mary Ryan, "Party Formation in the United States Congress, 1789 to 1796," *Wiliam and Mary Quarterly* XXVIII (1971), 540; Rudolph Bell, *Party and Faction in American Politics: The House of Representatives, 1789–1801* (Westport, 1973).

13. Ronald Hatzenbuehler, "Party Unity and the Decision for War in the House of Representatives, 1812," *William and Mary Quarterly* XXIX (1972), 383; Bell, "Mr. Maddison's War and Long-Term Congressional Voting Behavior," *ibid.*, XXXVI (1979), 90.

14. Alvin Lynn, "Party Formation and Operation in the House of Representatives, 1824–1837" (unpub. Ph.D. diss., Rutgers University, 1972), 437, 455; U.S. Congress, *Register of Debates*, 19th Cong., 1st Sess. (1826), 1546; George Nielsen, "The Indispensable Institution: The Congressional Party during the Era of Good Feelings" (unpub. Ph.D. diss., University of Iowa, 1968).

15. James Young, *The Washington Community, 1800–1828* (New York, 1966); Bogue and Mark P. Marlaire, "Of Mess and Men: The Boardinghouse and Congressional Voting, 1821–1842," *American Journal of Political Science* XIX (1975), 207–30. See also Ronald P. Formisano, "Deferential-Participant Politics: The Early Republic's Political Culture, 1789–1840," *American Political Science Review* LXVIII (1974), 473–87.

16. Nielsen, "Indispensable Institution"; Formisano, "Deferential-Participant Politics." The definitive study of the formation of the party system in the political environment of the 1820s and 1830s remains Richard P. McCormick, *The Second American Party System: Party Formation in the Jacksonian Era* (Chapel Hill, 1966).

17. Silbey, *Shrine of Party,* 142. A somewhat different emphasis appears in Alexander, *Sectional Stress and Party Strength.*

18. Gerald Wolff, *The Kansas-Nebraska Bill: Party, Section and the Coming of the Civil War* (New York, 1977); Bogue, *The Earnest Men: Radical and Moderate Republicans in the U.S. Senate during the Civil War* (Ithaca, 1981); Shade et al., "Partisanship in the United States Senate, 1869–1901," *Journal of Interdisciplinary History* IV (1973), 185–205; Jerome M. Clubb and Santa A. Traugott, "Partisan Cleavage and Cohesion in the House of Representatives, 1861–1974," *ibid.*, VII (1977), 375–402.

19. Clubb and Howard W. Allen, "Progressive Reform and the Political System," *Pacific Northwest Quarterly* LXV (1975), 144; Erik Olssen, "The Progressive Group in Congress, 1922–1929," *The Historian* XLII (1980), 216. See also, Charles M. Dollar, "The Senate Progressive Movement, 1921–1933: A Roll-Call Analysis" (unpub. Ph.D. diss., University of Kentucky, 1966). The quotation is in the abstract of Hilty's dissertation in *Dissertation Abstracts International* XXXIV (1974), 7152A. LaFeber, *Panama Canal,* 157–58.

20. Edward Countryman, "'Consolidating Power in Revolutionary America: The Case of New York, 1775–1783," *Journal of Interdisciplinary History* VI (1976), 672. Davis, "Partisanship in Jacksonian Politics"; Ershkowitz and Shade, "Consensus or Conflict?"; Levine, *Behavior of State Legislative Parties.*

21. Erickson, *Banking in Frontier Iowa,* 119; Phyllis F. Field, *The Politics of Race in New York: The Struggle for Black Suffrage in the Civil War Era* (Ithaca, 1982); Ershkowitz and Shade, "Consensus or Conflict?" 614.

22. Silbey, "The Civil War Synthesis in American Political History," *Civil War History* X (1964), 130–40; Bogue, "Senators, Sectionalism and the 'Western'

Measures of the Republican Party," in David M. Ellis et al. (eds.), *The Frontier in American Development: Essays in Honor of Paul Wallace Gates* (Ithaca, 1969), 20–46. Analysis by cluster blocs and Guttman scaling shows that, even when individual roll-calls did not meet the demands of high partisan polarity scores (for example, 90% of one party's representatives versus 90% of the other party's legislators on a single roll-call), the distribution of party members usually showed them in different and contrasting parts of the scale of attitudes from one another.

23. Bogue, *Earnest Men*.

24. David Brady, *Congressional Voting in a Partisan Era: A Study of the McKinley Houses and a Comparison of the United States House of Representatives* (Baton Rouge, 1968), 14.

25. Charles A. Beard, *An Economic Interpretation of the Constitution of the United States* (New York, 1913). Paul Goodman, "Social Status of Party Leadership: The House of Representatives, 1797–1804," *William and Mary Quarterly* XXV (1968), 465–74; Campbell, "Ethnicity and Wisconsin General Assembly." See also Ralph A. Wooster, *The People in Power: Courthouse and Statehouse in the Lower South, 1850–1860* (Knoxville, 1969); idem, *Politicians, Planters and Plain Folk: Courthouse and Statehouse in the Upper South, 1850–1860* (Knoxville, 1975); Terry L. Seip, "Southern Representatives and Economic Measures during Reconstruction: A Quantitative and Analytical Study" (unpub. Ph.D. diss., (Louisiana State University, 1974); Bogue, *Earnest Men;* David P. Thelen, "Social Tensions and the Origins of Progressivism," *Journal of American History* LVI (1969), 323–41.

26. Bogue, "Some Dimensions of Power."

27. Sheldon Hackney, "Power to the Computers: A Revolution in History?" *Proceedings*, Spring Joint Computer Conference of the American Federation of Information Processing Societies XXXVI (1970), 278. Silbey, "Clio and Computers: Moving into Phase II, 1970–1972," *Computers and the Humanities* VII (1972), 67–79.

28. There has always been something of an implicit theory present in traditional studies. As noted earlier, most researchers in the field proceed as if legislative behavior reflected political and social tensions at work outside of the legislative body. Congressmen voted in reaction to these tensions, either as delegates of specific interest groups, or due to their desire to be reelected. They needed, therefore, to have a voting record positively perceived by a majority of their constituents. Whichever the specific construct involved, there are theoretical assumptions in both as to why voting occurs as it does. There is also something of a nondevelopmental point of view in these studies; a strong implication that the particular forces examined always have explanatory value even though times changed and sociopolitical conditions were different. Parties, sections, and regions are always with us; they always have meaning, even if they have different weights at different times. Such ideas as these have never been well articulated, consciously tested, or clearly applied in most of the historical work reviewed here. But they are there. The quotation is from Bogue, review of Alexander and Beringer. *Anatomy of Confederate Congress*, in *Historical Methods Newsletter* VI (1973), 81. See Bogue, Clubb, and William Flanigan, "The New Political History," *American Behavioral Scientist* XXI (1977), 201–20; Zemsky, "American Legislative Behavior," in Bogue (ed.), *Emerging Theoretical Models in Social and Political History* (Beverly Hills, 1973), 57–76.

29. Bogue, Clubb, Carrol R. McKibben, and Traugott, "Members of the House of Representatives and the Processes of Modernization, 1789–1969," *Journal of American History* LXIII (1976), 277.

30. Clubb et al., "Partisan Cleavage and Cohesion"; David Brady et al., "The Decline of Party in the U.S. House of Representatives, 1887–1968," *Legislative Studies Quarterly* IV (1979), 381–407.

31. Bogue, *Earnest Men;* Clubb and Traugott, "Partisan Cohesion," 381ff.

32. Bogue, Clubb, and Traugott, "House of Representatives and Modernization."

33. Polsby, "The Institutionalization of the U.S. House of Representatives," *American Political Science Review* LXII (1968), 144–68; Polsby et al., "The Growth of the Seniority System in the U.S. House of Representatives, *ibid.,* LXIII (1969), 787–807. The quotation is on 807. See also Ray Gunn, "The New York State Legislature: A Developmental Perspective, 1777–1846," *Social Science History* IV (1980), 267–94. H. Douglas Price, "Careers and Committees in the American Congress: The Problem of Structural Change," in Aydelotte, *History of Parliamentary Behavior,* 28–62; Price, "Congress and the Evolution of Legislative 'Professionalism,'" in Norman Ornstein, *Congress in Change: Evolution and Reform* (New York, 1975), 2–23.

34. Walter Dean Burnham, *Critical Elections and the Mainsprings of American Politics* (New York, 1970); Richard L. McCormick, "The Party Period and Public Policy: An Exploratory Hypothesis," *Journal of American History* LXVI (1979), 279–98.

35. Robert Zemsky et al., "The Congressional Game: A Prospectus," *Social Science History* I (1976), 101–13.

36. Kousser, "Quantitative Social Scientific History," in Kammen, *Past Before Us,* 433–56; Bogue and Clubb, "History, Quantification and the Social Sciences," *American Behavioral Scientist* XXI (1977), 167–86. See also, for a different perspective, Lee Benson, "Changing Social Science To Change the World: A Discussion Paper," *Social Science History* II (1978), 427–41; *idem, Toward the Scientific Study of History* (Philadelphia, 1972).

37. W. Wayne Shannon, *Party, Constituency and Congressional Voting: A Study of Legislative Behavior in the United States House of Representatives* (Baton Rouge, 1968); Benson, *Toward the Scientific Study,* 327–33.

38. Harry Fritz, "The War Hawks of 1812: Party Leadership in the Twelfth Congress," *Capitol Studies* V (1977), 40.

39. David Donald, *The Politics of Reconstruction, 1863–1867* (Baton Rouge, 1965).

3. Parties and Politics in Mid-Nineteenth Century America

1. *Federal Union* (Milledgeville, Ga.), 30 January 1849.

2. Robert Barnwell Rhett to William Porcher Miles, January 1860, quoted in Harold Schultz, *Nationalism and Sectionalism in South Carolina, 1850–1860* (Durham, 1950), 213–14.

3. The attitudes of the leading figure of this group, John C. Calhoun, toward political parties is well examined in William Freehling, "Spoilsmen and Interests in the Thought and Career of John C. Calhoun," *The Journal of American History* LII (June 1965), 25–42.

4. See Calhoun to H. W. Connor, 2 February 1849, Library of Congress [LC], H. W. Connor Papers (photostats).

5. Frederick Jackson Turner, *The Significance of Sections in American History* (New York, 1932), 36–37.

6. V. O. Key, *Politics, Parties and Pressure Groups* (5th ed.; New York, 1964), 229.

7. Charles Sydnor, *The Development of Southern Sectionalism, 1819–1848* (Baton Rouge, 1948), 316.

8. Glyndon G. Van Deusen, "Some Aspects of Whig Thought and Theory in the Jacksonian Period," *American Historical Review* LXIII (January 1958), 305–22.

9. The "artificial" quote is from Richard P. McCormick, *The Second American Party System* (Chapel Hill, 1966), 353. A good representative of the standard historiographic treatment of the period is Avery O. Craven, *The Coming of the Civil War* (2nd ed.; New York, 1957).

10. Joel H. Silbey, "The Civil War Synthesis in American Political History," *Civil War History* X (October 1964), 130–40.

11. James S. Young, *The Washington Community, 1800–1828* (New York, 1966). In 1824 Andrew Jackson received 97 percent of the vote in Tennessee, 76 percent in Pennsylvania, and none in Connecticut, Massachusetts, and New Hampshire, among other states.

12. Charles Sellers, "The Equilibrium Cycle in Two-Party Politics," *Public Opinion Quarterly* XXIX (Spring 1965), 16–38; Richard P. McCormick, "New Perspectives on Jacksonian Politics," *American Historical Review* LXV (January 1960), 288–301; McCormick, *Second American Party System*; Walter Dean Burnham, "The Changing Shape of the American Political Universe," *American Political Science Review* LIX (January 1965), 7–28.

13. McCormick, *Second American Party System, passim*.

14. John Minor Botts, *To the Whigs of Virginia* (Washington, 1848), 14–15.

15. The breakdown in seats in the House was as follows:

Congress	27th		28th		29th		30th		31st	
	D	W	D	W	D	W	D	W	D	W
North	48	82	81	49	78	50	84	74	51	77
South	50	48	55	26	69	21	55	35	62	29

The fluctuations in the numbers result from changes in apportionment and from seats held by third parties.

16. The discussion of congressional behavior that follows is basically drawn from my book, *The Shrine of Party, Congressional Voting Behavior, 1841–1852* (Pittsburgh, 1967). The votes were brought together in a number of Guttman scales, an attitudinal segregating and measuring technique widely used in the social sciences. It allows the analyst to handle a large number of votes on the same subject matter and refine the shadings of attitudes on an issue into more than a simple yes or no dichotomy. The scalogram is discussed in *Shrine of Party*, 149–53, 221n.

17. There is a good description of the political skirmishing around the bill in Charles Wiltse, *John C. Calhoun, Sectionalist, 1840–1850* (Indianapolis, 1951), 266–72.

18. The breakdown in the House was:

	Scale Type	Democrats No.	Democrats %	Whigs No.	Whigs %
Low	(0–2)	91	67.4	—	—
Moderate	(3–5)	21	15.6	1	1.4
High	(6–7)	23	17.0	71	98.6

19. On the tariff issue in the Twenty-seventh Congress, for example, the Democrats were 94.6 percent united in the House, the Whigs, 70 percent. In the Senate, the figures were: Democrats 90 percent, Whigs 83.3 percent.

20. In the Twenty-seventh Congress, for example, the Democrats in the Senate were only 52.3 percent united against proposals to grant federal aid for internal improvements, while the Whigs were only 56.6 percent united. On the other hand, on similar votes in the House in the Twenty-ninth Congress, the Democrats were 65.5 percent united at one end of the scale, the Whigs 87.1 percent at the other.

21. There is a useful discussion of the Democratic problems on this bill, as well as of the whole congressional session, in Charles Grier Sellers, Jr., *James K. Polk, Continentalist, 1843–1846* (Princeton, 1966).

22. See George Harris to James K. Polk, 18 June 1841, Cave Johnson to Polk, 30 December 1843, LC, James K. Polk Papers; *Southern Banner* (Athens, Ga.), 11 January, 14 March 1844; *Courier* (Charleston, S.C.), 21 June 1841; U.S., Congress, House, *Congressional Globe*, 27th Cong., 1st sess., 1841, X, 54, 60.

23. For example, in the Thirtieth Congress, eighteen of forty-five northern Democrats in the House voted in the proslavery extension or moderate positions on the scale. At the same time, six southern Whigs broke with their Democratic colleagues in the Senate on the issue.

24. These votes involved matters of war policy and land distribution, among other things.

25. Benton supposedly made the remark to Charles Sumner around 1850. James G. Blaine, *Twenty Years in Congress* (2 vols., New York, 1884), II, 545.

26. *Charleston Mercury*, 22 January 1849.

27. This whole episode is treated in my "John C. Calhoun and the Limits of Southern Congressional Unity, 1841–1850," *The Historian* XXX (November 1967), 58–71.

28. Leslie Coombs to John Clayton, 22 January 1849, LC, John M. Clayton Papers; *The Diary of James K. Polk During His Presidency, 1845–1849*, ed. Milo M. Quaife (4 vols., Chicago, 1910), IV, 249–50, 281, 283.

29. Howell Cobb to Robert J. Walker, 2 June 1849, New-York Historical Society, Robert J. Walker Folder.

30. Thomas B. Alexander, *Sectional Stress and Party Strength* (Nashville, 1967), 98, 94.

31. Gerald Wolff, "The Slavocracy and the Homestead Problem of 1854," *Agricultural History* XL (April 1966), 101–12.

32. *Ibid.*, 111.

33. Dean Yarwood, "Legislative Persistence: A Comparison of the United

States Senate in 1850 and 1860," *Midwest Journal of Political Science* XI (May 1967), 193–211.

34. Sellers, "Equilibrium Cycle," 22. The whole concept of realignment and other electoral patterns is discussed in Angus Campbell et al., *Elections and the Political Order* (New York, 1966) and their *The American Voter* (New York, 1960).

35. Alexander, *Sectional Stress, passim.*

36. Letter, Henry Hiliard to the editors, *National Intelligencer*, 2 June 1857.

37. Alexander, *Sectional Stress*, 98.

38. *Richmond Enquirer*, 17 November 1856.

39. Lee Benson, *The Concept of Jacksonian Democracy: New York As a Test Case* (Princeton, 1961), 291n. Some of this is worked out and demonstrated in Michael Holt, *Forging a Majority, The Formation of the Republican Party in Pittsburgh, 1848–1860* (New Haven, 1969), and Ronald Formisano, *The Birth of Mass Political Parties: Michigan, 1827–1861* (Princeton, 1971).

40. All presidential election statistics are drawn from Sven Petersen, *A Statistical History of the American Presidential Elections* (New York, 1963), and Walter Dean Burnham, *Presidential Ballots, 1836–1892* (Baltimore, 1955).

41. The Cobb speech is quoted in Zachary Taylor Johnson, *The Political Policies of Howell Cobb* (Nashville, 1929), 143. The Wise remark is in *The Letters of Stephen A. Douglas*, ed. Robert Johannsen (Urbana, 1961), 429n.

42. Robert B. Rhett to William P. Miles, January 1860, quoted in Schultz, *Nationalism and Sectionalism*, 213–14.

43. Angus Campbell, "Voters and Elections, Past and Present," *Journal of Politics* XXVI (November 1964). This is well developed in his *The American Voter.*

44. William Bissell to William Martin, 5 February 1850, Illinois State Historical Library, William Bissell Folder.

45. *Daily Advertiser* (Rochester, N.Y.), 18 June 1850.

46. Horace Greeley to J. S. Pike, 28 April 1850, quoted in Jeter Isely, *Horace Greeley and the Republican Party* (Princeton, 1947), 34.

47. I am developing this theme in a book with the working title of "The Maintenance of the Democratic Party, 1850–1870."

48. In the off-year elections of 1865, the Democrats averaged over 47 percent of the vote in these three states in races for statewide offices. Two years later they won two of three such races contested and averaged 50.6 percent of the vote. Even in the bad Democratic year of 1866, they won over 49 percent of the vote in the New York gubernatorial race.

49. *Diary of Gideon Welles*, ed. Howard K. Beale (3 vols., New York, 1960), II, 427.

50. Blaine, *Twenty Years in Congress*, II, 407–8.

51. Allen Weinstein, "Party Politics and the Silver Question, 1875–1878," paper delivered at the Southern Historical Association Convention, New Orleans, 1968.

52. Robert Wiebe, *The Search for Order, 1877–1920* (New York, 1967); Burnham, "Changing Shape of the American Political Universe"; David Rothman, *Politics and Power: The United States Senate, 1869–1901* (Cambridge, Mass., 1966).

53. Donald Stokes, "Party Loyalty and the Likelihood of Deviating Elections," in Campbell et al., *Elections and the Political Order*, 127.

54. U.S. Congress, House, *Congressional Globe*, 30th Cong., 1 sess., 1847–48, XIX, Appendix, 775.

4. "The Salt of the Nation"

1. Lee Benson, *The Concept of Jacksonian Democracy: New York As a Test Case* (Princeton, 1961); Richard P. McCormick, *The Second American Party System: Party Formation in the Jacksonian Era* (Chapel Hill, 1966); William N. Chambers and Walter Dean Burnham, *The American Party Systems* (New York, 1967); Bernard Bailyn, *The Ideological Origins of the American Revolution* (Cambridge, Mass., 1967).

2. There are overviews of the work of the new political history in a series of essays by Allan G. Bogue, "United States: The 'New' Political History," in Walter Laqueur and George L. Mosse (eds.), *The New History: Trends in Historical Research and Writing Since World War II* (New York, 1967), 185–207; Allan G. Bogue, Jerome M. Clubb and William Flanigan, "The New Political History," *American Behavioral Scientist* XXI 21 (December 1977), 201–20; Bogue, "Recent Developments in Political History: The Case of the United States," in *The Frontiers of Human Knowledge* (Uppsala, 1978), 79–109; Bogue, "The New Political History in the 1970s," in Michael G. Kammen (ed.), *The Past Before Us: Contemporary Historical Writing in the United States* (Ithaca, 1980), 231–51; and, Bogue, "Numerical and Formal Analysis in United States History," *Journal of Interdisciplinary History* XII (Summer 1981), 137–75.

3. The lumper-splitter dichotomy is announced in Jack Hexter, *On Historians: Reappraisals of Some of the Makers of Modern History* (Cambridge, Mass., 1979), 241–42, quoting Donald Kagan.

4. Eugene Genovese, *The Political Economy of Slavery* (New York, 1965); Eric Foner, *Free Soil, Free Labor, Free Men: The Ideology of the Republican Party Before the Civil War* (New York, 1970); Daniel Walker Howe, *The Political Culture of the American Whigs* (Chicago, 1979).

5. John Higham, "American Historiography in the 1960's," in Higham, *Writing American History: Essays on Modern Scholarship* (Bloomington, 1970), 157–74.

6. Ronald P. Formisano, "Toward a Reorientation of Jacksonian Politics, A Review of the Literature, 1959–1975," *Journal of American History* LXIII (June 1975), 43.

7. Michael F. Holt, *The Political Crisis of the 1850s* (New York, 1978); Richard L. McCormick, "The Party Period and Public Policy: An Exploratory Hypothesis," *Journal of American History* LXVI (September 1979), 279–98; William Gienapp, "'Politics Seems To Enter into Everything': Political Culture in the North, 1840–1860" (paper presented as part of the Walter Precott Webb Memorial Lecture Series, University of Texas at Arlington, 1981).

8. The five-party system thesis is described in Chambers and Burnham, *American Party Systems*. The idea has been most recently used in Paul Kleppner (ed.), *The Evolution of American Electoral Systems* (Westport, 1981).

9. These patterns can be followed in the essays in Kleppner, *Evolution of American Electoral Systems*.

10. Frank Sorauf, *Party Politics in America* (Boston, 1968); Ronald P. Formisano, "Deferential-Participant Politics: The Early Republic's Political Culture, 1789–1840," *American Political Science Review* LVIII (June 1974), 437–87; and the essays by Formisano and William Shade in Kleppner, *Evolution of American Electoral Systems*, 33–111.

11. That view could be summed up, "new parties emerged and the old parties split into warring factions." David M. Ellis, *Landlords and Farmers in the Hudson-Mohawk Region, 1790–1850* (Ithaca, 1946), 268.

12. See, for example, the recent outpouring of books on the Free-Soilers, the Free Soil election of 1848, and related matters. Frederick J. Blue, *The Free Soilers: Third Party Politics, 1848–54* (Urbana, 1973); Joseph Rayback, *Free Soil: The Election of 1848* (Lexington, 1970); John Mayfield, *Rehearsal for Republicanism: Free Soil and the Politics of Anti-Slavery* (Port Washington, N.Y., 1980).

13. The quotation is from Bernard Bailyn "The Challenge of Modern Historiography," *American Historical Review* LXXXVII (February 1982), 6. The pattern of party continuity is described in Joel H. Silbey, *The Shrine of Party: Congressional Voting Behavior, 1841–1852* (Pittsburgh, 1967); and in Silbey, *A Respectable Minority: The Democratic Party in the Civil War Era, 1860–1868* (New York, 1977).

14. Benson, *Concept*; Holt, *Political Crisis of the 1850s*; Robert Kelley, *The Cultural Pattern in American Politics: The First Century* (New York, 1979); Paul Kleppner, *The Third Electoral System, 1853–1892: Parties, Voters, and Political Cultures* (Chapel Hill, 1979). I have summed up the literature on this subject in Joel H. Silbey, "'Let the People See': Reflections on Ethnoreligious Forces in American Politics" (unpublished paper, 1981).

15. William Shade, *Banks or No Banks: The Money Issue in Western Politics, 1832–1865* (Detroit, 1972); Kleppner, *Third Electoral System*.

16. Lee Benson and Joel H. Silbey, "Toward a Theory of Stability and Change in American Voting Patterns: New York State, 1792–1970," in Joel H. Silbey et al. (eds.), *The History of American Electoral Behavior* (Princeton, 1978), 78–105. See also, Benson and Silbey "American Political Eras, 1788–1984: Toward a Normative, Substantive and Conceptual Framework for the Historical Study of American Political Behavior" (paper prepared for delivery at annual meeting of the Social Science History Association, 1978).

17. Richard P. McCormick, *The Presidential Game: The Origins of American Politics* (New York, 1982).

18. Patricia Bonomi et al. (eds.), *The American Constitutional System Under Strong and Weak Parties* (New York, 1981), x.

19. McCormick, *Second American Party System*.

20. *Albany State Register*, September 25, 1850.

21. Howe, *Political Culture of the American Whigs*, 14.

22. Holt, *Political Crisis of the 1850s* is good on this. See also chapter I of Silbey, *A Respectable Minority*.

23. *American Whig Review* IX (June 1849), 553.

24. *Democratic Review* XII (May 1843), 485.

25. Silbey, *Shrine of Party*; Herbert Ershkowitz and William Shade, "Consensus or Conflict? Political Behavior in the State Legislatures During the Jacksonian Era," *Journal of American History* LVIII (December 1971), 591–621.

26. The presidential turnout figures are reported in *Historical Statistics of the United States from Colonial Times to 1970* (Washington, 1976), II, 1072. They were computed by Walter Dean Burnham. One state's voter turnout rates are reported in *Census of the State of New York, 1865* (Albany, 1866.)

27. This is the conclusion of most of the studies of popular voting already referred to. The findings are summed up in Silbey, *Respectable Minority*, chap. I.

28. Michael Les Benedict, "The Party Going Strong: Congress and Elections in the Mid-19th Century," *Congress & the Presidency: A Journal of Capital Studies* IX (Winter 1981–82), 37–60.

29. Edward Pessen, "We Are All Jeffersonians, We Are All Jacksonians: Or a Pox on Stultifying Periodizations," *Journal of the Early Republic* I (Spring 1981), 25.

See also Pessen, "How Different from Each Other Were the Ante-bellum North and South?," *American Historical Review* LXXXV (December 1980), 1139–40.

30. McCormick, *Presidential Game,* 166.

31. As Willie Lee Rose has written, "surely the politicians were not endlessly speaking and writing about issues for their own elite pleasure. They had a target." "Comment" [on Robert Kelley, "Ideology and Political Culture from Jefferson to Nixon,"], *American Historical Review* LXXXII (June 1977), 582.

32. On the Republican synthesis see Robert F. Shallhope, "Towards a Republican Synthesis: The Emergence of an Understanding of Republicanism in American Historiography," *William and Mary Quarterly* XIX (January 1972), 49–80.

33. *Democratic Review* XL (October 1957), 296.

34. See Howe, *Political Culture of American Whigs;* Silbey, *Shrine of Party* and *A Respectable Minority;* Holt, *Political Crisis of 1850s;* Kelley, *Cultural Pattern;* Ronald P. Formisano, *The Birth of Mass Political Parties: Michigan, 1827–1861* (Princeton, 1971); Shade, *Banks or No Banks.*

35. See, an example, Silas Wright to James K. Polk, July 21, 1845, in Ransom Gillett, *The Life and Times of Silas Wright* (Albany, 1874), II, 1648.

36. Troy, Ohio, *Investigator & Expositor* (September 1839), 42; R. McKinley Ormsby, *A History of the Whig Party* (Boston, 1859), 294; *Democratic Review* XL (July 1857), 7; Wooster Sherman to the Chairman, Tammany Committee, November 3, 1859, Isaac V. Fowler Papers, New-York Historical Society.

37. Formisano, "Toward a Reorientation," 51.

38. The quotation is the title of Horace Greeley's pertinent article in *The Whig Almanac, 1843,* 16–17.

39. See, for example, Albany, *The Rough Hewer,* May 28, 1840; Washington, *The Campaign,* July 10, 1852; "Taylor Whiggery Exposed" (n.p., 1848), 8; "Address to the People of Massachusetts" (n.p. [1852]), 8; *Democratic Review,* XIII (July 1843), 100.

40. *Democratic Review* XXXVII (April 1856), 316.

41. And so often did contemporary candidates and leaders of defeated factions.

42. This is, of course, the thesis of Robert Michels, *Political Parties* (New York, 1915; reprt. 1949).

43. Giovanni Sartori, *Parties and Party Systems: A Framework for Analysis* (New York, 1976), 25.

44. Albany *Atlas,* 22 February 1848.

45. "Speech of the Hon. John Minor Botts. . . ." (New York, 1859), 12; *Democratic Review* XI (July 1842), 96.

46. Andrew Jackson to James Gunn, February 23, 1835, in *Nile's Register,* 4 April 1835, 84.

47. "The Proceedings of the Democratic National Convention, Held at Baltimore, May 22, 1848" (n.p. [1848]), 6; *Democratic Review* XXX (May 1852), 472.

48. As a Whig writer put it in 1846, "without organization, method, discipline, agreement, in short *without party,* we cannot accomplish our purposes." *American Whig Review* IV (November 1846), 446.

49. Silbey, *Shrine of Party;* Ershkowitz and Shade, "Consensus or Conflict."

50. Gerald Pomper, *Elections in America: Control and Influence in Democratic Politics* (New York, 1968) chaps. 7–8; Benjamin Ginsberg, "Elections and Public Policy," *American Political Science Review* LXX (March 1976), 41–49.

51. *Congressional Globe,* 26th Cong., 1st sess., Appendix, 52.

52. The best book on the polity in this period which catches the changes under way is Morton Keller, *Affairs of State: Public Life in Late Nineteenth Century America* (Cambridge, Mass., 1977).

5. "Let the People See"

1. *New York Tribune* (weekly), September 11, 1852.

2. Greeley was much involved in battles with the Know Nothings in the 1850s who made their position quite clear. "Romanism as a political system, is the avowed and implacable foe of independent thought and action, of improvement, and of the rights of individuals and nation." *Albany Statesman*, May 25, 1857.

3. Nathan Glazer, "American Jews: Three Conflicts of Loyalties," in S. M. Lipset (ed.), *The Third Century: America As a Post-Industrial Society* (Chicago, 1979), 224.

4. Quoted in Debra Dash Moore, *At Home in America: Second Generation New York Jews* (New York, 1981), 213.

5. Bernard R. Barber, Review of Glenn Tinder, *Community* in *The New Republic*, June 28, 1980, 34. See also, Murray Friedman, "Religion and Politics in the Age of Pluralism," *Publius* X (Summer 1980), 45–75.

6. Ronald P. Formisano, *The Birth of Mass Political Parties: Michigan, 1827–1861* (Princeton, 1971), 9.

7. The classic volumes in the new political history include Lee Benson, *The Concept of Jacksonian Democracy: New York As a Test Case* (Princeton, 1961); Formisano, *Birth of Mass Political Parties*; Michael Holt, *Forging a Majority: The Forming of the Republican Party in Pittsburgh, 1848–1860* (New Haven, 1969); Richard J. Jensen, *The Winning of the Midwest: Social and Political Conflict, 1888–1896* (Chicago, 1971); Samuel T. McSeveney, *The Politics of Depression: Political Behavior in the Northeast, 1893–1896* (New York, 1972); Bruce Stave, *The New Deal and the Last Hurrah: Pittsburgh Machine Politics*, (Pittsburgh, 1970); John Allswang, *A House for All Peoples: Ethnic Politics in Chicago, 1890–1936* (Lexington, 1971); David Brye, *Wisconsin Voting Patterns in the Twentieth Century, 1900–1950* (New York, 1979); Robert Kelley, *The Cultural Pattern in American Politics, The First Century* (New York, 1979). Joel H. Silbey et al., *The History of American Electoral Behavior* (Princeton, 1978). Many seminal articles are included in Joel H. Silbey and Samuel T. McSeveney (eds.), *Voters, Parties and Elections* (Waltham, 1971).

Important articles describing and assessing the movement include Robert Swierenga, "Ethnocultural Political Analysis: A New Approach to American Ethnic Studies," *Journal of American Studies* V (April 1971), 59–79; Samuel T. McSeveney, "Ethnic Groups, Ethnic Conflicts, and Recent Quantitative Research in American Political History," *International Migration Review* VII (Spring 1973), 14–33; Richard L. McCormick, "Ethno-cultural Interpretations of Nineteenth-Century American Voting Behavior," *Political Science Quarterly* LXXXIX (June 1974), 351–77; Allan G. Bogue, "The New Political History in the 1970s," in Michael G. Kammen (ed.), *The Past Before Us: Contemporary Historical Writing in the United States* (Ithaca, 1980), 231–51.

8. Benson, *Concept of Jacksonian Democracy*, 165.

9. Samuel P. Hays, "Political Parties and the Community-Society Continuum," in William Nisbet Chambers and Walter Dean Burnham, *The American Party Systems* (2nd ed.; New York, 1975), 158.

10. Arthur Mann, *The One and the Many: Reflections on the American Identity* (Chicago, 1979), 73.

11. Quoted in Coleman J. Barry, *The Catholic Church and German-Americans* (Milwaukee, 1953), 11.

12. Paul Kleppner, *The Third Electoral System, 1853–1892; Parties, Voters and Political Cultures* (Chapel Hill, 1979), 197.

13. *The Know-Nothing Almanac for 1855* (New York, 1855), 26.

14. Alan J. Lichtman, *Prejudice and the Old Politics: The Presidential Election of 1928* (Chapel Hill, 1979), 10.

15. *The Democratic Review*, October 1855, 342; January 1856, 11.

16. Mann, *One and the Many*, 73.

17. Hays, "Community-Society Continuum,"158.

18. Kelley, *Cultural Pattern in American Politics*, 265–66.

19. Kleppner's two books are, of course, *The Third Electoral System* and *The Cross of Culture: A Social Analysis of Midwestern Politics, 1850–1900* (New York, 1970). I am also dealing here with two articles in anthologies: "From Ethnoreligious Conflict to 'Social Harmony': Coalitional and Party Transformations in the 1890s," in Seymour Martin Lipset (ed.), *Emerging Coalitions in American Politics* (San Francisco, 1978); and "The Greenback and Prohibition Parties," in Arthur M. Schlesinger, Jr., ed., *History of U.S. Political Parties* (New York, 1973), II, 1549–1696, and with an unpublished paper kindly shown to me by Professor Kleppner (and written with Stephen C. Baker), "The Impact of Depressions on Mass Political Behavior: The United States in the 1870s, the 1890s, and the 1930s."

20. Kleppner, *Cross of Culture*, 18.

21. Kleppner, *Third Electoral System*, 144.

22. *Ibid.*, 58. The dust jacket of this book reminds us that Kleppner's work challenges "the liberal-rationalist assumptions that have dominated political history."

23. *Ibid.*, 371.

24. As Allan Bogue has written "the challenge of modern research lies in assigning the proper weights to a number of independent variables rather than in the admission that there is more than one." "Billington's *Frederick Jackson Turner*: An Essay Review," *Pacific Northwest Quarterly* LXIV (October 1973), 177.

25. Philip Ennis, "The Contextual Dimension in Voting," in William N. McPhee and William A. Glaser, *Public Opinion and Congressional Elections* (Glencoe, 1962), 184.

26. Kleppner, *Third Electoral System*, 369–70.

27. *Ibid.*, 367.

28. Dale Baum, "The Political World of Massachusetts Radicalism: Voting Behavior and Ideology in the Civil War Party System, 1854–1872" (unpub. Ph.D. diss., University of Minnesota, 1978), 353.

29. Kleppner, *Third Electoral System*, 196–97.

30. *Ibid.*, 328; Kleppner, "From Ethnoreligious Conflict to 'Social Harmony'," 53; Richard L. McCormick, "Shaping Republican Strategy: Political Change in New York State, 1893–1910" (unpub. Ph.D. diss., Yale University, 1976), 241.

31. On outbreaks of violence, see Michael Feldberg, *The Philadelphia Riots of 1844: A Study of Ethnic Conflict* (Westport, 1975).

32. James Turner, "Recovering the Uses of History," *Yale Review* (Winter 1981), 223.

33. Joan L. Fee, "Religion, Ethnicity and Class in American Electoral Behavior," in William J. Crotty (ed.), *The Party Symbol* (San Francisco, 1980), 271.

34. Dale C. Nelson, "Ethnicity and Socioeconomic Status As Sources of Participation: The Case for Ethnic Political Culture," *American Political Science Review* LXXIII (December 1979), 1026-27.

35. See especially, Walter Dean Burnham, "American Voting Behavior and the 1964 Election," in Silbey and McSeveney, *Voters, Parties and Elections*, 366-95. *Time*, July 21, 1980, 9. The Associated Press story is in *The Ithaca Journal*, July 11, 1980.

36. The libertarian is quoted in the *New York Review of Books*, November 19, 1981, 21. Broder is in the *Manchester Guardian Weekly*, December 14, 1980, 17. See also *Time*, January 19, 1981, 86.

37. Mann, *The One and the Many*, 17-18.

38. Walter Dean Burnham, "The 1980 Earthquake: Realignment, Reaction, or What?," in Thomas Ferguson and Joel Rogers, *The Hidden Election: Politics and Economics in the 1980 Presidential Campaign* (New York, 1981), 106.

39. Mann, *The One and the Many*, 44; *Time*, July 7, 1980, 23.

40. *U.S. News and World Report*, July 7, 1980, 33.

41. Walter Dean Burnham, "American Politics in the 1980s," *Dissent* (Spring 1980), 150.

42. Morton Keller, *Affairs of State: Public Life in Late Nineteenth Century America* (Cambridge, Mass., 1977), 35.

43. Richard F. Schier, Review of Lipset, *Emerging Coalitions*, in *American Political Science Review* LXXIV (March 1980), 205.

44. Richard J. Jensen, "Armies, Ad-Men and Crusaders: Types of Interparty Election Campaigns," *The History Teacher* II (January 1969), 33-50; and Jensen, *Winning of the Midwest*.

45. Kleppner, *Third Electoral System*, 142.

46. Lichtman, *Prejudice and the Old Politics*. For more recent times see Benjamin Page, *Choices and Echoes in Presidential Elections* (Chicago, 1978).

47. Burnham, "American Politics in the 1980s," 150.

48. See, of course, Angus Campbell et al., *The American Voter* (New York, 1960) and the vast literature it has spawned.

49. Geoffrey Blodgett, "A New Look at the American Gilded Age," *Historical Reflections* I (Winter 1974), 235. One might ask where economic differences fit into this politics, under what conditions, whether they are primarily the concern of political elites and not the electoral masses, etc. It is a question that has to be answered and approached with these other matters in mind and well in hand. For some interesting reflections on such conditions see Lee Benson, "Group Conflict: A Critique of some Marxian and Tocquevillian Theories," in Allan G. Bogue (ed.), *Emerging Theoretical Models in Social and Political History* (Beverly Hills, 1973), 123-50.

50. Kleppner, *Third Electoral System*, 238.

51. See McSeveney, *Politics of Depression, passim* for the 1890s; and James L. Sundquist, *Dynamics of the Party System: Alignment and Realignment of Political Parties in the United States* (Washington, 1973) for the 1930s.

52. Walter Dean Burnham, "American Politics in the 1970's: Beyond Party," in Chambers and Burnham, *The American Party Systems*, 308-57.

53. James David Barber, *The Pulse of Politics, Electing Presidents in the Media Age* (New York, 1980).

54. For one example of the revision of our general understanding of the structure of voting due to contextual effects, see Lee Benson, Joel H. Silbey, and Phyllis F. Field, "Toward a Theory of Stability and Change in American Voting Patterns: New York State, 1792–1970," in Silbey, Bogue, and Flanigan, *History of American Electoral Behavior*, 78–105.

55. Burnham, "Voting Behavior and the 1964 Election," in Silbey and McSeveney, *Voters, Parties and Elections*, 391.

56. Burnham, "Politics in the 1970's," *passim.*

57. Christopher Lasch, "On Richard Hofstadter," *New York Review of Books* XX (March 8, 1973), 12.

58. *Congressional Record*, 97th Cong., 1st sess., S3929 (April 27, 1981).

6. "There Are Other Questions . . ."

1. There is no inclusive study of the Democratic party in these years. A useful overview is Michael F. Holt, "The Democratic Party 1828–1860," in Arthur M. Schlesinger, Jr., *History of U.S. Political Parties* (New York, 1973), 1:497–571.

2. The phrase is Eric Foner's and appears in the best study of this group, *Free Soil, Free Labor, Free Men: The Ideology of the Republican Party Before the Civil War* (New York, 1970), chap. 5.

3. Joel H. Silbey, "The Civil War Synthesis in American Political History," *Civil War History* X (June 1964): 130–40.

4. Eric Foner, *Politics and Ideology in the Age of the Civil War* (New York, 1980), p. 72.

5. Richard Sewell, *Ballots for Freedom: Antislavery Politics in the United States, 1837–1860* (New York, 1976), 138, 84.

6. Aileen Kraditor, "The Liberty and Free Soil Parties," in Schlesinger, ed., *History of U.S. Political Parties*, 1: 753.

7. Silbey, "Civil War Synthesis."

8. George Fredrickson, *The Black Image in the White Mind: The Debate on Afro-American Character and Destiny, 1817–1914* (New York, 1971); Eugene Berwanger, *The Frontier Against Slavery: Western Anti-Negro Prejudice and the Slavery Extension Controversy* (Urbana, 1967); C. Vann Woodward, "The Antislavery Myth," *American Scholar* XXXI (Summer 1962): 312–28; Joel H. Silbey, *The Shrine of Party: Congressional Voting Behavior, 1841–1852* (Pittsburgh, 1967).

9. Joel H. Silbey, *A Respectable Minority: The Democratic Party in the Civil War Era, 1860–1868* (New York, 1977).

10. The *Address* is reprinted in Joel H. Silbey, "The Election of 1836," in Arthur M. Schlesinger, Jr., ed., *History of American Presidential Elections, 1789–1968* (New York, 1971), 1: 623; *Washington Globe*, May 18, 1835.

11. Mount Vernon (Ohio) *Democratic Banner*, February 13, 1849, in Athens (Ga.) *Southern Banner*, March 1, 1849; *Detroit Free Press*, March 17, August 23, 1849; Spgingfield *Illinois State Register*, December 8, 1848. The party's national platforms are reprinted in Kirk H. Porter and Donald Bruce Johnson, *National Party Platforms 1840–1964* (3rd ed.; Urbana, 1965).

12. David M. Potter, *The Impending Crisis, 1848–1861* (New York, 1976), 79.

13. "Sketches of the Lives of Franklin Pierce and William R. King. . . ." (Washington, D.C., 1852), 8, 9; *Washington Globe*, October 14, 1835, May 28, 1836.

14. D. L. Gregg to Sidney Breese, February 15, 1848, Sidney Breese Papers, Illinois State Historical Society; *Congressional Globe*, 29th Cong., 2nd sess., Appendix, 159, 322; *Detroit Free Press*, December 31, 1847.

15. *Albany Argus*, November 1, 2, 1848; Springfield *Illinois State Register*, July 14, 1848; William Bissell to William Martin, February 5, 1850, Miscellaneous Papers, Illinois State Historical Library; Circular dated May 7, 1850, in William L. Marcy Papers, Library of Congress; Nahum Capen to William L. Marcy, May 23, 1851, Marcy Papers.

16. *Illinois State Register*, October 4, 1859; *Frémont—His Supporters and Their Record* (Washington, D.C. [1856]), 12; *Remarks on the Majority and Minority Reports of the Select Committee on Secret Societies of the House of Delegates of Maryland* (New York, 1856), 28.

17. Silas Wright to Thomas Ritchie, May 10, 1835, Martin Van Buren Papers, Library of Congress.

18. Charles Z. Lincoln, ed., *Messages from the Governors* (Albany, 1909), 3: 573, 582n, 589; Silbey, "Election of 1836," in Schlesinger, Jr., ed., *History of Elections*, 1: 590.
In related matters as well the Democrats remained consistent. As early as 1837, Democrats in the New York State legislature rejected decisively with their votes pro-black suffrage resolutions. At the 1846 Constitutional convention in that state they took the lead in resisting efforts to extend voting rights to blacks. Alan M. Kraut and Phyllis F. Field, "Politics Versus Principles: The Partisan Response to 'Bible Politics' in New York State," *Civil War History* XXV (June 1979): 101–18.

19. "Address of the Democratic Members of the Legislature to the People of Virginia," ([Richmond, 1836]), pp. 7, 10; *Federal Union*, October 3, 1836; Gideon Pillow to Martin Van Buren, March 2, 1836, Van Buren Papers.

20. Silbey, *Shrine of Party*, passim.

21. Chaplain Morrison, *Democratic Politics and Sectionalism: The Wilmot Proviso Controversy* (Chapel Hill, 1967), 22ff.; Ernest Muller, "Preston King: A Political Biography" (Ph.D. diss., Columbia University, 1957), 420.

22. Thomas B. Alexander, "The Dimensions of Voter Partisan Constancy in Presidential Elections from 1840 to 1860" (Paper presented as part of the Walter Prescott Webb Memorial Lecture Series, University of Texas at Arlington, 1981).

23. William Gienapp, "'Politics Seems To Enter into Everything': Political Culture in the North, 1840–1860" (Paper prepared as part of the Walter Prescott Webb Memorial Lecture Series, University of Texas at Arlington, 1981), 49.

24. *Ibid.*, 51.

25. Jonathan Nathan to Fish, January 3, 1844, Hamilton Fish Papers, New-York Historical Society; Azariah C. Flagg to "Dear Sir," October 14, 1844, Azariah C. Flagg Papers, New York Public Library.

26. Lee Benson, *The Concept of Jacksonian Democracy: New York As a Test Case* (Princeton, 1961), 208n. See also, Alan M. Kraut, "The Liberty Men of New York: Political Abolitionism in New York State, 1840–1848" (Ph.D. diss., Cornell University, 1975); Ronald P. Formisano, *The Birth of Mass Political Parties: Michigan, 1827–1861* (Princeton, 1971), p. 120–21.

27. *New York Tribune*, November 23, 1844.

28. Kraut and Field, "Politics Versus Principles," 110.

29. James Buchanan to William L. Marcy, November 21, 1850, Marcy Papers. See also, Joseph Rayback, *Free Soil: The Election of 1848* (Lexington, 1971); and Frederick Blue, *The Free Soilers: Third Party Politics, 1848–1854* (Urbana, 1973).

30. Keven Sweeney, "Rum, Romanism, Representation, and Reform: Coalition Politics in Massachusetts, 1847–1835," *Civil War History* XXII (June 1976): 116–37.

31. Ray M. Shortridge, "Voting For Minor Parties in the Antebellum Midwest," *Indiana Magazine of History* 74 (June 1978): 130.

These four states cast approximately one-third of the popular vote in the Northern states between 1840 and 1848.

32. Philip C. Davis, "The Persistence of Partisan Alignment: Leaders and Votes in New Jersey, 1840–1860" (Ph.D. diss., Washington University, 1978).

33. Paul Kleppner, *The Third Electoral System, 1853–1892, Parties, Voters and Political Cultures* (Chapel Hill, 1979), 65; Michael Holt, *The Political Crisis of the 1850s* (New York, 1978), 65.

34. As Thomas P. Alexander has written, "the voters rode out the stormy national controversies from 1848 through the compromise of 1850 and were still able to regroup for the 1852 presidential election very nearly in the party pattern of the elections preceding the sectional storm, those of 1840 and 1844. This is striking evidence of the power of party labels to direct the response of all but a small proportion of voters. The deviations of 1848 were substantial principally because of Van Buren's name and the comfort it gave to Democratically aligned voters aroused to cast a protest vote on either ideological or party factional grounds." Alexander, "Dimensions of Voters Partisan Constancy," 38.

35. *Argus*, November 28, 1848.

36. *Cass and Taylor: Is Either Worthy of a Freeman's Suffrage?* (n.p., 1848), 1.

37. John Y. Mason to Lewis Cass, September 25, 1848, Lewis Cass Papers, William E. Clements Library, University of Michigan.

38. Foner, *Free Soil, Free Labor, Free Men*, 165; Sewell, *Ballots for Freedom*, 263; David Donald, review of Sewell, *Journal of American History* 64 (December 1977): 798.

39. Dale Baum, "Know-Nothingism and the Republican Majority in Massachusetts: The Political Realignment of the 1850's," *Journal of American History* LXIV (March 1978): 959–86.

The estimates were computed by means of an ecological regression formula. See J. Morgan Kousser, "Ecological Regression and the Analysis of Past Politics," *Journal of Interdisciplinary History* IV (Autumn 1973): 237–62.

40. Ray M. Shortridge, "The Voter Realignment in the Midwest During the 1850s," *American Politics Quarterly* IV (April 1976): 193–222.

41. This material is drawn from a project on New York State voting patterns under way by Lee Benson and myself.

42. Shortridge, "Voter Realignment in the Midwest."

43. *Ibid.*, 219.

44. Richard H. Brown, "The Missouri Crisis, Slavery, and the Politics of Jacksonianism," *South Atlantic Quarterly*, LXV (Winter 1966): 70–71.

45. Leonard Richards, "The Jacksonians and Slavery," in Lewis Perry and Michael Fellman, eds., *Antislavery Reconsidered: New Perspectives on the Abolitionists* (Baton Rouge, 1979), 99–118.

46. Brown, "Missouri Crisis," 55; Daniel Walker Howe, *The Political Culture of the American Whigs* (Chicago, 1979), 147.

47. John McFaul, "Expediency vs. Morality: Jacksonian Politics and Slavery," *Journal of American History* LXII (June 1975): 24–39. The quotation is on p. 25.

48. Sewell, *Ballots for Freedom*, 227; Edward Pessen, "How Different from Each Other Were the Antebellum North and South?" *American Historical Review* LXXXV (December 1980): 1139.

49. Much of the material on political culture that follows stems from two papers: Lee Benson and Joel H. Silbey, "The American Votes, 1854–1860 and 1948–1984" (presented at the Annual Meeting of the Organization of American Historians, 1978); and, by the same, "American Political Eras, 1788–1984" (presented at the Annual Meeting of the Social Science History Association, 1978).

50. See, Silbey, *A Respectable Minority*, chap. 1, "A Party of Habits, Prejudices and Traditions."

51. See, for example, the description in Richard S. Alcorn, "Leadership and Stability in Mid-Nineteenth Century America: A Case Study of an Illinois Town," *Journal of American History* LXI (December 1974): 693; Gienapp, "'Politics Seems To Enter into Everything,'" *passim*.

52. The election pamphlets and "Addresses to the People," issued by each party throughout the period from the 1830s onward reflected these characteristics repeatedly. The question of what was at stake was clearly spelled out and the relationship of that to community norms and fears heavily stressed. See, as examples of such, Richard Rush, *To the Democratic Citizens of Pennsylvania* (n.p., 1844), and *Addresses and Resolutions of the Democratic State Convention of New York . . . January 26, 1848* (n.p. [1848]).

53. See Silbey, *Respectable Minority*, 7–11.

54. *The Utica Convention: Voice of New York* (Albany, 1848), 21; *Speech of Hon. John A. Dix, of New York, at the Mass Meeting . . . Newburgh . . . 26th July, 1852* (n.p. [1852]), 1.

55. *Official Proceedings of the National Democratic Convention, Held in Cincinnati, June 2–6, 1856* (Cincinnati, 1856), 22.

56. See Silas Wright to James K. Polk, July 21, 1845, in Ransom Gillett, *The Life and Times of Silas Wright* (Albany, 1874), 2: 1648.

57. As Giovanni Sartori has written: "To be sure, party members are not altruists, and the existence of parties by no means eliminates selfish and unscrupulous motivations. The power-seeking drives of politicians remain constant. What varies is the processing and the constraints that are brought to bear on such drives. Even if the party politician is motivated by crude self-interest, his behavior must depart—if the constraints of the system are operative—from the motivation. The difference is, then, that parties are instrumental to collective benefits, to an end that is not merely the private benefit of the contestants." Giovanni Sartori, *Parties and Party Systems: A Framework for Analysis* (New York, 1976), 25.

58. This comes through in both the correspondence and newspaper editorials written by mainstream Democratic sources. See, for example, Columbus *Ohio Statesman* in Richmond *Enquirer*, July 1, 1848; Washington *Union*, April 11, 1848.

59. *Address of Democratic Members to People of Virginia*, 14. John Niven describes one Connecticut politician of the time as "a fierce partisan, a Democrat who worshipped at the shrine of organization. Principle and party were so fused in

his mind that it was difficult for him to grasp new issues if they seemed to threaten the Democracy." Niven, *Gideon Welles: Lincoln's Secretary of the Navy* (New York, 1973), 225.

60. *Proceedings of the Republican Convention* [of Virginia] ([Richmond, 1839]), 10.

61. Preston King to Azariah C. Flagg, December 21, 1844; Michael Hoffman to Flagg, October 19, 1844, Flagg Papers.

62. Silas Wright to Benjamin Butler, May 15, 1844, Benjamin Butler Papers, New York Public Library; Azariah C. Flagg to Orville Hungerford, May 9, 1844, Flagg Papers.

63. See Silas Wright to Azariah C. Flagg, January 23, 1844; Michael Hoffman to Flagg, October 19, 1844; Preston King to Flagg, December 21, 1844; John A. Dix to Flagg, March 3, 1845, Flagg Papers. Silas Wright to Benjamin Butler, May 20, 24, 1844, Butler Papers. See also, John Niven's discussion of Gideon Welles's reaction to these events in Niven, *Welles*, 202, 220–21.

64. John A. Dix to Azariah C. Flagg, January 20, 26, 1845; Orville Robinson to Flagg, January 28, 1845, Flagg Papers.

65. *Illinois State Register*, April 2, 1847.

66. Wright to Polk, July 21, 1845, in Gillett, *Life of Wright*, 2: 1648.

67. Azariah C. Flagg to John Lawrence, October 27, 1845, Flagg Papers.

68. Quoted in Walter Feree, "The New York Democracy: Division and Reunion, 1847–1852" (Ph.D. diss., University of Pennsylvania, 1953), 246. See also Edwin Croswell to Horatio Seymour, October 22, 1849, Horatio Seymour Papers, New-York Historical Society.

69. *New York Evening Post*, October 14, 1848; New York *The Barnburner*, July 29, August 26, 1848.

70. Cleveland *Plain Dealer*, September 18, 1848; Columbus *Ohio Statesman*, in Richmond *Enquirer*, July 1, 1848; Alfred E. Burr to Gideon Welles, September 9, 1849, John M. Niles to Welles, September 17, 1846, October 28, 1848; William Pettit to Welles, October 28, 1848, Welles Papers, Rayback, *Free Soil*, 232.

71. *Detroit Free Press*, December 31, 1847.

72. *Proceedings of the Democratic and Free Democratic Conventions Held at Rome on the 15th, 16th and 17th Days of August, 1849* (Rome, 1849), 12, 14.

73. John Wentworth to E. S. Kimberly, June 27, 1848, E. S. Kimberly Papers, Chicago Historical Society, *Chicago Democrat*, December 22, 1848. See also, *Milwaukee Weekly Wisconsin*, June 28, 1848; *Ohio Statesman*, September 14, 1848; Cleveland *Plain Dealer*, June 12, September 18, 1848.

74. *Plain Dealer*, March 30, 1847.

75. *Address and Resolutions of The Democratic State Convention. . . . Syracuse, 1848* (Syracuse, 1848), 7; *Proceedings . . . Rome . . . 1849*, 18, 21, 38.

76. *Plain Dealer*, September 10, 1846; *Proceedings of the Democratic National Convention Held at Baltimore, June 1–5, 1852* (Washington, D.C., 1852), 61.

77. "One Idea" (n.p., [1848]), 3. *Barnburner*, July 29, 1848.

78. William Bissell to William Martin, March 5, 1850, Miscellaneous Papers, Illinois State Historical Society. See also, *Plain Dealer*, September 18, 1848; William Pettit to Gideon Welles, October 28, 1848, Welles Papers.

79. *Speech of Hon. Horatio Seymour, Delivered at Tammany Hall, . . . Sept. 28, 1855* (n.p., [1855]), 9.

80. *Address and Resolves of the Democratic Members of the Massachusetts Legislature of 1838. . . .* (n.p., [1838]), 2; *Speeches Delivered at Tammany Hall, New York City, Sept. 2,*

1852. . . . (n.p., [1852]), 7; Don E. Fehrenbacher, *Chicago Giant: A Biography of "Long John" Wentworth* (Madison, 1957), 139.

81. Isaac Holmes to Howell Cobb, August 21, 1847, in Ulrich B. Phillips, ed., "The Correspondence of Robert Toombs, Alexander Holmes Stephens and Howell Cobb," *Annual Report of The American Historical Association for 1911* (Washington, D.C., 1913), 88; *Washington Union*, June 17, 1847.

82. Lee Benson, *Merchants, Farmers and Railroads* (Cambridge: Harvard University Press, 1955), 138.

83. Nor do I believe that this lack of preoccupation with slavery related issues made the Democrats' concerns and behavior "artificial." See Richard P. McCormick, *The Second American Party System* (Chapel Hill, 1966), 353.

84. Stephen Maizlish, "The Triumph of Sectionalism: The Transformation of Politics in the Antebellum North, Ohio, 1844–1860" (Ph.D. diss., University of California, Berkeley, 1978), p. 224.

85. *An Appeal to the People of Massachusetts on the Texas Question* (Boston, 1844), 4.

86. Alfred E. Burr to Welles, August 9, 1849, Welles Papers.

87. John W. Lawrence to Azariah C. Flagg, October 23, 1845; John A. Dix to Flagg, March 5, 1847, Flagg Papers.

88. *Address of the Republican State Committee to the Electors of Rhode Island* (Providence, 1857), 1.

89. *Evening Post*, October 16, 1848.

90. See above, p. 88.

91. Foner, *Politics and Ideology*, especially chaps. 1–3.

92. Roger Peterson, "Reactions to a Heterogeneous Society: Voting Behavior in Pennsylvania, 1848–1860" (Ph.D. diss., University of Pittsburgh, 1973); Kleppner, *Third Electoral System*, chap. 3.

93. Baum, "Political Realignment of the 1850s," Davis, "Persistence of Partisan Alignment," 91ff.

94. Kleppner, *Third Electoral System*, p. 57; William E. Gienapp, "The Transformation of Cincinnati Politics, 1852–1860" (seminar paper, Yale University, 1969); Thomas Kremm, "Cleveland and the First Lincoln Election: The Ethnic Response to Nativism," *Journal of Interdisciplinary History* VIII (Summer 1977): 69–86.

95. Kleppner, *Third Electoral System*, chaps. 3, 21.

96. Robert Ernst, *Immigrant Life in New York City, 1825–1863* (New York, 1949), p. 168; Peterson, "Reactions to a Heterogeneous Society," 34.

97. Kleppner, *Third Electoral System*, 168.

98. Robert Imholt, "Beyond Slavery: The Transformation of Issues in the Politics of New York, 1852–1860" (Ph.D. diss., University of Kentucky, 1974).

99. Formisano, *Birth of Mass Parties*, 266.

100. The clipping is in the Daniel Ullman Papers, New-York Historical Society; Corning (N.Y.) *Weekly Journal*, October 29, 1857.

101. Gienapp, "'Politics Seems To Enter . . .'" 46.

102. Sewell, *Ballots for Freedom*, 169.

103. Robert Kelley, *The Cultural Pattern in American Politics: The First Century* (New York, 1979).

104. *New York Herald*, September 21, 1860; Thomas M. Cook and Thomas W. Knox, *Public Record of Horatio Seymour* (New York, 1868), 21; C. L. Vallandigham, *The Record of the Hon. C. L. Vallandigham on Abolition, the Union and the Civil War* (Columbus, 1863), 13.

105. Silbey, *Respectable Minority*, chap. 8.
106. Ibid., 245.

7. The Southern National Democrats, 1845-1861

1. *Congressional Globe*, 29th Cong., 1st sess., 1214, 1217.
2. See, for example Avery O. Craven, *The Coming of the Civil War* (2nd ed.; Chicago, 1957).
3. I have attempted to demonstrate the strength and meaning of the two national political parties in my *The Shrine of Party: Congressional Voting Behavior, 1841-1852* (Pittsburgh, 1967).
4. For example, during the first session of the Twenty-ninth Congress, 98.5 percent of the Whigs in the House of Representatives voted together on all land issues as did 78.5 percent of all Democrats. On the tariff issue the figures were Whigs 98.6 percent, Democrats, 85.5 percent. Similar unity percentages were present in the Senate. The manner in which the votes were brought together and measured is discussed in Silbey, *Shrine of Party*, chap. 1.
5. "Mr. Calhoun is in a false position, if a man ever was. He is crying 'wolf' when the Democratic shepherds at Washington, have already driven the wolf from the fold. . . ." *Columbus Times* in *Southern Banner*, (Athens, Ga.), April 27, 1847. See also the *Montgomery Flag and Advertiser*, March 30, 1847.
6. Isaac Holmes to Howell Cobb, August 21, 1847, in Ulrich B. Phillips (ed.), "The Correspondence of Robert Toombs, Alexander Holmes Stephens and Howell Cobb," *Annual Report of the American Historical Association for 1911*, 88.
7. *Charleston Mercury*, February 10, 20, July 27, 1847; *Richmond Enquirer*, April 22, 1847.
8. Wilson Lumpkin to John C. Calhoun, August 27, 1847, in Chauncey S. Boucher and Robert B. Brooks (eds.), "Correspondence Addressed to John P. Calhoun, 1837-1849," *Annual Report of the American Historical Association for the year 1929*, 395-97. Also see R. K. Cralle to Calhoun, April 18, 1847, Alexander Bowie to Calhoun, April 13, 1847, in *ibid.*, 1113, 1110-11.
9. The background of the anti-Calhoun element in the Southern Democratic party can be followed in Charles Wiltse, *John C. Calhoun, Nullifier, 1829-1839* (Indianapolis, 1949), 115 ff. Calhoun's opposition to the Mexican War also brought him condemnation from Southern Democrats. See the *Nashville Union*, February 23, June 5, 1847; *Southern Banner*, May 18, 1848; Milledgeville Federal Union, May 20, 1848.
10. See *The Address of the Southern Delegates in Congress to Their Constituents* (Washington, 1849), *passim*.
11. See the resolutions of Democrats in the Sixth Congressional District of Georgia, June 2, 1847, and of the Alabama State Democratic Convention, February 1848, both in the *Washington Union*, June 17, 1847, Feb. 25, 1848.
12. The leading Democratic newspapers, the *Washington Union* and the *Richmond Enquirer*, took this position repeatedly in this period.
13. After listing the policies they wished enacted a group of Georgia Democrats resolved that "we look to the ascendency of the democratic party of the Union alone for the maintenance of the foregoing doctrines. . . . That we insist on preserving its present organization by union and harmony of action between its Northern and Southern portions. . . ." *Washington Union*, June 17, 1847.
14. *Southern Banner*, February 2, 1847. There are similar comments in other Southern papers.

15. "The old party organization cannot much longer hold together. . . ." John C. Calhoun to Duff Green, November 9, 1847, in J. Franklin Jameson, ed., "Correspondence of John C. Calhoun," *Annual Report of the American Historical Association for 1899*, 740.

16. *Congressional Globe*, 30th Cong., 2nd sess., 83.

17. The proceedings of the meeting may be followed in the *Richmond Enquirer*, January 30, February 9, 1849; *Montgomery Flag and Advertiser*, January 27, 1849; Thomas Metcalfe to John J. Crittenden, January 14, 1849, John Jordan Crittenden Papers, Library of Congress; Robert Toombs to Crittenden, January 22, 1849, in Mrs. Chapman Coleman, ed., *The Life of John J. Crittenden.* . . , Philadelphia, 1873, I, 335–36.

18. A copy of the *Southern Address*, including the names of those who signed the document may be found in Richard K. Crall (ed.), *The Works of John C. Calhoun* (New York, 1888), VI, 285–313.

19. See *ibid*.

20. *Washington Union*, January 18, 1851, and various issues through the election of 1852; Horace Montgomery, *Cracker Parties* (Baton Rouge, 1950), chaps. 2–4.

21. Congressman George W. Jones of Tennessee wrote to Howell Cobb that he liked Franklin Pierce very much since the latter was a Democrat "after my own heart, no taint of protective tariff, internal improvements, banks, exclusive privileges, class legislation, extravagant expenditures of the public moneys abolition, free-soilism or sectional prejudices to mar or tarnish the brightness of his eschutcheon." Jones to Cobb, June 13, 1852, in Phillips "Correspondence," 301.

22. James A. Seddon of Virginia advocated that the Southern sectionalists return to the Democratic party in 1852 and commented that the "cursed bonds of party paralyzed our strength and energy when they might have been successfully exerted, and now as some partial compensation must sustain and uphold us from dispersion and prostration." Seddon to Robert M. T. Hunter, February 7, 1852, in Charles Ambler, ed., "Correspondence of Robert M. T. Hunter, 1826–1876," *Annual Report of the American Historical Association for the Year 1916*, 137.

23. William L. Yancey was beaten by Henry Hilliard in his race for re-election to Congress from Alabama; see Henry T. Hilliard, *Politics and Pen Pictures at Home and Abroad* (New York, 1892). In South Carolina Robert Rhett found the political atmosphere unpromising after 1850: "The cold water of Southern indifference had silenced many of the fire eaters in South Carolina. . . ." Harold Schultz, *Nationalism and Sectionalism in South Carolina, 1852–1860* (Chapel Hill, 1950), 38.

24. *Congressional Globe*, 35th Cong., 1st sess., 1965.

25. Quoted in Lillian Kibler, *Benjamin F. Perry, South Carolina Unionist* (Chapel Hill, 1946), 281 ff.

26. Quoted in Zachary Taylor Johnson, *The Political Policies of Howell Cobb* (Nashville, 1929), 143.

27. Quotes in support of this may be found in Henry T. Shanks, *The Secession Movement in Virginia, 1847ω1861* (Richmond, 1934), 119; Percy Scott Flippin, *Herschel V. Johnson of Georgia, State Rights Unionist* (Richmond, 1931), 65; Richard M. Johnson and William H. Browne, *Life of Alexander H. Stephens* (Philadelphia, 1878), 364; and in the speech of Thomas Clingman in the House of Representatives, May 8, 1860, *Congressional Globe*, 36th Cong., 1st sess., 1965.

28. *Ibid.*, 34th Cong., 1st sess., 67.

29. *Ibid.*, 36th Cong., 1st sess., 1484.

30. Horace Montgomery, "The Solid South Movement of 1855," *Georgia Historical Quarterly* XXVI (June 1942), 101–12.

31. Orr's plans can be followed throughout Schultz, *Nationalism and Sectionalism.*

32. See Howell Cobb to Alexander H. Stephens, July 21, 1857, Robert Toombs to Stephens, August 15, 1857, and Stephens's Address to Voters of the Eighth Congressional District of Georgia, August 14, 1857, all in Phillips, "Correspondence," 407, 409–21.

33. See Stephen A. Douglas to Robert J. Walker, July 21, 1857, in Robert Johannsen (ed.), *The Letters of Stephen A. Douglas* (Urbana, 1961), 386; George Fort Milton, *The Eve of Conflict Stephen A. Douglas and the Needless War* (Boston, 1934), 267.

34. Gerald Capers has caught what deserting his party meant to someone such as Douglas: "To an extrovert in his forties, holding the deep loyalties which the Senator did—and the chief of these, next to the nation, was the Democratic party—apostasy without great compulsion was impossible. When Pierce had banished him from the inner councils, he had stuck by the party; when Buchanan had been chosen over him, he gave his energy and his money without stint for the party success. When the new President similarly ignored him . . . he still gave the administration his support. . . . His recurrent affirmation of devotion to the party must be taken at face value. His brave speeches concealed an undercurrent of sorrow." Gerald Capers, *Stephen A. Douglas, Defender of the Union* (Boston, 1959), 169–70.

35. Avery O. Craven, *The Growth of Southern Nationalism, 1848–1861* (Baton Rouge, 1953), 297–98, 298n.

36. *Ibid.*, 299–302, contains a variety of quotes from Southern sources.

37. Henry A. Wise of Virginia wrote to Douglas's campaign manager in 1858, "I see you standing alone, isolated by a tyrannical proscription which alike foolishly and wickedly lop off one of the most vigorous limbs of the national Democracy. . . . I see you, in spite of this imputation, firmly fronting the foe and battling to maintain conservative nationality against embittered and implacable sectionalism. Fight on, fight on, never yield but in death or victory." Johannsen, *Letters of Douglas*, 429n.

38. See, for example, the speeches of Louis Wigfall and Willard Saulsbury, April 2, 1860, and of Thomas Clingman of North Carolina, May 8, 1860. *Congressional Globe*, 36th Cong., 1st sess., 1480–90, 1962–66.

39. *Ibid.*, 1484, 1490, 1965.

40. Robert Toombs to Alexander H. Stephens, February 10, 1860, Phillips, "Correspondence," 461.

41. *Congressional Globe*, 36th Cong., 1st sess., 1871–72.

42. Congressman James Orr of South Carolina noted in July 1860, after the Charleston convention, that the disruption of the Democratic party "extinguishes my ardently cherished hope of preserving not only our rights, but the Union itself." Quoted in Schultz, *Nationalism and Sectionalism*, 95n.

43. The Upper South's delegates stayed at Charleston. See William Hesseltine (ed.), *Three Against Lincoln: Murat Halstead Reports the Caucuses of 1860* (Baton Rouge, 1960), 74, 83–85, 88.

44. *Ibid.*, 88–90, 92; Milton, *Eve of Conflict*, 450 ff., traces the election of Gulf states delegates to Baltimore.

45. Capers, *Stephen A. Douglas*, 196–97; Roy F. Nichols, *The Disruption of the*

American Democracy (New York, 1947), 300 ff.; Howell Cobb to John B. Lamar, May 22, 1860, Phillips, "Correspondence," 480.

46. "From the Autobiography of Herschel V. Johnson, 1856–1867," *American Historical Review* XXX (January 1925), 318.

47. Douglas received 163,586 votes in the South in 1860 and carried Missouri. W. Dean Burnham, *Presidential Ballots, 1836–1892* (Baltimore, 1955).

48. They are noted in the various state studies of secession as well as in Ralph Wooster, *The Secession Conventions of the South* (Princeton, 1962).

49. Arthur C. Cole, *The Whig Party in the South*, The American Historical Association, 1913; Chauncey Boucher, "*In Re:* That Aggressive Slavocracy," *Missippi Valley Historical Review* VIII (June-September 1921), 13–79.

50. Montgomery, *Cracker Parties*; Charles Sellers, "Who Were the Southern Whigs?" *American Historical Review* LIX (January 1954), 335–46; Thomas P. Govan, "Americans Below the Potomac," in Charles Grier Sellers, ed., *The Southerner as American* (Chapel Hill, 1960), 19–39.

51. Flippin, *Herschel V. Johnson*; Schultz, *Nationalism and Sectionalism*; Laura White, "The National Democrats of South Carolina, 1852 to 1860," *South Atlantic Quarterly* XXVIII (October 1929), 370–89.

52. I have discussed some of the dangers of over-concentrating on the sectional forces for the country as a whole in "The Civil War Synthesis in American Political History," *Civil War History* X (June 1964), 130–40.

53. Charles Sydnor, *The Development of Southern Sectionalism, 1819–1848* (Baton Rouge, 1848), 316.

54. William O. Aydelotte, "Voting Patterns in the British House of Commons in the 1840's," *Comparative Studies in Society and History* V (January 1963), 154.

55. Milledgeville *Federal Union*, January 30, 1849.

56. In January 1860, Robert B. Rhett wrote to W. P. Miles complaining about the weakness and lack of courage demonstrated by Southern leaders. "The fact is that, from party contact at Washington, the courage of Southern representatives . . . oozes out. . . . So long as the Democratic party as a 'National' organization, exists in power at the South, and so long as our public men trim their sails with an eye to either the favor or enmity, just so long must we hope for no Southern action for disenthrallment and security." Quoted in Schultz, *Nationalism and Sectionalism*, 213–14.

57. This has been a traditional comparative variable in discussing differences among Southern politicians, particularly on the secession-disunion issue. For a recent use of it, see Wooster, *Secession Conventions*.

58. Those feuds are discussed in Nichols, *Disruption of American Democracy*, and Craven, *Growth of Southern Nationalism*, among other places.

59. Regionalism within the South is discussed in Frederick Jackson Turner, *The United States, 1830–1850, The Nation and Its Sections* (New York, 1935); Craven, *Growth of Southern Nationalism*; and more particularly in Charles Ambler, *Sectionalism in Virginia, From 1776–1861* (Chicago, 1910).

60. Alexander H. Stephens and Robert Toombs of Georgia were outstanding representatives of this group.

61. Charles Beard, *An Economic Interpretation of the Constitution of the United States* (New York, 1913); David Donald, "Towards a Reconsideration of the Abolitionists," in *Lincoln Reconsidered* (New York, 1956); George Mowry, *The California Progressives* (Berkeley, 1951).

62. Lee Benson, *The Concept of Jacksonian Democracy: New York As a Test Case* (Princeton, 1961). Professor Hays has been working for several years on a comparative analysis of voting behavior in Iowa and various urban centers.

63. Staughton Lynd, *Anti-Federalism in Dutchess County, New York* (New Orleans, 1962); Forrest McDonald, *We the People, The Economic Origins of the Constitution* (Chicago, 1958).

8. "The Undisguised Connection"

1. David M. Potter, *The Impending Crisis, 1848–1861* (New York, 1976), 251.

2. Paul Kleppner, *The Third Electoral System, 1853–1892: Parties, Voters, and Political Cultures* (Chapel Hill, 1979), 51. It should be noted that Lee Benson originated this idea in his widely circulated but unpublished 1954 essay, "An Operational Approach to Historiography." In that paper and at very many occasions since Professor Benson has influenced my ideas and approach to dealing with this problem.

3. Paul Kleppner, "Partisanship and Ethnoreligious Conflict: The Third Electoral System, 1853–1892," in Paul Kleppner et al., *The Evolution of American Electoral Systems* (Westport, Conn., 1981), 121.

4. Eric Foner, *Free Soil, Free Labor, Free Men: The Ideology of the Republican Party Before the Civil War* (New York, 1970), 270, 285–86. See also, Michael F. Holt, *Forging a Majority: The Formation of the Republican Party in Pittsburgh, 1848–1860* (New Haven, 1969), 222.

5. Glyndon G. Van Deusen, *William Henry Seward* (New York, 1967), 225–26; Potter, *Impending Crisis*, 256–59; Foner, *Free Soil*, chap. 7, "The Republicans and Nativism"; Richard Sewell, *Ballots for Freedom: Antislavery Politics in the United States, 1837–1860* (New York, 1976), 275–76, 348ff.

6. Foner, *Free Soil*, 254, 258–60.

7. Horace Greeley, *Recollections of a Busy Life* (Port Washington, N.Y., reprt., 1971); Thurlow Weed, *Autobiography of Thurlow Weed* (Boston, 1884); Frederick W. Seward (ed.), *Seward at Washington As Senator and Secretary of State* (New York, 1891), 3 vols.

8. New York *Tribune*, May 20, 1858, November 5, 1857, November 2, 1859, November 5, 1860; New York *Evening Post*, November 4, 1858.

9. Albany *Argus*, March 13, 1855, August 10, 1855, February 11, 1856, September 7, 1857.

10. Dale Baum, "Know-Nothingism and the Republican Majority in Massachusetts: The Political Realignment of the 1850s," *Journal of American History* LXIV (March 1978), 959–86. The quotation is on 986. Baum argues that the Know-Nothing voting support tended, rather, to drop out of the voting universe entirely.

11. DeAlva S. Alexander, *A Political History of the State of New York* (Port Washington, reissued 1969), II, 254, 255. Alexander was a Republican congressman from New York from 1897 to 1911. He was also a Civil War veteran.

12. Michael F. Holt, *The Political Crisis of the 1850s* (New York, 1978), 276.

13. The "undisguised connection" quotation is in *Utica Daily Observer*, October 28, 1858.

14. Gary W. Cox and J. Morgan Kousser argue that "New York is the single most important state from which to draw generalizations about the nineteenth century non-Southern electorate." Gary W. Cox and J. Morgan Kousser, "Turn-

out and Rural Corruption: New York As a Test Case," *American Journal of Political Science* XXV (November 1981), 3.

15. New York's politics in the 1850s have been extensively studied but much of the work remains unpublished and without the focus offered here. Among the most relevant of these works are: Hendrik Booraem, *The Formation of the Republican Party in New York: Politics & Conscience in the Antebellum North* (New York, 1983); Thomas Curran, "The Know Nothings of New York" (unpub. Ph.D. diss., Columbia University, 1963); Mark L. Berger, *The Revolution in the New York Party Systems, 1840–1860* (Port Washington, 1973); Karen Markoe, "The Origins of the Republican Party in New York State" (unpub. Ph.D. diss., Columbia University, 1971); Robert J. Imholt, "Beyond Slavery: The Transformation of Issues in the Politics of New York, 1857–1860" (unpub. Ph.D. diss., University of Kentucky, 1974); Lee Warner, "The Silver Grays: New York State Conservative Whigs, 1846–1856" (unpub. Ph.D. diss., University of Wisconsin, 1971). The "vindicative" quotation is in James Kelly to William H. Seward, January 25, 1855, William Henry Seward Papers, University of Rochester. See also D. W. C. Clarke to Seward, February 6, 1855, George Geddes to Seward, February 7, 1855, *ibid.*

16. The New York Whig (J. W. Taylor) is quoted in William Gienapp, "The Origins of the Republican Party, 1852–1856" (unpub. Ph.D. diss., University of California, Berkeley, 1980), 508–9; George Baker to William H. Seward, October 13, 1855, Seward Papers, Rochester.

17. Thurlow Weed to William H. Seward, July 23, 1855, George E. Baker to Seward, April 19, 1855, Seward Papers; William Henry Seward to Julius Rockwell, March 26, 1855, William Henry Seward Papers, New-York Historical Society; Albany *Argus*, October 20, 1855.

18. Thomas M. Monroe to Daniel Ullmann, June 13, 1856, Daniel Ullmann Papers, New-York Historical Society; Albany *Statesman*, January 12, 1857. See also S. G. Haven to Ullmann, February 29, 1856, Ullmann Papers. Booraem, *Formation of the Republican Party*, 215.

19. Caleb S. Henry to William H. Seward, November 6, 1856, in William Gienapp, "Origins of the Republican Party," 1181.

20. Booraem, *Formation of the Republican Party*, 221.

21. Imholt, "Transformation of Issues," 40; *Auburn Daily Advertiser*, October 21, 1857; Albany *Statesman*, June 2, 1857.

22. William Henry Seward to George W. Patterson, November 11, 1857, quoted in Imholt, "Transformation of Issues," 86, *Buffalo Express*, November 6, 1857; Albany *Atlas and Argus*, November 10, 1857.

23. New York *Courier and Enquirer*, June 17, 1858; *Jamestown Journal*, November 13, 1857.

24. *Madison Observer*, September 16, 1858; Ithaca *American Citizen*, December 2, 1857.

25. Bath *Steuben Courier*, August 17, 1859.

26. New York *Tribune*, January 19, May 20, June 19, 1858; *Buffalo Express*, October 27, 1857; *Syracuse Journal* in *ibid.*, September 6, 1858; Albany *Evening Journal*, October 31, 1857.

27. Foner, *Free Soil*, 254; Booraem, *Formation of the Republican Party*, 212.

28. Bath *Steuben Courier*, May 26, 1858; George W. Patterson to John A. King,

January 19, 1858, John A. King Papers, New-York Historical Society; New York *Courier and Enquirer*, September 18, October 15, 1858.

29. See, for example, New York *Courier and Enquirer*, August 12, 1858.

30. Albany *Atlas and Argus*, June 22, December 31, 1857; Paul O. Weinbaum, "Temperance, Politics and the New York City Riots of 1857," *New-York Historical Society Quarterly* LIX (July 1975), 246–70; New York *Tribune*, November 9, 1857; New York *Courier and Enquirer*, November 2, 1857; Benson, "Operational Approach to Historiography," 37; "Speech of Dewitt C. Littlejohn to Republican National Convention, 1856" in *Proceedings of the First Three Republican National Conventions of 1856, 1860 and 1864* (Minneapolis, 1856), 56; Louis D. Scisco, *Political Nativism in New York State* (New York, 1901), 231.

31. Albany *Argus*, March 13, January 6, August 10, 1855, February 11, 1856; *Atlas and Argus*, June 18, 1856, September 7, 1857.

32. Ithaca *American Citizen*, June 9, 1856.

33. Ithaca *American Citizen*, July 14, August 11, 1858; Albany *Statesman*, November 18, 1856; American Party, "Platform, Resolutions and Address, Adopted at the Annual Meeting of the State Council at Troy . . . 1857 (Troy, 1857), 2.

34. *Chenango American*, November 19, 1857; Albany *Statesman* in Ithaca *American Citizen*, December 9, 1857; "The Controversy Between Senator Brooks and '†John,' Archbishop of New York. . . ." (New York, 1855), 20; Charles Freeman et al., to Daniel Ullmann, September 20, 1855, Thomas Monroe to Ullmann, June 26, 1856, Daniel Ullmann Papers; Ithaca *American Citizen*, September 8, 1858; Humphrey Marshall to Millard Fillmore, November 16, 1857, Millard Fillmore Papers, Erie County Historical Society, Buffalo; Albany *Statesman* December 1, 1856, May 9, 1857; Auburn *Daily American*, February 1, 1858.

35. Curran, "The Know Nothings of New York," *passim*; Van Deusen, *Seward*, 156ff; Albany *Statesman*, April 11, December 19, 1856, September 1, 1857; Booraem, *Formation of the Republican Party*, 65.

36. Albany *Statesman*, December 6, 1856; J. Van Deusen, Jr., to Daniel Ullmann, July 9, 1855, Ullmann Papers.

37. Ithaca *American Citizen*, March 17, 1858; Albany *Statesman*, August 10, 1857.

38. H. R. Selden to John A. King, July 13, 1858, William H. Seward to King, January 28, 1858, J. Petrie to King, January 6, 1858, King Papers; William Beach to William Henry Seward, November 29, 1857, Theodore M. Pomeroy to Seward, December 16, 1857, William H. Carpenter to Seward, December 20, 1857, George E. Baker to Seward, January 12, 1858, Seward Papers, Rochester.

39. John A. King to W. H. Seward, February 1, 1858, King Papers; same to same, February 20, 1858, Seward Papers, Rochester; W. H. Seward to R. M. Blatchford, February 13, 1858, enclosed in Blatchford to Horace Greeley, February 22, 1858, Greeley Papers.

40. Steven Fram, "'Purifying the Ballot': The Politics of Electoral Procedure in New York State, 1821–1871" (unpub. M.A. thesis, Cornell University, 1983).

41. *Ibid.*, 98.

42. Albany *Atlas and Argus*, March 4, 1856, November 29, 1858.

43. Albany, *Statesman*, March 25, April 16, July 7, August 20, November 6, 1856, May 18, June 15, 1857.

44. Scisco, *Political Nativism*, 151; *Statesman*, January 15, 1857.

45. Van Deusen, *Seward*, *passim*, on his relationship with Hughes and the Irish

in New York; Michael Holt, "The Politics of Impatience: The Origins of Know Nothingism," *Journal of American History* LX (September 1973), 309-31. I have also been aided by Andrea Rothe, "Seward, the Know Nothings, and the Republican Nomination of 1860" (unpub. Senior Honors Essay, Cornell University History Department, 1978).

46. Albany *Statesman,* January 19, April 18, 1857; Auburn *Daily American,* April 12, 1858.

47. Daniel Ullmann, untitled clipping of speech at Albany, August 24, 1858, Ullmann Papers; Auburn *Daily American,* February 1, March 6, 1858; Scisco, *Political Nativism,* 228.

48. Albany *Statesman,* January 5, 1857; *Buffalo Express,* November 10, 1857, April 8, 1858; New York *Tribune,* March 4, April 3, 1858; Rochester *Democrat and American,* April 10, 1858; *Syracuse Journal,* n.d., in *Buffalo Express,* April 8, 1858; *Goshen Democrat,* April 16, 1858; *Addison Advertiser,* April 17, 1858, *New York Times,* April 6, 1858; Little Falls *Herkimer County Journal,* April 1, 22, 1858; New York *Evening Post,* April 9, 1858; Bath *Steuben Courier,* March 3, 1858; New York *Courier,* July 28, 1858.

Interestingly, in his discussion of what he suggests were few Republican concessions to the Know Nothings in New York, Foner does not mention the registry.

49. John A. King to William H. Seward, February 1, 1858, King Papers.

50. Charles Z. Lincoln (ed.), *State of New York, Messages from the Governors* (Albany, 1909), V, 53; New York State Assembly, 1858, *Documents,* IV, #109, 6; *New York Times,* April 6, 1858; *Herkimer County Journal,* May 6, 1858.

51. Albany *Statesman* in Ithaca *American Citizen,* December 9, 1857.

52. See Van Deusen, *Seward,* 193ff.

53. Auburn *Daily American,* May 15, 17, 21, 1858; *Poughkeepsie Eagle,* April 24, May 5, 1858; *Buffalo Express,* November 10, 1857; New York *Tribune,* April 21, May 31, June 1, 1858; *New York Times,* May 26, June 10 1858; John R. Thompson to Millard Fillmore, February 20, 1858, Fillmore Papers.

54. *Steuben Courier,* August 25, 1858; Batavia *Republican* in *Buffalo Express,* September 2, 1858; *Addison Advertiser,* August 25, 1858; New York *Tribune,* August 6, 26, 28, 1858; New York *Evening Post,* September 6, 1858; *Buffalo Express,* September 1, 1858; Auburn *Daily Advertiser,* September 2, 6, 1858.

55. *New York Times,* September 7, 1858; *Buffalo Express,* September 7, 1858; James Watson Webb to William Henry Seward, August 11, 1858, R. P. Baber to Seward, September 3, 1858, Seward Papers, Rochester; Imholt, "Transformation of Issues," 216; Albany *Evening Journal,* September 8, 1858.

56. John R. Thompson to Millard Fillmore, February 17, 1858, Washington Hunt to Fillmore, August 20, 1858, Fillmore Papers; *Poughkeepsie Eagle,* April 2, 1859; Auburn *Daily Advertiser,* April 9, September 1, 11, 15, October 6, 1858.

57. *Steuben Courier,* May 26, 1858; *Herkimer County Journal,* June 3, September 2, 1858; Imholt, "Transformation of Issues," 222-23; Preston King to N. S. Benton, July 25, 1858, King Papers; Rochester *Democrat and American,* September 11, 1858; T. A. Cheney to William H. Seward, June 21, 1858, Seward Papers, Rochester.

58. *Herkimer County Journal,* September 16, 1858; Albany *Evening Journal,* September 14, 1858; American Party, State Committee, "Address, September, 1858," copy in Ullmann Papers.

59. *Steuben Courier,* September 15, 1858; *Jamestown Journal,* September 17, 1858.

60. All platforms are in New York *Tribune*, September 18, 1858. The rest of the Republican platform focused on sectional issues.

61. New York *Tribune*, September 13, 1858. See also Huntington *Long Islander*, September 17, 1858.

62. *Buffalo Express*, September 11, 1858; New York *Times*, October 11, 1858; *Utica Daily Observer*, September 7, 1858.

63. New York *Tribune*, October 14, 1858.

64. Albany *Evening Journal*, October 19, November 11, 1858; Rochester *Democrat and American*, November 8, 1858; Rome *Roman Citizen*, November 1, 1858; New York *Courier and Enquirer*, September 11, October 15, 1858; *Jamestown Journal*, October 29, 1858.

65. Curran, "The Know Nothings of New York," 274–75, *Buffalo Express*, September 15, 1858; New York *Tribune*, September 10, October 18, 19, 20, 23, 1858; Albany *Evening Journal*, October 25, 1858; Huntington *Long Islander*, October 8, 1858; *Addison Advertiser*, October 6, 1858.

66. Benjamin Welch, Jr., to Thurlow Weed, September 13, 1858, Thurlow Weed Papers, New-York Historical Society; Van Deusen, *Seward*, 195.

67. Huntington *Long Islander*, October 29, 1858; Imholt, "Transformation of Issues," 263; Auburn *Daily Advertiser*, November 4, 1858.

68. Albany *Atlas and Argus*, September 24, 1858, for example.

69. Auburn *Daily American*, October 9, 1858.

70. Van Deusen, *Seward*, 196; New York *Tribune*, January 1, 1859. There also continued to be voices on the other side. See George W. Palmer to William H. Seward, November 12, 1858, Seward to Theodore Parker, November 19, 1858, Seward Papers, Rochester.

71. *Steuben Courier*, January 19, March 2, 1859; Huntington *Long Islander*, November 12, 1858; New York *Tribune*, November 4, December 20, 1858; *Buffalo Express*, January 4, 1859.

72. Lincoln, *Messages from Governors*, V, 92; New York *Courier and Enquirer*, January 5, March 20, 1859; *Buffalo Express*, January 6, March 15, 1859; Rome *Roman Citizen*, February 2, 1859; Albany *Evening Journal*, April 14, 1859; *New York Times*, March 30, 1859; New York *Tribune*, April 9, 1859.

73. R. L. Mecke to John A. King, February 1, 1859, King Papers.

74. Albany *Statesman*, April 14, 1859, quoted in *Steuben Courier*, April 20, 1859.

75. New York *Tribune*, April 9, 1859. Interestingly, a Republican minority of a Senate committee reported against the bill, repeatedly quoting Seward to make their point. New York State Senate, 1859, *Documents*, II, #84.

76. Derived from my analysis of the votes reported in the legislative journals.

77. New York *Tribune*, April 20, 1859; *Poughkeepsie Eagle*, April 16, 1859; *Buffalo Express*, April 16, 1859; Albany *Atlas and Argus*, April 26, 29, 1859.

78. *Chenango American*, February 24, April 21, 1859.

79. Albany *Atlas and Argus*, November 15, 1859.

80. *Chenango American*, September 2, 1858.

81. *Jamestown Journal*, April 1, 1859; Albany *Evening Journal*, March 14, 1859; *Poughkeepsie Eagle*, February 19, 1859; *Buffalo Express*, March 15, 1859.

82. Ithaca *American Citizen*, July 27, August 10, 24, 1859.

83. J. W. Reynolds to Daniel Ullmann, May 28, 1859, L. L. Pratt to Ullmann, May 31, 1859; William H. Goodwin to Ullmann et al., n.d., 1859, Ullmann Papers.

84. Ithaca *American Citizen*, August 31, 1859; Auburn *Daily Union*, June 17, August 19, 1859; Rochester *Democrat and American*, October 5, 1859.

85. Auburn *Daily American* in Ithaca *American Citizen*, June 22, 1859; Auburn *Daily Union*, June 17, August 19, November 5, 1859; Rochester *Democrat and American*, October 1, 5, 1859; *Steuben Courier*, July 27, October 12, 1859; *Buffalo Express*, November 10, 1859; Newburgh *Telegraph*, September 29, 1859; Huntington *Long Islander*, October 7, 1859; New York *Tribune*, October 12, 1859; Ithaca *American Citizen*, September 21, 1859; E. A. Warden to William H. Seward, August 13, 1859, George E. Baker to Seward, September 27, 1859, Seward Papers, Rochester.

86. Based on subtracting the difference between Democratic and Republican candidates' vote-totals with American support and without it.

87. Auburn *Daily Advertiser*, November 6, 1857; *Utica Daily Observer*, November 3, 5, 1858; Newburgh *Telegraph*, November 11, 1858; New York *Courier and Enquirer*, September 18, 1858.

88. Turnout is computed from the report in *Census of the State of New York for 1865* (Albany, 1867).

89. Baum, "Know Nothingism and Republican Majority." The source of this analysis are the voting returns from all the towns, wards, and election districts in the state. The ecological regression technique is discussed in J. Morgan Kousser, "Ecological Regression and the Analysis of Past Politics," *Journal of Interdisciplinary History* IV (Autumn 1973), 237–62.

Much of this analysis has been supplemented and/or confirmed by the careful work of William Gienapp on the movement of Know-Nothing voters into the Republican party in nine Northern states (including New York). I am grateful to Professor Gienapp for his willingness to share his insights with me. See Gienapp, "Nativism and the Creation of a Republican Majority" (paper presented to Annual Convention of the Organization of American Historians, 1984).

90. *Utica Daily Observer*, October 28, November 5, 1858.

91. Of course, a significant number of American voters in 1856 voted Democratic in 1860. That split, as noted, reflects the two streams of voters in the Know-Nothing party in 1856, the anti-Seward, anti-Republican sentiment, being quite potent.

92. Gienapp, "Nativism and a Republican Majority," 35.

93. Horace Greeley to Schuyler Colfax, October 24, 1859, Greeley Papers; Thurlow Weed to William Henry Seward, April 12, 1859, Seward Papers, Rochester; New York *Courier and Enquirer*, November 5, 1859.

94. Ithaca *American Citizen* in Auburn Daily Union, November 17, 1859.

95. Albany *Evening Journal*, November 17, 1859; *Poughkeepsie Eagle*, November 19, 1859; *Clinton Courier*, December 1, 1859; L. L. Pratt to Daniel Ullmann, May 31, 1859, Ullmann Papers.

96. Lincoln, *Messages from Governors*, V, 195–96; Z. Ellis to Daniel Ullmann, July 2, 1860, Ullmann Papers; "Speech of Daniel Ullmann at Lincoln and Hamlin Ratification Meeting, June 12, 1860," Ullmann Papers; New York *Tribune*, August 23, 1860.

97. J. J. Seaver to Daniel Ullmann et al., June 27, 1859; A. Myrick to same, July 4, 1859, Ullmann Papers.

98. William Gienapp, "Nativism and the Creation of a Republican Majority in the North Before the Civil War."

99. As emphasized in Kleppner, *Third Electoral System*.

100. Joel H. Silbey, "The Civil War Synthesis in American Political History," *Civil War History* X (June 1964), 130–40. Cf. to Foner, *Politics and Ideology*.

101. Dale Baum and Dale Knobel have recently examined voter movements in New York State between 1848 and 1860. They emphasize the number of former Know Nothings who did not vote Republican in 1860 and argue the continuing potency of their nativist convictions as the main reasons for their aloofness from Seward's party. While I disagree with the implication of that conclusion, and the tone and direction of their analysis more generally, I am struck by the very large area of agreement between us—as there should be, given the numbers. Dale Baum and Dale T. Knobel, "Anatomy of a Realignment: New York Presidential Politics, 1848–1860," *New York History* LXV (January 1984), 61–81. I am grateful to Professor Baum for sharing this essay with me.

9. "The Surge of Republican Power"

1. Thomas Pressly, *Americans Interpret Their Civil War* (Princeton, 1954), is the standard treatment of historiography to its date of publication. For assessments of more recent works, see Eric Foner, *Politics and Ideology in the Age of the Civil War* (New York, 1980), 15–53. In a special, and important, historiographic category is Lee Benson's "Explanations of American Civil War Causation: A Critical Assessment and a Modest Proposal To Reorient and Reorganize the Social Sciences," in *Toward the Scientific Study of History: Selected Essays of Lee Benson* (Philadelphia, 1972), 225–340. I have benefited from the critical and helpful comments of Ronald Formisano, Michael Holt, James McPherson, Phyllis Field, Andrew Rotter, Gerard Bradley, and Steven Fram on earlier versions of this essay.

2. Don S. Fehrenbacher, *The South and Three Sectional Crises* (Baton Rouge, 1980); Kenneth Stampp, *The Imperiled Union: Essays on the Background of the Civil War* (New York, 1980); William Barney, *The Road to Secession: A New Perspective on the Old South* (New York, 1972); William Barney, *The Secessionist Impulse: Alabama and Mississippi in 1860* (Princeton, 1974); Steven A. Channing, *Crisis of Fear: Secession in South Carolina* (New York, 1970); David Potter, *The Impending Crisis, 1848–1861* (New York, 1976); Michael P. Johnson, *Toward a Patriarchal Republic: The Secession of Georgia* (Baton Rouge, 1977); David Donald, *Liberty and Union: The Crisis of Popular Government, 1830–1890* (Boston, 1978); J. Mills Thornton, *Politics and Power in a Slave Society: Alabama, 1800–1860* (Baton Rouge, 1978); Peyton McCrary, *Abraham Lincoln and Reconstruction: The Louisiana Experiment* (Baton Rouge, 1978); Peyton McCrary, Clark Miller, and Dale Baum, "Class and Party in the Secession Crisis: Voting Behavior in the Deep South, 1856–1861," *Journal of Interdisciplinary History* 8 (Winter 1978), 429–57; Foner, *Politics and Ideology*; Michael F. Holt, *The Political Crisis of the 1850s* (New York, 1978); Thomas B. Alexander, "The Civil War as Institutional Fulfillment," *Journal of Southern History* 47 (February 1981), 3–32.

3. There are useful assessments of much of this literature, and of the secession process itself, in Stampp, *The Imperiled Union*, esp. 191–245.

4. Johnson, *Toward a Patriarchal Republic*, xx.

5. Foner, *Politics and Ideology*, 20.

6. Fehrenbacher, *South and Three Sectional Crises*, xi.

7. Willie Lee Rose, "Comment" [on Robert Kelley, "Ideology and Political Culture from Jefferson to Nixon"], *American Historical Review*, LXXXII (June 1977), 580–81.

8. Paul Kleppner, *The Third Electoral System, 1853–1892: Parties, Voters, and Political Cultures* (Chapel Hill, 1979), 144. See also Ronald P. Formisano, *The Birth of Mass Political Parties: Michigan, 1827–1861* (Princeton, 1971); Michael F. Holt, *Forging a Majority: The Formation of the Republican Party in Pittsburgh, 1848–1860* (New Haven, 1969); Paul Kleppner, *The Cross of Culture: A Social Analysis of Midwestern Politics, 1850–1900* (New York, 1970); Frederick Luebke (ed.), *Ethnic Voters and the Election of Lincoln* (Lincoln, 1979); and Joel H. Silbey, *The Transformation of American Politics, 1840–1860* (Englewood Cliffs, 1967). For the most recent overview of the new political history, see Allan G. Bogue, "The New Political History in the 1970s," in Michael G. Kammen (ed.), *The Past Before Us: Contemporary Historical Writing in the United States* (Ithaca, 1980), 231–51.

9. Formisano, *Birth of Mass Political Parties*, 330.

10. Rose, "Comment," 581.

11. The quotation is from I. W. Avery, *The History of the State of Georgia from 1850 to 1881* (New York, 1881), quoted in Joseph E. Parks, *Joseph E. Brown of Georgia* (Baton Rouge, 1976), 128.

12. Holt, *Political Crisis of the 1850s*, 8.

13. Rose, "Comment," 582.

14. Fehrenbacher, *South and Three Sectional Crises*, 3.

15. *Ibid.*, 56. Compare his treatment of the birth of the Republican party with that offered by the authors cited in note 8.

16. Eric Foner, "The Causes of the Civil War: Recent Interpretations and New Directions," *Civil War History* XX (September 1974), 201. See also Eric Foner, *Free Soil, Free Labor, Free Men: The Ideology of the Republican Party Before the Civil War* (New York, 1970), and his recent *Politics and Ideology* (1980).

17. Johnson, *Toward a Patriarchal Republic*, xv.

18. Fehrenbacher, *South and Three Sectional Crises*, 63.

19. *Ibid.*

20. Thornton, *Politics and Power*, 457.

21. William McLaughlin, "Pietism and the American Character," *American Quarterly* XVII (Summer 1965), 176.

22. Cf. Kleppner, *Third Electoral System*.

23. Ronald P. Formisano, "To the Editor," *Civil War History* XXI (June 1975), 188; Formisano, *Birth of Mass Political Parties*.

24. Thornton, *Politics and Power*, 206. The second quotation is from a review by William Freehling, *New York Review of Books* (September 23, 1971), 39.

25. Fehrenbacher, *South and Three Sectional Crises*, 63.

26. McCrary, *Lincoln, and Reconstruction*, 65.

27. Don S. Fehrenbacher, *The Dred Scott Case: Its Significance in American Law and Politics* (New York, 1978), 547; Fehrenbacher, *South and Three Sectional Crises*, 57.

28. John Rozett, "Racism and Republican Emergence in Illinois, 1848–1860: A Re-evaluation of Republican Negrophobia," *Civil War History* XXII (June 1976), 115.

29. Freehling, *New York Review of Books*, 39.

30. "The American political culture in the pre-Civil War years was dominated by a strong national party system, clung to tenaciously and with an intense

loyalty for ideological, social and symbolic reasons, with a vigor and devotion revealed on every election day." Joel H. Silbey, *A Respectable Minority: The Democratic Party in the Civil War Era, 1860–1868* (New York, 1977), 7.

31. Alexander, "Civil War as Institutional Fulfillment," 14, 20–21.

32. This phrase or its equivalent was used frequently in political discourse, especially in the South. For one such usage see the Milledgeville (Ga.) *Federal Union*, January 30, 1849, quoted in Joel H. Silbey, *The Shrine of Party: Congressional Voting Behavior, 1841–1852* (Pittsburgh, 1967), 105.

33. On this point, for one southern state, see Marc W. Kruman, "Parties and Politics in North Carolina, 1846–1865" (Ph.D. diss., Yale University, 1978). See also Holt, *Political Crisis of the 1850s*.

34. Foner, *Free Soil, Free Labor, Free Men*, and Formisano, *Birth of Mass Political Parties*, spell out the Republican ideology in great detail.

35. McCrary, Miller, and Baum, "Class and Party," 457.

36. *Ibid., passim.*

37. Robert Kelley, *The Cultural Pattern in American Politics: The First Century* (New York, 1979).

38. Clarksville (Tenn.) *Jeffersonian*, May 30, 1855; Washington *Daily Union*, June 7, 1854; Edgefield (S.C.) *Advertiser*, November 16, 1854; Athens (Ga.) *Southern Banner*, August 16, 1855; Mobile *Daily Register*, July 10, 1856, September 13, 1855.

39. Galveston *Tri-Weekly News*, July 17, 1856; Athens *Southern Banner*, January 25, 1855. Cf. Albany (N.Y.) *Argus*, August 21, 1854. In the discussion that follows, I will quote from both Northern and Southern Democratic papers. Most of the time, regarding this ethnocultural phenomenon, their sentiments were the same, expressed in similar language.

40. Memphis *Daily Appeal*, February 17, 1861; *Illinois State Register*, September 5, 1856; Albany *Argus*, December 30, 1856, May 5, 1857; Charleston *Mercury*, September 13, 1859; *Arkansas State Gazette and Democrat*, August 11, 1854.

41. *New York Herald*, October 26, 1860.

42. Washington *Daily Union*, January 27, 1857, Albany *Argus*, January 20, 1857.

43. Mobile *Daily Register*, October 9, 1857; Richmond *Enquirer* in Washington *Daily Union*, October 24, 1854.

44. *Atlas and Argus*, February 20, 1857. A part of this quotation is from a famous speech by Clement Vallandigham in 1863, but it reflects a perspective that antedated the war. See Frank Freidel, *Union Pamphlets of the Civil War* (Cambridge, 1967), II, 723.

45. James K. Paulding to John C. Calhoun, March 19, 1850, in Ralph M. Alderman, ed., *Letters of James K. Paulding* (Madison, 1962), 515.

46. Mobile *Daily Register*, October 6, 1855.

47. See, for example, Avery O. Craven, *The Growth of Southern Nationalism, 1848–1861* (Baton Rouge, 1953).

48. Washington *Daily Union*, May 20, 1857; *Illinois State Register*, October 4, 1859; Washington *Star*, November 9, 1855.

49. *New York Herald*, September 21, 1860; Washington *Daily Union*, September 23, 1856, May 20, 1857; Edgefield *Advertiser*, July 1, 1857.

50. *Atlas and Argus*, July 22, 1856, September 7, 1857, September 5, 1860; *Illinois State Register*, September 4, 1855.

51. McLaughlin, "Pietism and the American Character."

52. *Texas State Gazette*, April 16, 1859; *Atlas and Argus*, October 10, 1856, January 3, 1857.

53. David Nasaw, *Schooled to Order: A Social History of Public Schooling in the United States* (New York, 1979), 73.

54. *Atlas and Argus*, October 15, 1856; *Congressional Globe*, 34th Cong., 1st Sess., Appendix, 1151; New York *Herald*, September 23, 1860.

55. *New York Herald*, September 23, 1860.

56. New York *Journal of Commerce* in *Illinois State Register*, September 22, 1855.

57. *New York Herald*, September 28, 1860; *Atlas and Argus*, October 10, 15, 1856, January 3, 1857; Washington *Daily Union*, March 26, 1857; *Congressional Globe*, 34th Cong., 1st Sess., Appendix, 1264.

58. Washington *Daily Union*, December 13, 1854; *Atlas and Argus*, October 7, 1854, March 26, October 1, 1855, April 28, 1857; Washington *Daily Union*, November 7, 1854.

59. *Democratic Review* (March 1852), 271; Mobile *Daily Register*, October 12, 1855; Washington *Dailyi Union*, April 13, 1854; *Atlas and Argus*, January 3, April 28, 1857. Robert Kelley has summed up the implications of the attitudes expressed here very well. The sins that aroused the Democrats, he notes, "were social sins, not so much the sins of personal life." Robert Kelley, *The Transatlantic Persuasion* (New York, 1969), 418.

60. William Gienapp, "The Origins of the Republican Party, 1852–1856" (Ph.D. diss., University of California, Berkeley, 1980), 1172. I am grateful to Professor Gienapp for allowing me to see and quote from his unpublished manuscript, which will become the standard work on the subject of early Republicanism.

61. *Ibid.*, 1173.

62. The realignment is discussed in *ibid.*; Holt, *Political Crisis of the 1850s*; Formisano, *Birth of Mass Political Parties*; and Kleppner, *Third Electoral System*.

63. *Atlas and Argus*, June 23, 1857.

64. In that year the Republican-dominated Massachusetts legislature passed an amendment to the state constitution restricting—by delaying—the right of foreign-born citizens to vote and hold state office. Dale Baum, "Know-Nothing-ism and the Republican Majority in Massachusetts: The Political Realignment of the 1850s," *Journal of American History* LXIV (March 1978), 959–86, argues that the problem was more complex than the Democrats charged and that there was much less Republican support for the legislation than usually claimed. Nevertheless, the Democrats viewed it as a Republican measure and used it against that party in immigrant areas. See Gustave Koerner, *Memoirs of Gustave Koerner, 1809–1896* (Cedar Rapids, 1909), II, 74–76, 89–90.

65. The first part of the quotation is from a prewar speech by Horatio Seymour of New York, cited in Thomas M. Cook and Thomas W. Knox, comps., *Public Record of Horatio Seymour* (New York, 1868), 21. The second part is from an 1855 speech by Clement Vallandigham, "History of the Abolition Movement," in *The Record of the Hon. C. L. Vallandigham* (Columbia, 1863), 13.

66. Andrew D. White commented about the great New York Democratic leader Horatio Seymour that "if he hated New England as the breeding bed of radicalism, he loved New York passionately." The symbolism and reality of the Puritan threat became the crucial element ordering and organizing the Demo-

cratic ideology. Andrew D. White, *Autobiography of Andrew Dickson White* (New York, 1905), I, 106.

67. Foner, "Causes of the Civil War," 213.

68. Baton Rouge *Daily Advocate*, December 3, 1860.

69. *Congressional Globe*, 34th Cong., 1st Sess., Appendix, 987.

70. Washington *Daily Union*, January 20, April 16, 1857.

71. Thornton, *Politics and Power*, xviii.

72. Craven, *Growth of Southern Nationalism, 1848–1861*; Allan Nevins, *The Emergence of Lincoln* (New York, 1950), II, Potter, *Impending Crisis* (secession chapters completed and edited by Fehrenbacher).

73. As Robert Kelley puts it, pietist reformers in the Republican party "were determined to use governments—as in the days of the Puritan past—as divine instruments to reshape American life in accordance with the imperatives of the newly recharged faith." And their stance "exuded intransigence." They seemed intent to "face down" any Southern threats or bullying. Kelley, *Transatlantic Persuasion*, 418; Formisano, *Birth of Mass Political Parties*, 326.

INDEX